SKETCH MAP

EUROPE

as seen by the Reid family on
their tour in the Blue Kiwi

Gromitz
Sinksoor

Hamburg

Y

rt-am-Main

Würzburg

Nürnberg

Regensburg

Linz   Vienna

AUSTRIA

ALY

Padua

Venice

Reggio

gna

Florence

Rome

A CARAVAN CLOSE BEHIND

Our artist, while reading the manuscript, found himself drawing the Little Man, who had popped up all over Europe and endeavoured to block, thwart, misdirect and generally upset the plans and progress of the Reid family. His mischievous pertinacity and many disguises have made him a part of the story—so we think it only right that his portrait should be allowed to appear throughout the pages, along with the sketches of buildings and events which were our original idea of illustrations for the book. Should anyone think he shows a facial resemblance to any member of the Reid family— why worry. We all have approximately the same allotment of features—as even Shakespeare noticed.

A
CARAVAN
CLOSE BEHIND

by

Joyce Reid

Illustrations by
W. Haythorn-Thwaite

Collins
AUCKLAND · LONDON
1965

FIRST PUBLISHED 1965

COLLINS BROS. & CO. LTD
P.O. BOX NO. 1   AUCKLAND

Registered in Australia for transmission by post as a book
PRINTED IN AUSTRALIA BY HALSTEAD PRESS, SYDNEY

FOR MY HUSBAND

Introduction

It would not have happened but for a chance remark made by a woman we knew slightly. She was describing a trip by caravan she had made in Europe some years previously; this was, she said, the ideal way to travel.

At the time my husband was about to go on Sabbatical leave from his university, and we were planning to take the four youngest of our seven children to England. We had some vague hope that we might be able to visit Continental countries briefly, but, with so many of us, had not dared hope we would be able to travel very far—the cost, we thought, would be prohibitive. But the mention of a caravan opened up a new field of ideas. Like most New Zealanders, we had spent many holidays by the sea, and were used to the "baching" life, but we had never been camping, nor had we driven a car with a caravan in tow. Still, we thought about it a good deal, and the more we thought of it the more we liked it; but at the beginning I for one did not dream that for six months the caravan would be our home, and that in it we would explore eight countries. It was an unforgettable experience. Apart from all the joys and excitement of travel, it was a unique opportunity, living in such close quarters and sharing so much as a family, to become better acquainted with our children.

We arrived in England in December, in a fog. A bleak but exciting Christmas in London, and not long afterwards we found a house in Purley, Surrey, where we settled down for the first five months; my husband to get on with the work he had come to England to do, the three younger children to go to school, Gerard, aged seventeen, in a job, and I to cope with the mysteries of housekeeping in England. I learned to deal with burst pipes in cold weather, to take the washing to the laundrette, and how to cook kippers, and I found that street markets were fine places to shop if you watched what went in the paper bags. After the first shock I became used to being addressed by barrow boys and waitresses as "dear" or "love", accepted the fact that in England refrigerators and washing machines are regarded as luxuries, and exploded the myth that the English don't speak until they are introduced. We made many friends and, having bought a car, spent many happy days exploring the countryside of Surrey, Sussex and Kent, with a couple of times a week, visits to London to go to the theatre, or to ramble about that most exciting of cities. London is—London, and can never be adequately described.

One day in January John and I went to see the Outdoor Life Exhibition at Olympia. We had never imagined that camping could be made so comfortable. The blue and orange Continental tents, the folding camp furniture, the various kinds of cookers were all new to us at the time, although later they were to become quite commonplace. The tent, we learned, has come a long way from the time when it was a cumbersome canvas affair, difficult to erect and comfortless in use. Modern tents are of light, brightly coloured fabric, usually with floors of the same material, built on folding metal frames, in various styles and sizes; often divided into several rooms, with clear plastic windows in the fabric walls. They are, in fact, small portable houses, put up or taken down in a twinkling, yet strong and weatherproof, and when packed taking up astonishingly little space. We made a few purchases—two folding beds of French manufacture, and a waterless cooker which became my delight. I used it all those months in Purley, later in the caravan, and even now, back in my all-electric New Zealand home, it is still my favourite method of cooking.

We collected all the literature about caravans we could find, joined the Caravan Club and studied its monthly magazine with the greatest of interest, travelled about a good deal to visit caravan dealers and inspect 'vans of different kinds, talked with people who had travelled that way, and finally settled for a Bluebird. It was 17 feet by 6 feet, painted pale blue with bright red curtains. Inside, the walls were pastel pink and the woodwork blonde. It had four bunks, which became seats by day, a gas-stove and gas-lights, a sink, a toilet, storage space under the bunks, cupboards under the sink, a wardrobe which would have been adequate for two but was taxed with clothing for six, and a folding partition which could divide the caravan into two rooms. Since there were only four bunks and six of us, we also bought a small orange tent. The children, filled with patriotic zeal, inscribed K I W I in large silver letters along both sides of the caravan, and that became its official name, although more often it was referred to as the Monster, or other unflattering titles.

Over the next few months we gradually acquired all we would need for our mobile home—cutlery, china, folding tables and chairs, ice-box, and sleeping-bags, which experienced caravanners advised us were much more practical than ordinary bedding and easier to stow by day. We also visited all the European embassies in London, and came away equipped with piles of maps, including "camping" maps, for each country, showing camping sites, graded according to their merits, with directions for finding them.

The Caravan Club issues two books listing recommended camp sites, one for Britain, one for the Continent, with valuable information about facilities available, the cost per night, and so on. The Automobile Association, for a small fee, arranges the necessary carnets, tickets, customs forms and other necessary formalities of foreign travel, and also supplies maps and information. Insurance provided something of a problem, since British insurance companies allow cover for only three months' foreign travel, and it was our intention to be abroad almost twice that time. However, we decided to leap that obstacle when we came to it. In the meantime, we felt reasonably well equipped.

Winter passed; the wonderful English spring broke over the land in all its dramatic unexpectedness. No wonder English poets so often celebrate the spring: no wonder the Christian mystery of Easter rebirth and resurrection gains extra significance in a northern clime. To one who had known only the seasons of northern New Zealand it was startling. One day snow, sleet and lowering skies: the next, suddenly, everywhere, flowers —crocuses, golden forsythia, little white wood anemones, then the brief glory of daffodils, and masses of bluebells, like smoke curling among the trees in the woods, and the chestnuts starred with their candles.

We were ready to move on.

Chapter I

WE left Purley on 31st May, Ascension Day, and, encouragingly, gloriously sunny.

All the morning, while we completed packing, there had been a stream of callers—the man to check the inventory of the house, the man to shut off the water, the man to cut off the telephone—the electricity; friends to say good-bye; the carrier for the luggage we were leaving in storage. In the midst of all this I tried to leave the house as tidy as we found it, which was not helped by having the electricity cut off before I had finished with the vacuum-cleaner. So when a gipsy appeared with her little bunch of wild flowers and her whining, sing-song voice, "Buy the gipsy's flowers, lady" I was rather brusque, and said I was busy as we were just leaving. It was the wrong thing to say.

"Buy the gipsy's flowers, lady, and you'll have a lucky journey. I'm a little Welsh gipsy, I know these things. The gipsy can bring you luck. Buy the gipsy's flowers and your journey will be lucky. Gipsies know about journeys. Buy the gipsy's flowers, lady."

She could obviously keep on like that all day, so I bought her flowers to be rid of her, wondering how a Welsh gipsy differed from any other gipsy, and why she should be presumed to know more than others.

A scrambled lunch of cold food out of paper bags, and a very welcome visitor, my friend K., bringing—blessings on her —a large Thermos of scalding hot coffee.

And so, we were ready. We posed for a snapshot beside the caravan, then into the car and away, through the golden afternoon, heading south-west: through Redhill, on through the smiling Surrey countryside, with everywhere chestnuts in flower, into Hampshire, all hopfields and blossoming orchards, past the little village of Chawton, where Jane Austen's house still stands, and so, in the late afternoon, to our first camp site, on the outskirts of Winchester.

We bumped across the entrance into a neat green field beside a service station. We were the only ones there, for which

1

we were rather glad as, inexpertly on this our first attempt, we made our camp. John and Gerard unhitched the caravan from the car, let down the legs, and unlocked the door. With something like dismay we surveyed our mobile home. At first glance it looked chaotic. Everything was stacked on the floor, and places had to be found for our belongings before we could get in to set up the table and cook a meal. First, out came the cylinder of bottled gas, which was placed on the ground and connected to the lead-tube, John and Gerard each having his own idea how it should be done, and getting in each other's way, but it was done at last. Next came the bucket, to be placed under the caravan to catch the waste-water from the sink. In the meantime, Miriam and I were stowing away china and cutlery in the cupboard under the sink.

I was relieved to find all the china was intact, for I had feared bumping along the roads might cause breakages. The only casualties were the gas-mantles of the lights, which, being very frail, had shattered en route, and one of the glass lamp-shades, which had fallen off and broken. Throughout the whole trip we were to have problems of this kind with the lights. The opaque glass shades rattled loose and the mantles broke. We tried dismantling the whole lights before moving, but it was very difficult to handle the brittle mantles without breaking them; then Gerard suggested leaving the light fittings in place and tying polythene bags over them, which worked sometimes, but at others we found glass shade and pulverized mantle in the bottom of the bag. It was wise to carry candles. However, on this first night we had spare mantles so were not worried.

Then came the business of deciding where everything was to be kept, and where everyone was to sleep. This being England, no tents were allowed on the site. The curious gentility of the English is something I find quite incomprehensible: the strange rules as to what may or may not be done. For instance, on caravan sites it is forbidden to erect tents or to hang out washing. Apparently camping is acceptable only so long as you pretend it is not really camping. A caravan might conceivably be merely a parked vehicle, but a tent is obviously camping, so mustn't be seen. Washing is indecent, so must never, never be hung out to dry. Why it is less reprehensible to wear clothing damp and risk rheumatism, or just leave it dirty I have never discovered.

So there we were, with four bunks and six people, and not

allowed to use our tent. By leaving the dividing partition folded
back we could just fit one of the folding beds in the space left.

"You'll have to sleep in the car," we told the youngest. "Do
you mind?"

He said no, but his anxious little face belied him—he was
obviously not happy about being left alone outside. Gerard
and Miriam were busily pulling apart the folding table and
fitting it across the two single bunks at the front of the caravan.
I could not at first see what they were doing, until they exclaimed, "Look, there's room for Nicky here!" And so there was.

The two bunks were really padded seats facing each other
on opposite sides of the caravan. A folding table which could
be removed fitted between them, and by taking the squabs
off the seats, turning the table sideways and resting the ends
on the bunks, then placing the squabs on the table they had
made a bed wide enough for three. With the folding bed and
the double bunk at the back of the caravan this made room,
cramped though it was, for all. Nicky's relief was obvious and
touching.

That matter settled, we put table and seats back in place
and went on with the job of storing things away. It wasn't
easy. Everybody wanted to help, and just as one had decided
the cupboard under the double bunk was ideal for linen and
clothing, someone else started to fill it with shoes and books.
In addition, the space in the caravan was small, and we kept
bumping into each other. At last I told the two youngest,
Godfrey and Nicky, aged eleven and ten, to go outside and
play.

At the back of the caravan, where the roof curved down, was
a comfortable little space with a small table hinged to the wall
just big enough to take John's typewriter; here, he announced,
he would be able to work, and proceeded to arrange his books
and papers conveniently.

I put the ice-box outside under the caravan, and was about
to put a pile of John's clothes in the cupboard under the bunk,
when he said:

"Don't put them there."

"Why not?"

"Because every time I want anything I'll have to stoop right
down."

"Where shall I put them, then?"

"Just leave them on the seat."

3

I did so, and picked up one of the sleeping-bags, rolled into a great sausage and tied with tapes.

"Don't undo that," said John. "They're tidier left done up."

"Yes, but they won't fit in the cupboard."

"Well, leave them on the seat."

After this had happened several times I surveyed the littered seats, and said:

"Do you know what you have done? You have arranged things so that nobody has anywhere to sit but you!"

With laughter we stowed everything away. The sleeping-bags, we found, were best laid out flat along the seats with the squabs on top of them. Here they were out of sight and took up no space.

When we called the two boys in they arrived looking as if they had fallen into a flour bin. They had been playing a wonderful game—climbing a bank and sliding down, and as the soil was almost pure chalk they were white from head to foot.

When we went to bed that night we decided that with so many in so small a space ventilation was important, and left the windows open. In the grey dawn we awoke to the loud shrill chorus of the birds. It was enchanting, but we were stiff and chilled to the marrow, and rather dismayed to realize that even our thick sleeping-bags were not proof against the cold. From then on we forgot about hygiene, kept all the windows tightly shut, except the small skylight, and were wonderfully snug, in the traditional English fashion. In that climate it is necessary to live in a fog. But we had survived our first night, had learned a great deal about caravanning, and felt we were really on our way.

Winchester is steeped in history. The statue of King Alfred, watching over the city that was his capital, is modern, but everywhere else are reminders of the past. The huge Cathedral, once the biggest in Christendom, and still, after St Peter's in Rome, the longest, contains the tombs of Saxon kings and of William Rufus: the baker's shop where I bought bread has a plaque on the wall commemorating the fact that it is on the site of William the Conqueror's palace, destroyed in the wars between Stephen and Matilda: the place-names ("Manor of God Begot") speak of the past. The passage of time can bring its ironies: in the Cathedral the inscription on Jane Austen's tomb praises her virtues, but her contemporaries did not consider it worth while to mention her work; that was left for a plaque erected by more recent admirers! and a statue of Joan of Arc gazes for ever at the tomb of that Bishop of Winchester who was one of her accusers.

From Winchester we went on into Dorset by way of the New Forest, driving through a cool green tunnel of trees, catching frequent glimpses of wild ponies, many with tiny foals. The West Country in summer is just as the romantically-minded visitor always imagines England to be—all of a picture-postcard prettiness, with thatched cottages, old-fashioned gardens, and everywhere wild flowers—hawthorn, buttercups, wild roses and many others. One of the prettiest and quaintest of the villages in Dorset is Tolpuddle, which must have changed very little since the days of the Tolpuddle Martyrs, whose memory is kept alive by the Martyrs' Chapel and a row of houses called T.U.C. Cottages.

This is Thomas Hardy's country, the Wessex of his novels, and in Dorchester, the county town, his statue sits benignly smiling on the world, while close by is a statue of another Dorset writer, the clergyman William Barnes, whose poetry caught the true cadences of the West Country dialect.

Dorchester that warm sunny Saturday morning was extremely busy. It was market day, and people from miles around seemed to have come into town to do their week-end buying. The narrow streets were crowded, with a quite surprising volume of motor traffic nosing cautiously between market stalls, piles of fruit and vegetables, pedestrians, and vendors shouting their wares.

I was delighted by the soft, drawling West Country accents; it was a pleasure to saunter through the market listening to the voices of the people; even a pleasure to lose the way and have to ask directions when the answer came from a Dorset man, "Tur-rn ri-ight aat the church and stra-aight up the hill"— but we were surprised at the speculation aroused by our own accent. We pulled into a camp site not very far from Dorchester, again at a garage, and while we made camp, much more quickly and easily this time, we asked the garage proprietor to grease the caravan chassis, which had developed an excruciating squeak. Through the windows came the voices of the two men as they worked.

"Australians, do you think? Their car's got Surrey number-plates."

"No-o-o. They're not Australians, they're from Yorkshire."

Astonished, we looked at each other. We were used to being taken for Australians or Canadians, but Yorkshire? We could only conclude the men could never have travelled far from their own county.

Later John and I walked downhill to the nearby little village of Frampton. It was so remote from London it was hard to believe it was in the same country. The birds were singing loudly, and the sinking sun was a great red ball in a pink and purple sky. Everywhere was the smell of Dorset, a rich, rural aroma made up of earth and flowers, cows and mud. The few passers-by we met all nodded and said, "Evenin'." An old grey stone church watched over the little cluster of houses and shops that was the village, and on the green some young men were playing cricket, a group of girls looking on. As we watched, a policeman's helmet appeared, gliding along the top of a hedge, and then the policeman on his bicycle came into view. He dismounted and stood watching the game for a few moments, then leaned his machine against the hedge, took the ball and bowled. A policeman playing cricket on a village green—what could be more English?

Chapter II

FROM Dorset into Devon, and the first difficulty we had encountered.

We had been driving along the top of a ridge, high up in the windy air; above us nothing but the sky, white clouds scudding across the blue; below, falling away on each side of the road the widespreading countryside, cloud shadows gliding across the checkerboard fields, with here and there a little village clustered about its church. Then downhill into Devon, with its thatched roofs, and pink and blue and white wild flowers in profusion along the verge of the road, occasional clumps of gorse or hawthorn, and beyond this fields gold with buttercups.

"I can't understand it," said John. "There's a blue monster following us."

"It followed us yesterday, too."

"It seems we can't shake it off."

"I hope not."

We came to a fork in the road. A signpost said "Sidmouth" for both ways. The route on the map seemed to go left, so we took the left-hand fork, only to find it went more and more steeply uphill, a slope that to us looked almost perpendicular. The car gallantly did its best, but six people and over a ton of caravan were just too much. The engine coughed and died. The road was too narrow to turn car and caravan—in fact, too narrow to turn a car. Though it is possible to reverse with a caravan it is a tricky business: John at this stage had not tried to do so, and did not care to begin on such a hill. There was nothing for it but to unhitch, turn the caravan by hand, drive the car on to a suitable place for turning, and come back.

"Everybody out," called John.

We all scrambled out of the car, and he coasted a few yards to bring the caravan level with a gateway in which we could turn it, then, while he and Gerard unhitched, the younger children and I stood at the back of the caravan, lower down the slope, braced ready to take the weight when it was detached from the car. Never had the blue monster looked so monstrous

7

as it looked to us then, and I had a vision of the heavy caravan careering off down the hill, leaving four mangled bodies in its wake. There was a terrifying moment before the brake went on, when the whole mass of the caravan seemed to be barely held by our united efforts. We defied gravity for a few seconds till John and Gerard could come and help us, and then, under the watchful eye of an old lady peeping through her lace-curtained window, spun it broadside to the slope and partly in the gateway. John drove the car on till he could turn, came back and re-hitched the caravan, and we sailed safely down again to the

bottom of the hill. Here we stopped for a while, still a little shaken, and rested. A furniture van drove up and two cheerful young men got out.

"Do you need help?"

"No thanks, we're just resting," said John. "What's that road like?" indicating the one we had not taken.

"A bastard, but the other's worse."

Thus encouraged, we drove on to Sidmouth, over a road hardly less winding than the first but not so terrifyingly steep. We stopped at a place called Dunscombe Farm, high on a cliff-top, with the land dropping in deep folds to the sea far below. It was here that we heard our first cuckoo.

Sidmouth, unlike many English seaside resorts, has a quiet dignity which I found appealing. In such places as Blackpool or Southend, the atmosphere is that of a vast fun-fair, and the sea is incidental: in Sidmouth, as befits the coast of Drake's and Raleigh's Devon, the sea is dominant. As we strolled on the promenade curving around the bay, where lobster-pots and fishing-nets were drying on the sea-wall, the air was redolent with the exciting scent of the ocean—until we smelled it again we had not realized how we had missed it. Around the promontory from the town of Sidmouth we found a quiet little bay —red cliffs above, one or two cottages on the beach, few people in sight. Here Godfrey and Nicky decided was the perfect place for a dip; to them the only reason for going to a beach is to swim. In no time they were in their bathing suits and dashing across the pebbles and into the water. It was their first and last sally into the sea in England—they shot out again faster than they went in. They had not known that the temperature would be so much lower than that of Auckland Harbour. The English seaside, they decided, is quite pleasant for playing ball, or building sandcastles, or even for sailing in boats, but definitely not for swimming.

In the long evening twilight we took a walk in a big circle, along Devon lanes, between high hedgerows colourful with blue-bells, purple clover and little yellow spotted flowers like tiny orchids, catching glimpses here and there of the red fields beyond, through one or two picturesquely squalid villages, and back to where we started.

From Sidmouth we went to Taunton, where we stayed one night, then across Sedgemoor, site of the last battle on English soil—peaceful now, with cows grazing knee-deep in golden buttercups—and so into Somerset, "where the cider apples grow," and to the most fascinating place in all England, Glastonbury, the Isle of Avalon.

We camped a few miles out of the town, in an apple orchard, the blossom just giving way to leaf, which we shared with a cow, a flock of geese, hens, a rooster, and two Manx cats. The geese stuck their heads in the caravan door and looked at us with bright, enquiring eyes. The cow walked around the caravan and gazed at us, then, deciding we were harmless, ambled off again. The cock, a handsome, brightly-coloured fellow with long greeny-black tail feathers, strutted about and crowed cheekily at the gander, but as soon as the gander approached him, he fled. Nicky delightedly rushed at the cats, and all the time we were there he was to be seen carrying them about or playing with them in the grass.

"They're my friends," he explained. "They belong to the Pussy Brigade."

Although the children had from time to time had pets— white mice, guinea-pigs, budgerigars—we had never regarded ourselves as animal lovers, and it had just not occurred to us

9

that our youngest child might have a particular interest in cats, but from then on he left us in no doubt of it.

The farmer and his wife were an elderly couple, more or less retired, and they told us they had let most of their land for grazing, retaining only the orchard and a small poultry farm. Most of the work was done by their daughter. I enjoyed going over to the farmhouse to buy milk, fresh eggs, or a dressed chicken with fresh herbs from the garden for stuffing. The house was very old, its walls seeming to lean together for support, out of plumb, and the stone floors of the kitchen and dairy were worn into deep hollows by generations of feet. It stood in a pretty, old-fashioned garden, sedately filled with wallflowers and granny-bonnets (which Mrs C., the farmer's wife, called granny-nightcaps), sweet-scented lilac, sage and thyme. Mrs C. was always ready for a chat, in her softly slurred Somerset voice, and full of questions about New Zealand, where, she told me, her brother had emigrated fifty years before, only to be accidentally killed soon after arrival.

I should have been content to stay a long time in that peaceful place. In the mornings Godfrey and Nicky were up very early and away to watch Miss C. milk the cow—an interesting novelty for city children—then back again with still-warm milk for breakfast. The children played and we loafed most of the mornings, then in the afternoons, off into Glastonbury.

Near the town a large sign said "GLASTONBURY, the ancient Avalon", and I was so excited I could scarcely contain myself.

"Avalon! Imagine being in Avalon!"

"What's so marvellous about Avalon?" asked Gerard.

"Surely you know! King Arthur's Avalon!"

"Oh, that."

What, I wondered, is the matter with the present-day young? Have they no sense of romance? Does nothing excite them at all? They might just as well have stayed at home.

But I was wrong; Glastonbury cast its spell on all of us alike.

The place has almost too much to be taken in on one visit. It goes back so far into the past—beyond Arthur, beyond the Romans and Boadicea, to the prehistoric lake-dwellers. It is the cradle of Christianity in England: long before Augustine landed in Kent there was a flourishing Christian community at Glastonbury. Before that, for the Britons it was the Isle of Glass, the dwelling of fairy-folk and a place of mystery. St Patrick

10

came here. Kings and saints were buried within its Abbey walls, including, they say, King Arthur and his Queen Guinevere. It was reputedly the hiding place of the Holy Grail: the Holy Thorn, according to legend planted by Joseph of Arimathea, still blooms at Christmas: in the Middle Ages the Abbey was renowned and powerful, and pilgrims came in great numbers from all over Christendom. On those golden, sun-lit afternoons we seemed to have slipped right back into history. There was an enchantment about the place that we found nowhere else in England.

We climbed the Tor, crowned with its broken tower, all that remains of the ancient church of St Michael, and looked out on the gentle, park-like countryside. From that height the outline of the former lake, when Avalon really was an island, can still be clearly seen, though it is now all green meadowland. We stood there for some time, among the docile cows wandering about the summit, with the scent of thorn-trees wafted to us on the breeze, then we slipped and slithered down the slopes, and almost fell over a pair of lovers, lying in the long grass making little posies of wild flowers—buttercups, daisies, purple clover and delicate quivering grasses.

We wandered about the town; we saw the George and Pilgrims Inn, once the hostel attached to the Abbey to accommodate pilgrims, and we visited the Museum, poring for a long time over the relics of the lake-dwellers, strange, long-ago people who made artificial islands on which to build their circular houses, and who have left behind them such surprisingly sophisticated artifacts. Who would have thought that in prehistoric times they would have had safety-pins?

The Abbot's Tribunal was the court-house where the Abbot heard legal cases. At the dissolution of the Abbey, Henry VIII gave it to one of his supporters, who used it as a dwelling, and who presumably was the one who had Henry VIII's arms and the Tudor rose carved in stone over the door. No doubt having been given a fine home he wanted to display his gratitude and loyalty. Here, too, the sense of the past was very strong. Upstairs, it was easy to imagine the sittings of the Abbot's court, but in the stone-flagged kitchen, and the quiet little garden at the back, I could almost see an Elizabethan household going about the daily business of cooking, eating, talking, walking in the garden. I was struck, too, by the similarity of the kitchen to that of the farmhouse where we were camped.

11

But, enthralling and moving as all these places are, the heart and centre of Glastonbury is the ruined Abbey. Awed and subdued we walked about among the broken arches, meditated by the thorn-tree, looked at the site of King Arthur's tomb, went down into the crypt of Joseph of Arimathea, saw the well of the Holy Grail, and peeped into the great ovens of the Abbot's kitchen. The Abbey must have been huge, as can be deduced from the foundations that remain. Under Henry VIII it was torn down, the stones carted away for road-making. It is heart-rending to see, all ravaged and despoiled, so much beauty, built so lovingly, with such attention to detail, to the glory of God. We stood for a long time gazing at the magnificent carvings about the one Norman doorway that remains—angels, saints and kings in profusion, a sermon in stone.

"Deliberate destruction—it makes you so angry," said Gerard.

Nicky's eyes were getting bigger and bigger, his lips trembling; he looked very close to tears. At last he burst out with the only possible comment.

"Rotten ol' Henry the Eighth!" he said.

Chapter III

ACCORDING to our maps, Old Sodbury seemed a good place to spend a few days—in the Cotswolds, within easy distance of both Bristol and Bath—but when we arrived there we were disappointed to learn that there was no room in the camping ground because it was full for the Whitsun holiday week-end. However, the owner of the ground, Mr M., suggested that, as his home was on a quiet side road with little traffic, there was no reason why we should not camp on the grass verge near his gate, and we could obtain water from his house. This was the only occasion in England that we camped elsewhere than on an approved site, but it was scarcely less convenient than some of the other places.

Camping in England, generally speaking, is far less comfortable than it is on the Continent—or, for that matter, in New Zealand. On the Continent camping is really big business. Most countries are eager to woo the tourist, and are awake to the fact that all tourists are not necessarily prepared to pay for luxury hotels. Accordingly, "campings"—the English word is used almost universally—are very numerous and are made as attractive as possible. There are usually excellent showers and washrooms, toilets, shops and sometimes restaurants on the site; laundry tubs, ironing rooms and occasionally even washing machines. Some have modern kitchens with coin-in-the-slot stoves, and, in France in particular, it is possible to buy ice for the ice-box. All this makes camping very pleasant, and the result is that summer sees thousands of people touring, some with caravans, others with elaborate and easily-erected tents. Many of them are young people without much money, but just as many are people who once would have stayed in hotels or pensions, camping, not because they cannot afford other accommodation, but because they prefer the greater freedom and the opportunities to visit remote places. The host countries have profited considerably. In Austria, where tourism is the major industry, and in Italy, where it makes the difference between national financial stability and instability, camping, and the

13

money campers spend, are quite important to the economy. In a lesser degree this is true of other countries. Only Britain seems unaware of the potential. There very little effort is made to cater for the camper; the general attitude seems to be that all he needs is a space for his caravan. Of course, there are some well-equipped camp sites, but they are few and far between. In seven weeks touring England we found only two with showers; most had toilets, but some had not, and, except in London itself, such refinements as laundries were unknown, and as a matter of fact, the washing of clothes was frowned upon. In Scotland we fared better, but England's camps were so poor that to camp on the roadside at Old Sodbury was really no great hardship.

Whatever the shortcomings of our camp, our instinct that Old Sodbury would be a good base from which to explore proved to be correct. In whatever direction we went, whether in the car or on foot, we found something interesting or beautiful.

Nearby is the town of Chipping Sodbury, built around its big market place, and almost every other building an inn. Chipping Sodbury is remarkably consistent. In most English towns ancient mingles with modern: old buildings house self-service stores or Woolworth's; new houses stand cheek by jowl with old: but here all seem of the same period—shops with small-paned windows, inns with wide arched entrances to cobbled coachyards. It must have changed very little in two hundred years. The Catholic church of St Laurence is the most unusual church I have ever seen. It was once a coaching inn, the Swan. The arched entrance is still there, but the yard has become a cool walled garden with a stone cross in the middle. Inside, the upper-storey floors have been removed, so that the walls of the church extend right up to the rafters, disproportionately high for its small floor space, which seats only about a hundred. Not far away is the manor house of creamy-beige Cotswold stone, where Tyndale translated the Bible. In another direction lies an ancient Roman camp, all grass and buttercups, clumps of hawthorn, and black-faced sheep, but with the earthworks still clearly visible, and the spaces which once were gates.

Mr M., who was over eighty, seemed to enjoy having campers so close to his home. He frequently came over to chat and tell us stories of the district, bringing old photographs to show us. His family had lived there for generations. When he was a child, he told us, his father had kept the village store where we

14

had bought our groceries, and his grandfather had been in service at Dodington House—the mansion whose gates we could see nearby—for seventy years, starting at the age of seven! It was quiet and peaceful in Old Sodbury. Few cars came up the narrow road by which we were camped. Every morning we were awakened early by the loud dawn chorus of the birds, and once, at sunrise, John and I sat at the window and watched a baby rabbit gambolling about near the caravan. We called softly to the children to look, but by the time they were awake it had frisked up its little tail and disappeared through the hedge.

One evening we were at dinner when a homing pigeon mistook the open skylight of our caravan for its loft, and came fluttering in about our heads. Gerard and Godfrey, after a great deal of jumping about and climbing on seats, finally caught it and put it out the door, but it promptly came in again. When we closed the skylight it refused to go away, but continued to sit disconsolately on the roof. At last the boys coaxed it down and into a box, and, examining its ring, found it had come from Birmingham. I asked Mr M. what we should do with it, and he rang the police. Shortly afterwards a police car came roaring up and took the bird into custody, much to the delight of Godfrey and Nicky.

"Isn't it exciting?" they said gleefully. "Just like Z-Cars!"

The day we spent in Bath was fine and warm—according to the weather report 72 deg. F., which is not really very hot, but after the rigours of the English winter it seemed almost tropical. Bath responded with what for England was mad abandon—men walked about the streets in their shirtsleeves, and all the girls looked very pretty in light summery dresses without the usual coats or jackets. It gave the city a gay, holiday atmosphere, and thereafter it became a family joke that summer in England that year was the day we went to Bath.

We went from the Guildhall through the market to see "the nail"—a flat-topped pillar on which payment for purchases was formerly placed: hence, "pay on the nail". We visited the Abbey Church with its "Jacob's ladder" façade; we went into the elegant Pump Room, all blue and gold and white, where eighteenth century fashion gathered for balls under the autocratic rule of Beau Nash, and which Jane Austen celebrated in her novels, and we went down to the Roman Baths, so extraordinarily well preserved after two thousand years. How the Romans, shivering

15

in the English climate, must have enjoyed those warm baths! It is believed that the many ancient jewels and coins found there and now displayed in the Museum, were tossed into the water as thank-offerings. Gerard, an enthusiastic coin-collector, was fascinated by the display, and had to be almost dragged away. We could not leave without ceremonially "taking the waters"—and found that, like all hot mineral springs, it tasted foully of bad eggs.

On the morning of the Whitsun Bank Holiday we left Old Sodbury, headed for Stratford-on-Avon. Mr M. came out in his dressing-gown to shake hands with us all. "I'm sorry you're going," he said. "You're the most sociable people I've known." I think he had enjoyed telling us his stories of the past as much as we had enjoyed hearing them. His wife, who was badly crippled by arthritis and seldom left the house, also hobbled out to say good-bye.

"I envy you going to Stratford," she said, wistfully. "I love Shakespeare, and I used to go sometimes to see the plays, but now I'm past travel."

We were looking forward very much to Stratford. Apart from the thrill of visiting Shakespeare's town, we had the pleasurable anticipation of seeing four plays at the Memorial Theatre, for which we had booked seats six months ahead. There was also a more mundane reason for wanting to reach Stratford. The camp site there, according to the camping guide, was one of the best in England: perhaps instead of our usual sponge in a basin we might find baths or showers; I might even be able to press some of our crumpled clothes. The iron I carried had never been taken out of its box because we had never found electric points to plug it in. So it was with high hopes we went from Gloucestershire, through Wiltshire, Oxfordshire, and into Warwickshire, by way of Burford and Cirencester, to Stratford-on-Avon on a Bank Holiday.

The wonder was that so small a town could hold so many people. They milled about in their thousands, picnicking on the lawns and river-banks, crowding the pavements, crossing the roads in crowds and bringing the traffic to a standstill, pouring into souvenir shops and historic places in tightly packed droves. Charabancs and double-decker buses kept pouring in from every part of the country: from Southern Counties, from Yorkshire and Lancashire, from Scotland and Wales. Every British accent could be heard in the crowd, and many foreign languages as well.

"No good trying to do any sight-seeing today," said John, as we forced our way through the press of people. "Better to wait till after the holiday."

We were to spend a week in Stratford, so this seemed much the best plan: instead of going out in the afternoon we would stay at the camp, and I thought it would be a good opportunity to do some ironing, so that we would not look too crumpled when we went to the theatre that night. Accordingly, I went in search of the proprietor to enquire about an ironing-room, or, at the least, an electric point. I found her mopping the lavatories. Wearing a smart suit, fur stole, flowered hat, stiletto heels and gloves, she worked with a deprecating air, as if to make it quite clear the task was beneath her, and she was really not used to this sort of thing. I put my request as politely as I could, and was greeted with an icy stare.

"Are you an Australian?" she demanded.

"No," I said, "a New Zealander."

"I don't like Australians," she snapped. "And New Zealanders are as bad. They ask for things like ironing-rooms—and they steal the toilet paper."

Stratford is a memorable experience. It is easy to be cynical about the Great Shakespeare Industry. One is constantly amused —or exasperated, according to one's temperament—by the phoniness and vulgarity, the Gifte Shoppes selling busts of Shakespeare, "Present from Stratford" plates and ash-trays, and genuine Elizabethan cocktail cabinets; by signs on old buildings, such as "Judith Shakespeare's House—Hamburgers"; by the sentimental talk of the guide in Anne Hathaway's Cottage— which almost certainly wasn't Anne Hathaway's—"and here is the very settle where Anne and Will used to sit when he came courting." But when all the dross is discounted much pure gold remains. Nothing can alter the fact that it *is* Shakespeare's home-town. The streets may now have traffic-lights and streams of cars, but they are the same streets that he once walked; he did attend the Grammar School, and he is buried in the Church of the Holy Trinity under a very bad doggerel inscription. Shakespeare may or may not have been born in The Birthplace, but there is still the Warwickshire countryside that inspired so much of the poetry, the trees and flowers, the swans on the river and the cuckoo's call. And above all, there is the theatre. It was an unforgettable experience to go each evening to see the plays superbly performed. It was the first time any of the

17

children had seen Shakespeare on the stage, and John and I felt they were to be envied such a perfect introduction as *A Midsummer Night's Dream* in Stratford in summer. I, too, had an enviable evening. One night the play was *Measure for Measure*, which I had never seen or read before, and of which I knew nothing. So, in the twentieth century, to all intents and purposes, I saw a new Shakespeare play, seeing it as the original audience must have done, with no preconceived ideas, and not knowing what would happen next. It was exciting. The long light summer evenings made it delightful, during the intervals of the plays, to stand on the theatre balconies above the Avon, watching the swans, the young people flitting about on the water in canoes and punts, and the occasional rowing skiff with the coxswain calling the strokes.

One afternoon we drove to Coventry to see the new Cathedral. On the outskirts of the city some evidences of the heavy war-time bombing were still to be seen, but the centre rose, like the phoenix chosen as its symbol, spick-and-span new. We parked in a multi-storey carpark, and joined the queue being pushed into and around the Cathedral, which had been opened only a few weeks and was still attracting crowds of visitors. It was not the ideal way to see it—I should have preferred time to stand and stare—but it was infinitely better than not visiting it at all, and I should have been sorry to have missed it. The new building is extremely impressive in its simplicity and its use of colour, and it was a brilliant conception to join the new to the ruins of the old by means of a colonnade, thus expressing continuity. The roofless Chapel of Forgiveness in the old Cathedral, with its charred cross among the broken arches and traceries, and the inscription "We Forgive" is very moving.

"I'm convinced," said John, "that there's a Little Man on the job putting these things in front of us to hold us up."

We had left Stratford that morning heading north. Since the caravan was cumbersome and streets in English towns are often narrow, we had intended to avoid cities as much as possible; but something had gone wrong in the map-reading department, and we found ourselves, in the middle of a busy week-day, crawling at a walking pace through the centre of the manufacturing city of Wolverhampton behind the largest vehicle I had ever seen. We had seen many motor transporters before; huge trucks with as many as a dozen new cars packed neatly

18

on them like eggs in a crate, but this one surpassed them all. It had at least twenty-four wheels, and its superstructure projected far out beyond the chassis to left and right, effectively blocking at least two traffic lanes. Perched high on each side was a man talking into a telephone—presumably giving instructions to the driver. Preceded by motor-cycle police and followed by a truck, it ambled through the heart of the city at all of three miles an hour, and our car and caravan lumbered along behind while all the traffic of Wolverhampton got hopelessly snarled. To make matters worse, the road went uphill, and at a slow pace with frequent stops we had little impetus for dragging the caravan. Once the car stalled, but started again immediately. A few paces on, brake, slowly forward, brake again.

"What on earth is that thing in front?" demanded John, and the boys leaned as far out the windows as they could, trying to see what load could possibly require such an enormous carrier.

"It's a road-roller transporter!"

Oh well, road-rollers have to be manufactured somewhere, and when they are made they have to be taken somewhere else. It was just our bad luck to be caught there. Nothing for it but to keep on and hope it wouldn't be long. On, stop, on again. At last the leviathan turned off to the left, and we were free. It had taken three-quarters of an hour to come less than a mile. Being able to increase speed was a great relief to us and, I suppose, to the long line of traffic that had formed behind us.

But the Little Man hadn't finished yet. After Wolverhampton, still travelling uphill, we found ourselves behind a big truck loaded with huge flagons labelled "CAUTION—CORROSIVE". They were packed around with straw, but all the same they didn't look any too secure, and it was an uncomfortable feeling to have them jolting up the hill only a few feet before, and

19

slightly above, our faces. We had horrid visions of one flying off and spraying us with sulphuric acid, or whatever substance it was.

It was many miles further north that we happened along just after an accident. On a bend, police were directing traffic around a truck, and the whole of the road and the grass verge were smeared red. We all stared in fascinated horror, thinking somebody must have been decapitated at least: but no one had been hurt. Swinging too fast round the corner the truck had lost part of its load, and dozens of jars of raspberry jam had smashed on the road.

No doubt about it, the Little Man had had a busy day.

As we advanced into the Black Country I expected unrelieved ugliness, and was pleasantly surprised to find that this was not the case at all. The towns tend to be grim, but there is still the green countryside; the stone houses are more uncompromisingly plain than those in the south, and it is perhaps true that there are fewer flowers, but when we were there lilacs and laburnums made bright splashes of purple and gold in cottage gardens, every field was edged with hawthorn, white or faintly rosy, and masses of scarlet poppies bloomed along the roadside. Even the slag heaps, those strange, man-made monuments to the Industrial Revolution, change the countryside, but do not deface it as much as one would expect. They are as huge as mountain ranges, and might in fact be mistaken for them, were it not for their unnaturally straight lines.

I feel that the "realist" novelists and playwrights who depict North Country working-class life as an unbroken confinement in squalid homes and dingy streets are less than honest. I do not for a moment deny that there is much poor housing and unemployment in the north of England, but it is also a fact that the city worker in search of fresh air and country scenery does not have to go far or spend much money to find them. They are never more than a bus ride away.

Rudyard Lake is in Staffordshire, about eight or nine miles from the silk-manufacturing town of Macclesfield—a narrow streak of water, two miles long, set deep in wooded hills. Kipling's parents liked this place so much they gave their son its name, but oddly enough he himself never visited it. On the Saturday afternoon we were there many people were spending the half-holiday in the sunshine, the young ones paddling canoes or sailing small boats on the green weed-covered water, their parents sitting on the banks fishing, the children running about playing among the trees. It was a quiet and peaceful scene, and worlds away from city streets and factories.

If it had not been for the children we would not have found another, smaller lake at Bosley, about five miles nearer to Macclesfield, where we stayed two days. Godfrey and Nicky came bursting into the caravan: "Mummy, Daddy, come and see our island. It's a beauty place—come on!" So we followed them, picking our way over muddy ground churned up by cows, to their "island", which was really not an island, but a little peninsula where bluebells and ferns covered the ground under trees and rhododendron bushes in full wine-purple bloom. Out in the lake thousands of white petals from the hawthorns round the shore had been carried by currents to the centre, where they had banked up to form what looked like a snowy island. Everything was still, the quiet water reflecting back the quiet sky. The boys were right, it was a beauty place.

"Isn't it good?" said Godfrey. "We've been playing Robin Hood here."

Since we had been in England, they had discovered Robin Hood, and every piece of wooded land became Sherwood Forest.

I enjoyed posting letters in Bosley because it was a pleasure to visit so quaint a post office. It was a semi-detached cottage. One entered by a garden gate and walked up a crazy-paved path between flower-beds, then rang the door-bell, when the postmistress would open the door and accept a telegram, or sell stamps, or stationery, or sweets.

From Bosley we went on into Lancashire, by way of Knutsford —the original of Cranford, no longer a quiet little village, but a large and bustling town—through Wigan, surely the dreariest and ugliest place in all England, and stopped for one night at Garstang, a grey stone village deep in the folds of hills. The next morning we continued, still heading north; skirted the city of Lancaster, and on through the rugged grandeur of the Westmorland fells. In the car as we went we were playing "animal, vegetable or mineral".

We played a variety of games in the car when we were on the road—quizzes, riddles, making up limericks on place-names we passed, "number-plate bingo"—which consisted of shouting "Bingo" on seeing a car with digits already agreed upon in its number-plate. None of them were ever played for very long, for usually we found the scenery far too interesting, but at times

21

when the children were tired or hungry or inclined to be quarrelsome a game could smooth things over.

"Something partly vegetable, partly mineral," said John.

"Is it big?"

"Yes, fairly big."

"Have I ever seen it?"

"Yes, frequently."

"Can I see it now?"

"You could if you looked at it."

"The car?"

"No."

"I know—the caravan."

"I've got one—I've got one," shouted Godfrey. "Let me have a go."

"It's not your turn. Miriam guessed the last one."

"I don't care," said Miriam. "I don't want to play, anyway."

"Can I? Can I? Can I have a turn? I've got a beauty. You'll never guess it."

"Well, if Miriam doesn't mind."

"You'll never guess this. It's a *beauty*. Ready? Well, it's animal."

"Is it big?"

"Yes."

"Has it fur?"

"Yes."

"Four legs?"

"No, no legs."

"A seal?"

"No, it lives on land. It's a *beauty*."

"A platypus?" I ventured, sure I would be wrong.

"No. I told you you wouldn't guess it," said Godfrey gleefully. Everybody thought hard. Nobody could guess.

"Do you give in? Do you?"

"All right, we give in."

"Well, it's an ape."

"An ape? But you said it had no legs."

"Well, an ape doesn't have feet. It has four hands."

"Don't be silly, Godfrey. Of course an ape has legs."

"It does not. It has four arms."

After that continuing the game seemed pointless.

Kendal; grey houses, curved stone bridge beneath green trees

—the scene, smudged by rain, was like an impressionist water-colour, just glimpsed as we passed; then came the prolonged climb over the Westmorland fells to Shap. Here the road winds up to a height of 1,300 feet. Through the soft, misty rain we went up and up, over the rugged fells with great outcroppings of rock, and stone walls dividing the land. Here and there were shaggy sheep and shaggy long-horned Highland cattle. Our pace was a crawl, for as usual large, awkward, slow-moving vehicles were in front of us. There was a car-transporter carrying eight cars, then several petrol tankers, then a truck with a formidable load—an enormous four-bladed ship's propeller, so huge it stood high in the air above the driver's cab and overhung the sides of the truck to a considerable width. A police motor-cycle escort preceded it, and we crawled slowly up behind, those wicked-looking blades towering threateningly above us. Up and up and up, then quickly down the other side, and so to High Hesket, where we camped in pouring rain and a blustery wind that shook the caravan. Every now and then there was a bump and a shudder as the wind forced in the aluminium body, which immediately sprang back with a loud report.

As we arrived, another party was getting ready to leave. They had a "baby" car, towing a lilliputian caravan, but in the party there were two men, two women and six children. How they all fitted in the caravan, let alone the car, was a mystery. I could only conclude some of them must have sat on the roof; but when they left I was busy cooking lunch and did not see them go, so I'll never know. Late in the evening, in howling wind and pelting rain, another party drove in—a motor-cycle and side-car combination with a pillion passenger, and camping gear hanging all over the machine. The two figures on the cycle wore leggings, leather jackets and crash helmets, and I thought at first they were two youths, but they turned out to be a young married couple with a baby boy in the side-car. Battling against the gale they struggled to put up a pup-tent and prepare baby food on a primus. When I told the young wife I thought she was very brave to travel so with a baby she looked surprised, and said she was having a lovely holiday!

23

Chapter IV

"SOUTH of the Border, down Cumberland way," sang the children in the back seat of the car.

"Hardly *down*, a thousand feet up in the fells," I said.

"Well, we're below the Border, anyway."

We were on our way to Scotland, and for John and me it was an emotional moment. Both of us had Scottish ancestors, and even though a century had passed since they left their native land we were romantically—or sentimentally—excited at seeing the country. In soft, misty rain we sped through Carlisle and on towards the border.

"You tak' the high road, and I'll tak' the low road," sang John suddenly, and we all joined in. We sang all the other Scottish songs we could remember—"Will Ye No' Come Back Again", "Ye Banks and Braes", "Scots Wha' Hae". Then the Border, and how brave looked the bright gold and red Scottish flag, flying in the rain! As we crossed we all cheered, then burst into laughter that was close to tears.

There is not very much of Gretna Green—an unimposing white building with an inscription boasting "The first house in Scotland—10,000 marriages in this room since 1830"—hotels, motels, a few houses with notices offering bed and breakfast, that is all. Marriages are still the town's chief industry. Even though couples can no longer be married immediately, but must wait the prescribed period of residence, they still come here in large numbers, most no doubt attracted by the glamour attached to the name, but there are still some, surprisingly enough, who are runaways; usually foreigners who for one reason or another cannot marry in their own countries.

We stopped briefly at Ecclefechan, home of my forefathers: a small town of whitewashed stone houses, a church, a surprisingly large hotel, a few shops: its only imposing feature a seated statue of its most famous son, Thomas Carlyle. We had intended to make another stop at Crawford, but the wind and the rain continued, the countryside looked bleak, and we decided to push on to Glasgow.

24

Ugly, dirty, likeable Glasgow! Nowhere else have I known such kindness and hospitality. People we had not met before threw their hearts and their homes open to us in a way that was quite overwhelming. The Scots, we felt, are the kindest people in the world. The camp site, behind a garage on the Cumbernauld Road, and sheltered by trees, had hot showers, which were a delight to us after English camps, and a large sleek cat, which pleased Nicky.

"Another member of the Pussy Brigade," he cried, and swooped upon it.

Adjoining was a bottled-gas depot, so we were able to replenish our depleted supply of gas-mantles; not very far away was a laundromat, the most up-to-date and efficient I had yet found, and afterwards newly-met friends invited me to iron the freshly-laundered clothes at their house, so for the first time since leaving Purley we were able to face the world in an uncrumpled state. All of this added greatly to our sense of well-being.

One day John and I were taken by a woman doctor to whom we had had an introduction—herself a graduate of Glasgow—to visit the University. It was examination time, and here and there in the grounds and corridors were groups of students, their heads together, holding post-mortems on their papers. Universities are always interesting to us, and Glasgow we found particularly absorbing as we visited the War Memorial Chapel, the Museum with its collection of early surgical instruments and microscopes (including Lister's) and the Art Gallery with its fine Whistlers. Afterwards we were caught in a traffic jam, and arrived back at the caravan much later than we had expected. The young ones had intended to hire a boat and go for a sail on the little loch nearby, but as we returned four laughing faces were at the caravan windows. They had not been out, they told us; they couldn't—the caravan door had locked on the outside. They did not seem to mind, however; in fact they all regarded it as a very great joke, which surprised me, as I felt I should not have been so cheerful in their situation. We opened the door and went in, very contrite for having left them so long.

"What did you do, shut up all that time?" I asked them.

"Oh, we played games, and told jokes, and then we all went to sleep."

"It was an adventure, really," added Miriam.

As a matter of fact, it would not have been difficult for them to climb out the window; I think they really enjoyed the "adventure". But still, they had missed their sail on the loch.

"I'll tell you what we'll do to make up for it," said John. "We'll all go to a cinema tonight."

"In that case," I said, "it'll have to be a quick dinner. Salad and salmon and canned fruit."

I made the salad and then looked in the knife-box. No can-opener. Everybody helped—we looked on shelves and in cupboards, got down on the floor and poked under the table, opened boxes and suitcases, hunted through books—Godfrey even looked in my handbag—but it was nowhere to be found. At last I borrowed one from people in another caravan. But by that time it was too late for a cinema. However, we had promised the children an outing, so drove into the city and parked near the Central Station. It was still broad daylight, but at that hour there was very little traffic and few people about. What was surprising, in the heart of a big city, was that while there was no noise of traffic, the air was loud with the chattering of birds. Thousands of them were perched on every building, every ledge and window-sill, and this no doubt accounts in part for the dirty appearance of Glasgow. John and I would have been quite happy just to walk about looking at the streets and shops, but the children were obviously bored, so, seeing a news-reel theatre, we took them there to see the hour-long programme—fortunately cartoons as well as news-reels. When we came out at ten-thirty we were astonished to find it was still daylight, for we had forgotten that Scotland in summer is almost the Land of the Midnight Sun. John got into the car, and automatically switched on the lights, thinking rather of the hour than the conditions, but several other drivers flashed their lights at him to show he shouldn't, so he quickly switched them off again.

"Did you enjoy the pictures?" John asked Nicky.

"Oh yes, Daddy, it was lovely. You can be a captain in the Pussy Brigade." It was Nicky's highest accolade.

The missing can-opener turned up under my mattress—nobody knew how it got there! Perhaps the Little Man was responsible!

Loch Lomond is as beautiful as the songs and stories describe it. We drove out of Glasgow, along the Clyde past the huge cranes of the ship-building yards, through pleasant green country to Balloch, then on along the shore of the loch to Luss, a neat little village of trim grey stone cottages facing each other across a broad street, each wreathed in masses of climbing roses—pink and gold and apricot and red—brightening the grey, drizzly day with their riotous colour. Far across the grey waters of the loch Ben Lomond towered mysterious and forbidding, its peak hidden by clouds, and on its slopes a white streak like a chalk mark which was a distant waterfall. Then back the way we had come to Balloch, where we embarked for a boat trip on the loch, in a motor-launch called the *Lomond Gael*. By contrast with the lowering sky and steely water, the grassy banks were a brilliant green; beyond them the misty mountains, here and there a castle with candle-snuffer towers appeared and disappeared briefly as the boat sped over the water and threaded among the numerous small islands.

As we came ashore again we met an old photographer near the wharf. He had a large sign—"You Can Wear the Kilt Like Us"—and a painted screen, showing two comic kilted figures with holes where their heads should be. The customers stood in pairs behind the screen so that their own heads repaired the omission, and the resulting photograph showed them kilted and bandy-legged. Miriam and Nicky were eager to be photographed, so we stopped and waited while the photographer arranged them in position and clicked the camera.

Did we know Timaru, he asked, when he learned we were New Zealanders. A nice place, Timaru. He had visited New Zealand? Yes, indeed, he told us in his pleasant Scots voice, he had spent a year there, photographing scenery for a publishing firm; and he went on to describe a younger, more raw New Zealand than the one we knew. Christchurch had been his base, he said, and he often walked over the hills to Lyttelton to see the refrigerated ships loading. From the way he said it we gathered that refrigerated ships must have been something of a novelty. We asked how long ago this had been, and the answer

27

was in 1905. He must have been at least eighty, but with his outdoor complexion and vigorous speech and manner seemed twenty years younger.

We left him, and went off to look about the little town of Balloch, stopping at a café for tea. Here Godfrey somehow managed to knock over a tray of glasses, which shattered on the floor with a startling crash, much to our embarrassment; but the proprietor made light of it, and when John tried to pay for the damage vehemently refused, with true Scottish generosity. ("Och, the wee boy couldn't help it!")

There have been more successful expeditions than the one we took to Stirling. It was Sunday, dull and overcast. John announced he was tired of sight-seeing; he proposed to spend a quiet day in the caravan writing. Perhaps I could take the family out somewhere? So I rashly promised Nicky I would take him to the Art Gallery. But later the prospect of a day alone in the caravan did not seem so inviting to John, and he suggested a drive to Stirling. This was welcomed by everyone but Nicky. "It's not fair," he sulked. "Godfrey wanted to see the shipyards and he did; but when I want to see an Art Gallery we have to go for a drive."

However, he was somewhat mollified by the promise of a castle, and even became quite cheerful as we went through the Trossachs.

Stirling Castle stands in a fine commanding position, but the building itself I thought unimpressive, at least from a distance. We could not get very close to it because the roads were marked "No Entry". Instead we went into the town.

"First tea," said John, "then we'll see if we can find a way to the castle."

Sunday tea had become a ritual in the months we had lived in England. Unless the weather was very bad—and sometimes even when it was—Sunday had meant a drive in the country and sooner or later we stopped for tea. In England it is always possible to find a tea shop—it might be an ancient cottage with oak beams and uneven floors, or it might be a modern Tea Shoppe, all chrome and cacti, or sometimes a farmhouse where the meal was served at the family dining-table, but there was always hot tea, bread and butter, cakes and scones with jam and cream. It was a pleasant custom we had come to enjoy, and to look forward to, and on this particular day, with lowering sky and a chill in the air (although the calendar said it was midsummer), tea would have been particularly welcome. But we were in Scotland on the Sabbath. No shop or restaurant was open, no people were about, and Stirling seemed almost a ghost town. Even the castle, when we reached it, did not appear to be open: so we headed back towards Glasgow.

"See, you're not fair," grumbled Nicky. "Godfrey saw ships, but I couldn't see pictures. Oh no, you don't care. And you said I could see a castle, and I didn't. Nobody cares about *me*. It isn't fair. And we haven't had tea, either."

"Never mind, Nicky," I said. "I'm sorry you were disappointed, but we couldn't help it. And anyway, you saw the outside of the castle, and William Wallace's statue."

"I didn't want William Wallace's statue. I wanted to see paintings. I *told* you it's not fair."

Fortunately, by now we were at the Field of Bannockburn, which created a diversion, and talk of ancient battles kept him occupied the rest of the way back to Glasgow.

It was a surprise to me to find how close together Glasgow and Edinburgh are. I should have known better, of course, but, thinking vaguely of the four hundred miles between Auckland and Wellington, expected the trip to take the best part of a day, and was surprised to find it took only about an hour. Nowadays there are many commuters, living in one city and working in the other, and while we were there a "silly season" newspaper correspondence was being carried on discussing a suitable name for such people. Popular suggestions were either Edinwegians or Glasburghers!

In Edinburgh, perhaps because the weather was fine, we were even more struck by the long hours of daylight than we had been in Glasgow. One bright, sunny evening we drove to Queensferry to see the Forth Bridge. As we stood on the shore of the Firth, looking up at it, it was breathtakingly impressive. A train passed over it, and as the sun caught the windows each brilliant flash was duplicated in the quiet waters below. Looking at the sunlit scene it was hard to realize it was nearly ten o'clock at night. Later, I was sitting in the caravan writing letters, while Godfrey and Nicky played outside, when John suddenly said, "Shouldn't those boys be in bed?" and looking at my watch I was astonished to find it was eleven o'clock, but still quite light. When I was a child I used to wonder why the little boy in R. L. Stevenson's poem "had to go to bed by day"; but in Edinburgh, what else can parents do?

29

Speaking of Stevenson, a visit to his birthplace in Edinburgh was very rewarding. We were the only visitors, and the curator gave us the run of the house, with its interesting collection of relics and manuscripts; but it was saddening, not long afterwards, to learn that it had been closed to the public because the paucity of visitors did not justify the expense of keeping it up.

Edinburgh is blessed above most cities in the magnificence of its situation. Nothing could be more dramatic than the great craggy rock, crowned with the castle, rising in its very heart, or the rugged grandeur of Arthur's Seat, and the effect is enhanced by the contrast of the classic lines of the important buildings. One may or may not agree with the oft-quoted description of Princes Street as "the most beautiful street in Europe", but it is certainly satisfying, when shopping, to see an almost theatrical backdrop of castle, crags and trees, instead of just more shops, on the opposite side of the street. I had not known, till I saw some growing around the Royal Scots Greys Memorial in Princes Street Gardens, what a handsome flower the Scottish thistle is. Taller than a man, with great silver-grey leaves and huge purple blooms, it is worthy to be a national emblem.

Nicky was not disappointed this time: we visited the National Gallery, of which the children all approved, and the Gallery of Modern Art, which they emphatically disliked, though John and I enjoyed it. It is curious how conservative in taste the young can be.

The Botanical Gardens are a botanist's paradise, with the thousands of different specimens, and the many glass-houses at varying temperatures to simulate all the climates of the world, but to the mere sight-seer without specialized knowledge they appear somewhat lacking in colour.

No one could visit Edinburgh without taking the steep, cobbled road up to the Castle. It is a place of high romance. Here all Scotland's turbulent history is crystallized and preserved. Everywhere are reminders of the past, from the plaque at the gate marking the spot where witches used to be burned, to the great banqueting hall, the apartments of Mary, Queen of Scots, including the tiny room in which she bore her son; the Scottish crown jewels, the clothing that belonged to Bonnie Prince Charlie; the elaborate World War Memorial Chapel, and the tiny ancient St Margaret Chapel, once desecrated by being used as a powder magazine, now lovingly restored and kept decorated with fresh flowers by Scotswomen named Margaret.

We were sorry to leave Edinburgh—and Scotland—and when at the border we saw a large sign reading "Haste Ye Back to Scotland" we all vowed some day we would return.

Chapter V

WHEN first we had arrived in Scotland Godfrey and Nicky started counting the kilts they saw, but soon gave up because they lost count. But though we frequently saw the kilt, not once did we hear the pipes—for that we had to wait till we were back in England. It was at Whitley Bay in Northumberland.

We had left Edinburgh in the late morning, stopped for a picnic lunch high on a cliff-top above the sparkling sun-lit North Sea, and arrived in the late afternoon at the caravan park at Old Hartley. Almost as soon as we arrived Nicky made friends with a fluffy Chow dog, but he was not, he was careful to explain, disloyal to his Pussy Brigade.

"This is an honorary member," he said, fondling the dog. "He's a spy for the Pussy Brigade, and he finds out all the secrets of the Doggy Brigade."

The camp was a smooth sloping lawn on a cliff-top. Far below, the North Sea came rolling in in great breakers, and off-shore was a small island with the tall column of a lighthouse. Away to the south, along the coast, the town of Whitley Bay, softened by distance, looked unreal and mysterious in the evening air, a white dome, vaguely reminiscent of the Taj Mahal, floating like a bubble above its roof-tops. But when we went there we found that the reality of Whitley Bay was very different.

At first sight, the place repelled. The motor-road ran along the front: on one side, a wide stretch of grass and beyond it the sea; on the other, the pavement so crowded with people it was hard to move, many of them wearing funny hats inscribed "Kiss Me Quick" or "Swinging"; candy floss, mechanized bingo parlours in dozens, pin-ball machines, Whitley Bay rock, shell-fish stalls, dodgems, merry-go-rounds, helter-skelters, souvenir shops selling "presents from Whitley Bay"; vulgar postcards, fish and chips, noise. The big white dome, so ethereal in the distance, topped a fun-fair called "Spanish City", loud with the sound of merry-go-round calliopes, showmen shouting, and screams from the "big dipper" and the helter-skelter. That was one Whitley Bay. But there was another. Crossing the stretch of grass, where

32

girls with bird's-nest hairdos and long-haired boys in skintight jeans sprawled about in each other's arms, we found, on a lower level, a broad promenade of pink and cream checkerboard flagstones, with a graceful balustrade, and below the beach of fine yellow sand. Thousands crowded the beach, and here were the respectable family parties, quietly and decorously enjoying a Sunday at the seaside; the youngsters with buckets and spades, the parents sitting on deck-chairs looking at the sea. To our New Zealand eyes they all looked ludicrously unsuitably dressed, the men in dark suits, the women obviously in their Sunday best. Even though there were so many people on the sand, the contrast between the loud, noisy, raffish life above and the quiet of the beach was quite startling. We, too, sat on the beach and gazed at the sea, and lulled by the waves, the cries of the gulls, the voices of children at play, were beginning to feel peacefully somnolent, when, suddenly, the skirl of the pipes, and the band came swinging along the promenade, kilts and scarlet jackets bright in the sun. As if on a signal, all the people on their deckchairs sat up and eagerly turned their heads; the children dropped their spades and ran to fall in behind—and so did we. Along the promenade, and into a sort of small arena, and here the following crowd settled itself on the grassy slopes to enjoy the concert. There is no music more exciting than the pipes, so to sit in the sun for a couple of hours and listen, watching the figure marching and Highland dancing, we found delightful, and we were somewhat amused to think that we were in England, not Scotland.

Later, we found there was still another Whitley Bay. Back from the sea, behind the activity of the front, behind the rows of boarding-houses with names like "Bella Vista" and "Sea View" was the all-the-year-round Whitley Bay, a small town with churches and shops, houses and schools. In winter life in Whitley Bay must be no different from life in other small English towns.

It was not my idea of the perfect place for a summer holiday, but I can understand the appeal of such resorts in England. The climate is so uncertain that no one, planning a holiday, can be sure of sunshine and suitable weather for outdoor activities. It must be comforting to know there are always the amusement arcades, the "Spanish ballroom", the pubs and the bingo parlours, where mechanical fountains shoot out coloured balls while attendants intone numbers like priests performing some esoteric rite.

I was really glad to have seen Whitley Bay on a summer Sunday, and thousands of North Country folk at play, for it had, I felt, given us a deeper insight into the life of Britain and a better understanding of her people.

Sometimes I wondered if the rural English lived on confectionery and beer. Time after time, driving through the country, we came to a village and looked about for shops to buy food; but the village consisted of a church, a cluster of houses, a pub, a sweet-shop. No other businesses at all. What the inhabitants ate was a mystery. Did they live off the land? Or did they go to the nearest big town to buy food? It was impossible to tell. This was the state of affairs as we went from Northumberland into Yorkshire, through cornfields spangled with scarlet poppies. We had not a great deal of food, and I wanted to do some marketing, but when we passed through towns there was no parking, and in villages no shops, except confectioners. At one village, Thormanby, there were no shops at all, but I felt this lack was more than compensated for by the view of a great white horse cut in a distant hillside. So shopping had to wait till we arrived at our next camping place, Stamford Bridge, where, in 1066, Harold was victorious in a battle against the Danes, only to be defeated and lose his life at Hastings a few weeks later.

From Stamford Bridge it is a very short distance to the historic city of York. We were to see it first in the evening, and perhaps at that hour of the day, when the sun was low, the shops shut, and the bustle of business ended, its antique aspect was accentuated. Certainly we could easily imagine what life in the Middle Ages must have been, when little cities snuggled within their walls, close about their great cathedrals. Looking up at the fantastic traceries and gargoyles of the Minster, the topmost pinnacles gilded by the last rays of the sun, one could almost imagine five centuries had rolled back, and the narrow streets and low arches had known no traffic save the foot passengers and occasional carts for which they were designed. The city walls of York are almost intact, and we walked a considerable distance on them, looking down, on the inside, on gracious houses with formal rose gardens clustered about the Minster; on the outside, on the more modern streets, shops, flats and factories where the city extends beyond its original limit. On that summer evening many of the streets and squares of York were bright with flowers —masses of scarlet and orange and royal blue in flower-beds, in baskets hanging from lamp-posts, in window-boxes on buildings. These are seen more often in Continental cities than in English ones, but the adornment was very becoming to York.

We walked down the Shambles, the former meat-market, a crooked street of Tudor houses, so narrow that people facing each other in windows on opposite sides can shake hands across the street. Here at No. 36 (now a Catholic chapel) lived Blessed Margaret Clitherow, a prosperous butcher's wife who in 1586 suffered the horrible death of being crushed between stones for the crime of harbouring a fugitive priest.

> "She held her hands to, like in prayer;
> They had them out and laid them wide
> (Just like Jesus crucified) ;
> They brought their hundred weights to bear. . . . . .
>
> When she felt the kill-weights crush
> She told His name times-over three;
> *I suffer this* she said *for Thee."**

As we paused before the house, musing on the brutalities of the Tudor age, and the courage of such people as Margaret Clitherow, the quiet of the evening was shattered by upraised voices, and two drunken women erupted fighting from a public-house at the end of the street. Probably such violent scenes were common enough in the reign of the first Elizabeth—Margaret herself may have seen them many times.

From York on to Lincoln by way of Doncaster, where the famous St Leger race is run, and here we were surprised to find the motor-road went through the racecourse, so that as we drove along we had grandstands on one side of us and the track on the other. We wondered what happened on race days: whether they closed the motor-way and sent the traffic on a detour, or whether vehicles just kept on going through the crowds.

The part of Lincolnshire through which we travelled is as flat as a plate, save for the hill on which stands the city of Lincoln, dominated by the great golden-cream Cathedral.

"It's the most magnificent I've ever seen," I exclaimed.

John laughed.

"You and your cathedrals," he said. "Every one you see is the best!"

---

*By Gerard Manley Hopkins.

It was true, I did get excited by each new one, and I never tired of visiting them, but all the same, thinking back to all the English cathedrals I saw—I exclude Continental ones—Lincoln in my mind still stands supreme. Westminster Abbey has been spoiled and vulgarized with the numerous monuments; Chichester is melancholy; Canterbury, Winchester and York are all in their different ways impressive; Coventry pleases as an expression of the twentieth century; but Lincoln has real beauty, which moved me deeply. It is in a much better state of preserva-

tion than most of the others, and the stone is a warm, rich colour. The riotous wealth of stone-carving, the prophets and saints and Biblical scenes in profusion on the exterior, and the glorious angel choir within, are a marvellous expression of the exuberance of the medieval craftsmen who poured everything they had into the work they raised to the glory of God—not forgetting their sense of fun, which led some anonymous stone-mason to put a ridiculous little imp among the swaths of fruit and leaves in the choir. Among the tombs is the tiny one of a child, said to be that of the little St Hugh, who, according to one of the *Canterbury Tales,* was murdered by the Jews. The story is almost certainly apocryphal, and now an inscription above the little sarcophagus asks God to pardon those who spread calumnies.

The fact that the story was so widely believed shows the extent of anti-semitic feeling in the Middle Ages. Jews lived in constant fear of robbery or attack, so built their houses as strong as fortresses—which evidently is the reason the twelfth century Jews' houses in Lincoln still stand while those of their contemporary neighbours have disappeared. One of them, the house of Aaron, who was reputed to be immensely wealthy, is said to be the oldest dwelling in Europe—though perhaps the claim may be open to challenge.

The camping ground at Lincoln was an asphalt yard behind the post office vehicle maintenance workshops. It employed a quite large staff, and soon after seven in the morning we were awakened by the tramp of numerous feet as the men, with cloth caps, and small haversacks on their backs, passed the caravan on their way to work.

From Lincoln we went on through Holland, which is well-named, for it is extraordinarily like the Netherlands—flat country criss-crossed by canals, windmills, and now and again fields of flowers making bright splashes of colour.

At West Winch, a few miles out of King's Lynn, we camped in the yard of the Chequers Inn.

What do they know of England who have never been in an English inn? In every village and hamlet, in every suburb or neighbourhood, the pub is the club and community centre, a refuge for the lonely or a meeting-place for friends. The size and furnishings may vary, but the atmosphere is always the same—a homely cosiness and warmth. Here one can spend an evening gossiping or playing darts, or sometimes in summer sitting in the garden in the long twilight. Drinking to excess is rare—in fact in all the time we were in England I can remember only once having seen anyone really intoxicated—and quite often one will see whole families, grandparents, parents and children, quietly enjoying an evening together. It is an interesting fact that in England, while juvenile delinquents, "Mods" and "Rockers" frequent coffee houses, the more respectable youths and girls meet in pubs; the boys perhaps drinking beer, the girls orange juice or "Baby Cham". For the visitor there is no better way to get to know a village or district than to spend an evening in the "local". I have many happy memories of such evenings in the course of our wanderings. There was the Red Lion in a Somerset village, cosily Dickensian, with warming-pans on the walls and thick carpets on the floor, where a group of farm boys—better educated I should say than an earlier generation of farmers—talked knowledgeably of crops and the relative merits of different makes of farm machinery, while their girl friends, smart in a slightly out-of-date style, listened and drank orange juice. There was a small rural pub where nobody—except us—ordered anything. The host knew what each customer wanted and had it ready before he was asked. Here a long conversation went on about somebody who had five acres right down to the brook. It got nowhere, and was mostly repetition.

"Five acres, he has, right down to the brook."

"That's right, down to the brook."

"Yes, five acres."

"I didn't know he had five acres."

"Yes, down to the brook."

There was an inn in Hampshire where eggs and butter and home-baked cakes were sold.

"This is more a fa-a-armhouse than a pub," explained the proprietor, as he counted out our eggs.

At the Dog, in Old Sodbury, there was an extensive garden where, one summer evening, John and I sat in the long twilight, while swallows flicked and darted in the air above, and children ran about and played cricket on the lawn, under the eyes of their parents.

At a little pub in Staffordshire, where a collection of potted plants covered shelves, tables and counter, even extending to the hearth, on which more plants grew out of old boots enamelled white, and where the windows stood open to a garden bright with peonies, we were entertained by an overheard conversation. A pretty young woman was telling a group of friends about a fancy dress ball she had attended. Four "blokes", she said, had gone dressed as undertakers, with top hats and black gloves, and carrying a coffin with dummy feet sticking out at the end. They were unable to take a taxi because the coffin would not fit in, so they were obliged to walk to the ball carrying it on their shoulders. Her description of how old ladies collapsed in hysterics and strong men fainted as they passed lost nothing by her North Country accent.

One evening we were at a rather smart pub on an Essex river, patronized largely by yachtsmen and fishing enthusiasts, when suddenly the babble of conversation was broken as a group of people in evening dress burst in excitedly to say they were on a treasure-hunt, and hoped local people who knew the district better than they did might help them. Their clue was a mythical sea-creature. The whole company gathered around, trying to think of a pub, a house or a street with Neptune or Triton in the name; then someone remembered there was a Mermaid Antique Shop not far away; with laughter and thanks they went hurtling off on their quest.

Once we saw an incident which could have happened nowhere but in England. A man with a white miniature poodle came into a pub and ordered two Guinnesses, then proceeded to drink one and feed the other to the dog by dipping his fingers in it and holding them out to be licked. Nobody took the slightest notice and as a matter of fact it would hardly be considered eccentric behaviour in a country where dogs are worshipped, where they are taken into restaurants and sometimes even pushed around in prams.

Though the Chequers Inn yard was listed as a camping place, we had the impression not many caravans used it, and our arrival was an unusual event; for the innkeeper and his wife treated us as very special guests, fussing about us, and asking what they could do to make us more comfortable, their little daughter stood by with big wondering eyes, watching all we did, and asking questions, and a half-grown collie dog dashed about energetically barking and getting under our feet as we made camp. Even the rooster in the fowlhouse caught the atmosphere of excitement and crowed madly. Later in the evening when John and I went over to the inn for a glass of cider we found the bar had a homely, family atmosphere. A youth and a little girl of about ten played darts, a middle-aged couple and a younger couple with a pretty, red-haired baby sat talking, while the baby toddled about the room on chubby, unsteady little legs and was fed potato crisps by her father.

King's Lynn has existed for centuries in constant conflict with water, a conflict in which the town seems to be the victor. In spite of floods—successive high-water marks are recorded by plaques on the wall of St Margaret's church—this ancient port on the Ouse has a solidity that seems to suggest no inundation could affect it very much, and there are still a surprising number of antique buildings, solidly constructed to withstand whatever might come.

D

After we had visited the Tudor Guildhall, with its curious checkerboard front, the old Customs House, and the graceful Merchants' House with its observation tower, we wanted to do some shopping, but it was early closing day and none of the shops were open. While we were hesitating, wondering what to do next, an elderly man with a hearing aid came along the street.

"No shops open today," he said. "Early closing. It wasn't like that in my day—we really worked then. A butcher, I was, for fifty years; in a shop just round the corner there. Times have changed now—people don't work any more. Do you know, we did our own killing then: we started at daylight, and we never closed the shop till midnight. When I was a boy most of the business was done after eleven at night—people came in on their way home from work for fourpenny pieces—lovely meat it was, better than your rump steak now! Only fourpence. Yes, fourpenny pieces. No refrigerators then, either. Oh, but you don't get the good meat any more. Your modern stuff wouldn't keep like that if you didn't have a frig." And shaking his head over a decadent age, he shuffled on.

At this point it began to rain: we looked about for shelter, and, more to get under cover than for any other reason, we made for the Art Gallery and Museum. It proved to be rather an oddity, which charmed with its quaint artlessness. The building, erected in the nineteenth century in Victorian Gothic as a church for a now defunct sect, later became a gallery, without losing its ecclesiastic appearance. The collection was the oddest jumble imaginable—farm implements and fossils mixed up with snuff boxes and stuffed birds; medieval pilgrim badges and a blue enamel and pearl watch which had belonged to Fanny Burney, who was born in King's Lynn. Quite the strangest exhibit was a ship's biscuit which a sailor gave his sweetheart in 1830! Among the pictures, a Canaletto, an Alfred Munnings, and for the rest, local views by local people of varying degrees of competence.

During our first few months in England John had made several visits to Cambridge, and had come to know the university town fairly well, but the rest of us had not seen it; so there we went, travelling across the flat Norfolk countryside by way of the Isle of Ely, just glimpsing the octagonal tower of the Cathedral in passing.

Cambridge was a riot of roses—in all the college courts, everywhere, in every imaginable colour; deep sulphur yellow and purple as well as pink or red; shot or streaked, huge single blooms or miniatures in clusters. John had seized the opportunity of a quiet day alone in the caravan to work, and the children and I spent the day in the city. I found much that was impressive, particularly the round church of the Holy Sepulchre, with its endearing jumble of styles, and the incomparable fan-vaulting and stained glass of the King's College Chapel. We spent a considerable time in the Fitzwilliam Gallery, where Nicky covered me with embarrassment. Leaning over a case to look at some priceless exhibits, he dropped a florin on the top of it. The coin hit the glass with a ringing clang which in the hush sounded appalling; the few people moving about in reverent silence all jumped and turned to see what had happened; and an attendant, relaxed in a chair leaped up as if shot. No damage was done, fortunately, and I sharply told Nicky to keep his money in his pocket. As with a very shamefaced Nicky we continued our promenade, I was uncomfortably conscious that wherever we went the attendant seemed close behind. Quite sure he suspected us of having designs on some of the works of art, I was on the point of taking my unruly brood away, when he came up to us and addressed the boys, "There's a lot of armour downstairs. You'd like that, wouldn't you? Yes, I thought so—most boys do. When you've finished here you might go down; it's very interesting." With a friendly nod and a smile he left us, and I sighed with relief.

Our caravan was parked in a suburb of Cambridge which sounds like a girl's name—Cherry Hinton. Here John had been working all day, and he felt a need to get out for a while, so after dinner he and I decided to go for a walk and perhaps visit the local pub. We told the children we would not be long. Nicky looked up from his book to say in a loud voice:

"Godfrey, don't you hint to them about bringing us back potato crisps!"

Who could resist so delicate a plea?

In Essex we spent a week-end at Hullbridge, on the River Crouch, a very popular place for boating. Here the caravan park was occupied for the most part by permanent residents; and they spared themselves no trouble to make their caravan homes look like houses. Each sported a television aerial: pot plants and statuettes stood in windows, and house-names adorned doors: some were surrounded by picket fences, inside which were

41

miniature flower-gardens with masses of roses, garden furniture, and sometimes even fish-ponds complete with plaster gnomes and rabbits. We had the impression there was a certain amount of rivalry and keeping up with the Joneses; but there was a very happy atmosphere about the place. Everybody was interested in boats, and that week-end a regatta was being held. There was a playground with swings and see-saws, and Godfrey and Nicky told us they enjoyed it because all the other children were so friendly and eager to play with them. It was not very far to the popular seaside resort of Southend, and here one day Gerard took the younger children by bus. They returned with a black plaster cat which Gerard had won at hoop-la.

"It's the mascot of the Pussy Brigade," said Nicky, and placed it carefully on a shelf in the caravan. There it stayed for the rest of our travels, but was eventually broken on the ship coming home to New Zealand.

And so—back to London.

It was seven weeks since we had set out: by now London had put on her summer dress and was lovelier than ever. In all the parks flowers bloomed and people sat about in deck-chairs; the stone of the buildings glowed warmly in the sun; as we drove down Whitehall we caught the glint of helmets and flash of colour at the Horse Guards; in Trafalgar Square the fountains were playing and the tourists feeding pigeons wore bright summer clothes. It all gave one's spirits a lift, and my heart was full of affection for that enchanting, sprawling, dirty, loveable city. To make the cup full to overflowing, at the bank we found a huge pile of letters from home, the accumulation of weeks, including the children's Correspondence School lessons from New Zealand.

On such a long trip the children's education was a problem which could not be ignored. After the term they had spent at English schools there were eight months before we were to return to New Zealand—too long, we felt, to be without formal lessons. The New Zealand Correspondence School, which provides education for outback children in New Zealand, was very helpful, and agreed to supply the necessary courses, although of course, owing to the distance and our constantly changing address it was not possible to send their work back for marking and criticism. However, this was not a serious matter. The seven weeks touring Britain, we had agreed, was to be their summer holiday—from now on they must study for part of each day.

Idleness had begun to pall on all of them, so the arrival of the big parcel of school material was hailed with delight, and when I supervised their lessons no teacher had more willing pupils.

After the discomfort of most English camp sites, the London one at Crystal Palace was a joy. For once, tents were permitted as well as caravans, and these gave the place a cheerful, holiday appearance. Best of all, there was hot water in plenty, showers, laundry and ironing-rooms, and shops. Although we did not know it at the time, it was a foretaste of Continental camping. The people were cosmopolitan, of every race and colour. The boys enjoyed identifying the plates on the cars.

"E—that's Spain; F—France; and look, there's a D—that's Germany."

For the first time we learned how easily children surmount language difficulties. Very quickly Godfrey and Nicky made friends all over the camp. They brought a Dutch boy to the caravan for tea; a pretty little Irish girl stopped by to say hullo in her attractive accent; and two dark-eyed, olive-skinned little boys from a caravan with plates in Arabic script played ball with them for hours. These children, I learned later, were from Tunisia. One evening Godfrey left their game and came running to me to say:

"Mummy, those boys asked me what I think of de Gaulle."

Apparently in North Africa even the very young are interested in politics.

"What did you say?" I asked.

"Oh, I just said I didn't know."

I was curious as to the language in which this exchange took place. There must be some kind of children's lingua franca that adults don't know.

One young girl we dubbed the Compulsive Washer. Never at any hour could one enter showers or laundry without finding her there. She seemed to spend her days taking showers and washing her hair and her clothes. I am quite sure she could have seen little of London but the camping ground. One day I got into conversation with her and she told me she was from Sweden. Rather hesitantly she asked, "Are you English?" When I said no, a New Zealander, she relaxed, and in her careful English went on, "Every summer I travel to a different country, and always I say, 'Some day I come back.' But England—no, never again!"

"Why?" I asked. "Don't you like England?"

"I can't keep clean," she wailed. "London is so dir-r-rty. My clothes—my hair—it's all so dirty!"

I understood, though by then I had come to accept it, but I remembered my first few days in London six months before when I had been unable to believe I would ever get used to the grit and grime; but acceptance soon comes. It is said white shoes and white gloves mark the foreigner—no real Londoner would dare wear them.

One evening there was a knock at the caravan door, and a cheery voice, said:

"My name is Smith—I'm from Hawkes Bay. I saw the Kiwi on your caravan and thought I'd introduce myself. Come over and meet my wife and little boy." We all passed a very pleasant evening in homeland gossip.

We spent four days in London, attending to business matters, making last-minute arrangements for our Continental tour, and seeing friends before our departure from England.

We were lunching with an old friend one day in the restaurant of a department store. We had not met for years, and there was a great deal to talk about. The waitress hovered about rather more than was necessary, and at last in a lull in the conversation addressed John.

"Excuse me, sir, are you a missionary?"

Rather bewildered, John said, "No. Why?" and she went on, "I heard you talking about overseas, and overseas for us means missionaries. My son is a missionary in Borneo, and I thought you might know him."

We were sorry to have to admit none of us had ever been to Borneo.

Very early one morning we headed south through Kent, on our way to Dover and the Channel ferry.

Nowhere but in England, on a main arterial motor-way, would one see a sign: "Caution. Children Playing". This oddity had been occasioned by what was at the time a minor *cause célèbre*. Gipsies had for years camped in Darenth Wood, in Kent, but not very long before had been evicted. In protest at losing their traditional ground they had made themselves as awkward as possible by squatting on the motor-way, and nobody had been able to move them. The matter had been taken up in Parliament, and one M.P., incensed at what he considered an injustice to a harmless minority, had moved in with them and announced that he would stay there until they were allowed to return, or found a suitable alternative place. So there they were, gathered around their camp-fire at the side of the road, their children playing on tricycles and pedal-cars in what looked like imminent danger of being mown down by passing traffic. Their caravans were drawn up on the grass verge, some modern motor-drawn caravans like our own, others the traditional painted gipsy wagon with a chimney, drawn by horses. One appeared to have been burnt out.

In Kent we were on familiar ground, for we had come to know it well in our first few months in England; but now it was summer. The cherry orchards we had last seen in blossom were laden with fruit, and the hop-vines had grown high. The oast-houses and farms were as picturesque as ever.

We stayed two nights at Dover, which gave us time to spring-clean the caravan, to take the washing to a laundrette, and to stock up with food in case we found ourselves unable to do so after our arrival, for we were not sure what conditions would be at our first stopping-place on the Continent. We also visited historic Dover Castle, and explored the town and country round about, before embarking, very early in the morning, on the Channel car ferry. It was a grey, drizzly day, but the weather did not damp our spirits. As we watched the white cliffs—which really are white—receding behind us we were filled with excitement and anticipation of the adventure ahead of us.

Chapter VI

"DADDY," asked Nicky, "how do you say Pussy Brigade in French?"

"Brigade des Poussiquettes, I suppose," replied John.

We were standing on the deck, watching through the drizzle for the first glimpse of France. At first there was just sea and sky, and then we saw a sandy beach lined with gaily painted sheds, which even in the rain looked welcoming. No doubt on a fine day there would have been crowds of holiday makers. Then Calais, and the bustle of disembarkation. We drove off the ship into a strange town where people drive on the right, and at the first intersection almost collided with a rubbish truck, which, in what we later learned was the French manner, shot without warning from a side-street. The French dustmen, in their berets and blue blouses, obviously accustomed in that place to queer foreigners who drive on the wrong side of the road, thought it was a huge joke, and roared with laughter, one of them shaking a reproving finger at us as they passed.

Out into the country, and I was quite irrationally surprised and delighted to find that France looked so French. The men and women working in the fields, using horses and hand tools rather than farm machinery, might have come from Millet paintings. The names of the little cobbled towns through which we passed were all reminders of World War I, as were the scarlet poppies which starred the fields. Just outside Armentières we had a puncture and had to stop while John and Gerard, under the politely curious gaze of several young mothers and toddlers, changed the wheel. Then on again to Lille.

Lille—a pleasant, attractive enough city, no doubt, but for us it was a headache. It is easy enough to read a map in the country; even in a city it looks simple; but the trouble was the maps we had did not show one-way streets. As we bumped and rumbled over the cobblestones, along the broad Boulevard Louis XIV, through squares and streets, each time we thought we should turn a No Entry sign blocked the way. Round and round, and no way out. Hampton Court maze we had found

46

child's play, but Lille was a real puzzle. In heavy traffic one cannot stop and ask the way, one must just watch the signs. But street-names were no help, and there were no finger-posts pointing to Brussels. We turned past a café, tables and chairs on the pavement, and a gendarme with his high peaked cap standing on the corner. He watched us pass with interest, for a car towing a large caravan with K I W I along its sides must have been very conspicuous in the middle of a busy city. Around another corner—and another—and we found ourselves turning the same corner again, going in the same direction, the gendarme still standing there whistling. He glanced at us casually at first, then started and stared; open-mouthed with astonishment he pivoted slowly, watching us down the street. We all burst out laughing.

"He probably thinks we're advertising boot polish," I said.

"I don't care what he thinks—how on earth do we get out of this town?" muttered John.

"Trapped in Lille," said Gerard. "Round and round until we starve—or run out of petrol!"

"That's what I'm afraid of," said John. "If we did we couldn't pay for more."

We had not changed our British currency for French at Calais because we intended going straight through to Belgium, so we did not want to incur any expenditure in France.

Lille was a busy town, and cobblestones, heavy traffic, and towing a large caravan, all on his first day driving on the right, meant it was not exactly a joy-ride for John. It seemed we had been circling for hours, though it was probably not so very long, and then at last, on our fourth trip up the Boulevard, we decided to try a new tactic. Instead of following what *seemed* to be the road out of the city, we deliberately turned what *seemed* the wrong way, and, at last, there we were on the motor-way, headed towards the Belgian border. At the frontier we changed our money, and on to Tournai.

"We've been in three countries in one day," boasted Godfrey. "You don't do that very often."

At Tournai the camping was in a park close under the old city wall, near a canal, where shipping went up and down. There was no office and no caretaker, and we were at a loss as to where we should register and whom we should pay, but a Frenchman camping there told us just to go in and park, the ground was under police supervision. This, we learned, meant that each evening two gendarmes came to check passports and collect money. At the time, we thought this must be the usual Continental custom, but as a matter of fact we never again experienced such an arrangement. "Campings" may be privately owned or municipal, but in either case there is usually an office and someone in charge to accept registrations. Prices vary from camping to camping, the better equipped ones usually charging more than the others; prices being calculated as so much per vehicle, per tent and per person. We did not ever find them very expensive, and later, when we came to check up expenditure, we found that the cost of camping grounds had averaged out at about twelve shillings a day for our whole party.

The next day, on towards Brussels. All went well as we bowled merrily along through the sunlit country, past comfortable looking homes, each with a little shrine in a niche on the front wall.

"The Little Man must be resting today," said John. "He's tired after that masterpiece in Lille."

As we passed out of French-speaking Hainault into Brabant, Miriam, who had been teaching herself Dutch, suddenly exclaimed in surprise:

"Do you know what? I can read the signs. I didn't know they spoke Dutch in Belgium!"

"They don't," said John. "It's Flemish."

"Well, I can read it. It's like Dutch."

Far sooner than we expected we found ourselves on the outskirts of Brussels. We circled the city, catching brief and tantalizing glimpses in passing, then out into the country again, to Grimbergen, where we were to camp. It was a little town of narrow streets and substantial houses, clustered around the great Abbey church, which watched over them like a hen with her chickens.

We liked the camping as soon as we saw it—brightly-coloured tents and caravans among cherry- and pear-trees laden with unripe fruit, with wheatfields beyond—and were delighted to find there a recreation room, showers and laundry tubs. At once I swooped about the caravan gathering up any soiled clothing I could find, while John went off to cash travellers' cheques and buy food, and, the next day being Godfrey's birthday, the other three set off to buy him presents. The town was Flemish-speaking, and John had difficulty finding a shop where they spoke French—or admitted to speaking it—but the children came back well satisfied with their purchases, having apparently managed successfully. Perhaps Miriam's Dutch helped.

At the camping a sign said—in five languages—that children must not run about or play ball, but that there was a playground in the Abbey grounds. To us, coming from England, and remembering Canterbury, Glastonbury and other places, "abbey grounds" suggested a field with ruins. How different was the reality! No ruined abbey here—this one was very much alive. We passed through an archway in a long stone wall, and what a happy scene greeted us!

The Abbey buildings surrounded a sunny quadrangle, dotted with flower-beds, and crowded with children—sturdy, well-dressed, well-cared-for children—playing on swings and see-saws, or just running about, while their parents sat at little tables in the sun, eating ice-cream or drinking beer. An elderly monk, wearing a smock over his habit, and smoking a big cigar, walked about supervising the children.

John and I strolled over to the bar, where a group of monks were dispensing the beer, and found that only one of them spoke French. In answer to John's questions he told us they were selling Grimbergen beer, served in special Grimbergen glasses—tall, stemmed glasses with the Grimbergen crest. The Abbey did not actually brew it, but had the sole rights to sell it.

We bought two foaming glasses, and took them to a table in the sun. The beer was very dark, sweet and heavy, tasting like pumpernickel. We felt at peace with the world, sitting in the sun, sipping the beer and watching the children. All the town seemed to have gathered there to gossip and relax. At the next table a young mother rocked her baby with one hand, ate ice-cream with the other, and chatted animatedly all the time to her husband, who spoke little, merely nodding from time to time. There were loud shrieks from a little boy who had fallen and hurt his knees. From somewhere in the Abbey a basin and towels were brought, and the dirt washed off to show no injury at all. His tears instantly stopped, and he ran off again to play. A little girl with flying dark curls climbed to the top of a slide, and shouted in Flemish to another child, who replied in French.

"The children seem to understand each other," I remarked.

"But a lot of the adults don't speak French," said John. "It's Flemish in most of the shops."

"What happens? Is this generation more bilingual than the

49

last, or have all Belgians talked together as children and forgotten later?"

"Perhaps they only pretend not to understand—a matter of regional pride."

Whatever the explanation, here in the Abbey grounds, Fleming or Walloon, it was all one to the children. The monk with a cigar suddenly blew a whistle. All the children stopped playing and turned to him, while he reprimanded a bigger boy for getting on a swing meant for babies. The culprit shamefacedly got down, and the games went on as before.

My thoughts went back to Glastonbury and Canterbury. Once they, too, must have been like this, the heart and centre of their communities, providing recreation and hospitality as well as education and spiritual care for the people. The Middle Ages seemed very close, and I remembered again with approval Nicky's remark, "Rotten ol' Henry the Eighth."

On Godfrey's twelfth birthday we went to Brussels for the day, bumping in the car over cobblestones and tramlines all the eight miles from Grimbergen. It was a beautiful warm, summer day, and we were all in a holiday mood, ready to enjoy everything the city had to offer.

Brussels has an air of order and grace that is very pleasing. Every street seems a carefully designed vista that carries the eye forward to some imposing baroque building, with everywhere a wealth of chubby, smiling stone cherubs. Never before had I seen so many at once, and of course, pride of place in this stone nursery goes to Brussels' "best-loved citizen", the famous Manneken-Pis. The people of Brussels delight in him and want others to share their pleasure—in fact, they take it for granted it is he visitors have come to see. One has only to stop and consult a street map for some helpful citizen to come up—"Manneken-Pis?"—and point out the way. He is always the focus of a dozen tourists' cameras. He is a charming little fellow—no mother could fail to see in him her own little son, and to my mind his robust baby innocence is far less offensive than the more usual type of fountain, with water pouring from nose or mouth. If he had been in England the Victorian age would have seen him destroyed, but the Belgians are more realistic about the bodily functions, and instead of hiding him away as something shameful they make a pet of him, and provide him with a wardrobe of uniforms to wear on festal days. After their first gasp of shocked surprise, Godfrey and Nicky were enchanted by him, and it was astonishing how frequently for the rest of the day his name was dragged into the conversation, doubtless on the principle that chances to use a forbidden word with impunity come all too rarely to be missed.

I found it hard to tear myself away from the shops selling real Brussels lace. I wanted to go completely crazy and buy all in sight, but it was expensive, and besides, I asked myself, where could I put it in the caravan?

In the cobbled expanse of the Grande Place the flower-sellers' stands made brilliant splashes of colour; the sun gleamed on the gilded façades of the quaint old buildings, and on the spire of the Hotel de Ville, the winged, golden St Michael, poised high against the pale blue sky, watched over his city. I think Brussels must look its best in summer. Lunch at a sidewalk café, then on we went to the Royal Palace, in time to see the changing of the guard; and how pleasant it was, after so much walking in the hot sunshine, to go into the cool green shade of the gardens opposite the Palace, and sit for a while contemplating the statues and trees, and small boys sailing boats in the fountains.

Next, to the Cathedral, cool and dim after the sunlight. Here for the first time we encountered a device used quite widely in Europe—a mechanical guide. By dropping a coin in a slot and pressing the appropriate button the visitor can hear a recorded description of the Cathedral in one of several languages. It makes sight-seeing very easy. "Turn to your left and you will see the beautiful Renaissance window, and note that the stone tracery dividing the window into two halves is pierced, so that a ray of sunlight will fall on a brass rod set in the floor exactly at noon throughout the year." All heads turn and nod slightly in unison. It is true. The hole in the tracery can be seen, and if the shaft of light does not now fall on the bar, we accept that it did an hour ago, at noon. "Observe the magnificent baroque pulpit." That fantastic baroque pulpit. Of all we saw in Brussels Cathedral that is what remains most vividly in my mind—a masterpiece of wood-carving, all twisting and twining foliage, tree-trunks, animals and birds in a wild profusion, about Adam and Eve, being driven out by the angel, while the grinning skull of Death looks on, and above Our Lady holds the Infant Jesus, her foot on the head of the serpent.

Out of dimness into sun-dazzle, and then, a sharp contrast. From the Cathedral, dating back to Charlemagne, hallowed by centuries of worship, to the Atomium, as modern as tomorrow. This strange, gleaming structure, built for the World Fair, looks like nothing so much as a Martian from Wells's *War of the Worlds.* The likeness is almost terrifyingly apt at close quarters; at a distance, its science-fiction head seen peering over the trees, it is even more like a monster just landed from outer space.

Back we went in the evening to Grimbergen and the caravan, and for a peaceful hour or so listened to the Abbey carillon spilling its sweet, gentle melodies over the quiet countryside, reminding us that Belgium is a land of bells. Godfrey looked up from writing in his diary to say, "This is the best birthday I've ever had."

"I'm glad you've enjoyed it, but now it's time for bed."

Godfrey and Nicky were in a playful mood. It took a good deal of firmness to get them into their tent, and even then there were giggles and chatter, sounds of scuffling and bumps against the fabric.

"Quiet, you boys. Go to sleep!"

Dead silence for all of three seconds, and then smothered giggles and more scuffling. To exhausted parents it was only mild consolation to know we were not the only harassed ones. From another tent some yards away came similar sounds, and suddenly we heard an English voice explode:

"For God's sake, you kids—*shut up!*"

We smiled wryly. Other people's children behave no better. "They're a bit over-excited," I said. "It's been a big day."

"I suppose they'll remember all this," said John.

"Of course they will. They're old enough to get a great deal out of travel. I'm sure it will be of enormous value to them."

Wearily, I started to tidy the caravan. Godfrey's diary lay open, face up on the floor where he dropped it. I picked it up, and saw the entry for the day, evidence of the cultural value of travel.

"My birthday. Got some presents. Saw the Manneken-Pis."

By the time we left Grimbergen the weather had changed, and it was in heavy rain that we arrived at Antwerp. The camping was on the River Scheldt at St Annaplage, which had the slightly sad aspect of all beach resorts in the rain—cafés with umbrellas furled and chairs stacked out of the wet; souvenir and "fritten" (potato chip) stalls open but doing little business; the only sign of life youngsters twisting to a juke-box in the shelter of a bar.

We had not been there very long when a young man came over and introduced himself as a New Zealander, and he proved to be the son of an Auckland acquaintance. He told us he had been abroad eighteen months, and had met so many New Zealanders he was beginning to wonder if anybody was left at home! This was our experience also. For a country with a small population it is quite astonishing how ubiquitous Kiwis are: we found fellow-countrymen turn up in the most unexpected places.

Armed with a guide-book we set out to see the places of interest in Antwerp, but, finding ourselves outside a gallery with posters advertising an exhibition of the fantastic in seventeenth century Flemish art—"toegang frisj"—promptly abandoned our original plan, and spent a pleasurably gruesome afternoon among the gaping hell-mouths, the last judgments and the towers of Babel of Bosch and other artists of his school. It was extraordinary how often these same subjects occurred, and I was interested to notice they appeared again in the stone carving round the doors of the Cathedral.

Chapter VII

I WAS doing the washing at the Rotterdam camping, one of a row of women campers standing at tubs. As it was our first Dutch camp I was not sure what the practice was, and tried to ask the German woman next to me whether it was permitted to hang out laundry, but she did not understand English. I tried my elementary French with no more success, so turned to the Dutch woman on my other side, but she did not speak English either. Next I tried to ask a man who was mopping the floor, and though he did not speak English he understood my signs, and indicated I could hang it where I wished. Then, pointing to me, he asked "English?" I replied, "New Zealand", and his face lit up. "Ah, ja. Nieuw Zeeland—na Australie." A pause, then, "Emigra-at."

"Ja," I said. "Emigrate to New Zealand", and we stood beaming at each other. I still did not know whether he intended to emigrate to New Zealand, had friends who had done so, or simply knew of New Zealand as a place to which people did emigrate, but to a certain extent we had succeeded in communicating, and were well pleased with ourselves.

During the time we were in the Netherlands this was the only occasion on which I met with any language difficulty. The old fairy-tale about English being all that is necessary on the Continent is simply not true in most countries. It may be possible to get by completely in English if one stays at hotels that cater for tourists, it may be possible to find English speakers in the main European cities; but it was our experience over several months in the by-ways and smaller places that very few of the people speak any language but their own, and to get the most out of European travel one, or preferably two, extra languages are an enormous advantage. The only exception was the Netherlands, where we found almost everyone we met spoke English, many of them with no accent at all.

In this matter of languages we were not as well equipped as we should have liked to be, although perhaps better than many Antipodeans and Americans we met. John's French, although he would be the last to make claims to be a linguist, is reasonably

54

good; Gerard and Miriam's school French, small though it was, proved quite useful, and even I, though I learned it a long time ago and had forgotten most of it, was surprised to find that in a pinch I could usually dredge up the right French words. Miriam had been teaching herself Dutch, and I had for a year or so been learning Italian. Though none of us—except John—could really carry on much of a conversation in a language other than our own, we found we knew enough to shop, to order a meal and to ask the way. If the experience of travel had done nothing more for the children than to arouse their interest in languages I feel it would have been well worth while. It is all too easy for youngsters who never come into contact with people speaking tongues other than their own to dismiss the learning of languages as a dry academic study of no real value. But when they meet and make friends with children in other countries it all becomes vital and alive, and they find it has a purpose.

Gerard's first evening in Rotterdam was a case in point. While we were in Antwerp he had made friends with a Dutch boy of his own age named Harie, and they arranged to meet again in Rotterdam. We had scarcely arrived at the camping when Harie roared up on a motor-cycle and whisked Gerard off on a sightseeing tour. Gerard told us later they were headed towards the city when they saw a rather lost looking youth obviously trying to find his way, so they stopped and asked if they could help him. He did not speak Dutch or English, but Gerard tried his school French, and learned he was an Italian who also spoke French. He was looking for a student hostel, and Harie offered to take him there. They had scarcely left him when they met another lad looking for the same place, this time a Swede who spoke German, but not Dutch, English or French. They took him to the hostel, and for the third time headed towards the city, only to be stopped by still another boy—a German who could speak English. When they arrived at the hostel once more the woman who opened the door must have found the situation amusing, for she did not speak, she just stood there shaking with laughter, and the boys decided it was unusual enough to warrant a celebration, so they all went out to dinner together. There they were—five teenagers, a German, a Swede, an Italian, a Netherlander, a New Zealander; with about a dozen languages between them, but no two speaking exactly the same languages. It was, Gerard told us, an hilarious meal, the conversation carried on by a sort of chain translation round the table amid a great deal of laughter.

55

E

The camping at Rotterdam was well set out, with hedges planted to form bays, so that each tent or caravan could have a certain amount of privacy—if an unoccupied bay could be found. Late-comers had to be content with the open space in the middle. On the opposite side of the road, facing the camp gates, was what appeared to be a row of neat little bungalows. Actually they were house-boats moored on a canal, each with its little bridge to the front door, its letter-box, its curtained windows with flowers or ornaments on the sills, and its name above the door—"Donald Duck", "Notre Bonheur". It was in fact a suburban street, but the little homes rested on water instead of on earth.

We had not been there very long when a Dormobile pulled into the empty space next to us, and we found ourselves greeting the Smiths, the New Zealand family we had last met in London. After the usual remarks on such occasions about it being a small world, we discussed what was to be seen in Rotterdam, and they suggested we should all go the following day—Saturday—to Kinderdijk, to see the windmills. We were very glad they did, for Kinderdijk is unique, and we found it a fascinating experience.

It was a sunny day, and there was a strong wind. We walked along a dyke, on each side water covered with yellow water-lilies and reeds in which the breeze rustled and sang. Here and there along the dyke people sat fishing, and ahead were the windmills, more than twenty of them, their sails whirling around, making a picturesque frieze against the sky. Until then I had vaguely imagined—if I thought about it at all—that the Dutch windmills were used to grind flour, and it was a surprise to learn that the purpose of the Kinderdijk windmills was quite different. Built between 1738 and 1740, they were part of an ingenious scheme for draining the land; one round in the perpetual battle the Dutch must wage against the encroaching sea. The windmill operates a water-wheel, which in turn operates a sluice, which runs off the water. All but two of the mills are still occupied as dwellings.

We paid our money and went into one of the unoccupied mills, up dark, precarious ladders, round an enormous central wooden shaft and great cogged wheels, like a giant piece of wooden clockwork, making the whole building creak and shake with its rumbling movement, until we came to the topmost chamber, right under the thatch, where it was too low to stand, and we all had to squat on the floor. Here a young man explained the working of the mill, and showed how the brake could be operated.

Other parties kept coming up the ladder, till we were packed like sardines, and I was afraid somebody would fall through the unglazed window, across which the sails kept passing with a murderous "S-s-swish—s-s-swish—s-s-swish." But nothing untoward happened, and down we went again, and boarded a flat-bottomed boat, hauled across the reedy water on a rope, to visit another mill. This one was occupied. Everywhere were evidences of family life—tools propped up outside the door, a fresh-caught fish in a basin on a table; on the upper floors washing spread to dry, cupboard beds, wooden shoes in a row. Despite the fact that visitors were invited to inspect the mill, one felt an intruder in a stranger's home, and I for one was not sorry to escape outside, to stand in the windy sunlight watching the water boiling and foaming through the sluice, to listen to its bubbling, the swish of the sails, the singing of the reeds. Before we left we were shown a stork's nest with young ones in it.

Rotterdam suffered severely in the war. Bombing completely razed the heart of the city, leaving intact only the historic Stadthuis, which now stands like an antique jewel in a modern setting. The rebuilt heart of Rotterdam is a perfect example of how imagination can create a shopping district that is a thing of beauty and also good for business: in such surroundings one's money is almost charmed out of one's pocket. So successful has it been that many new towns in other parts of the world have been modelled on it. There are no roadways or traffic: instead, parking places on the periphery, and in the centre itself broad flagged pavements where shoppers can stroll at will among flower-beds, statues, fountains and cages of singing birds, looking at shops gay with hanging flower-baskets. It is possible to take one's time, without fear of being mown down by cars; there are no petrol fumes and no noise save the song of the birds and the voices of passing people. In the evening when the shops are closed it is still a pleasant place to stroll. The cafés are open, and there is music, and a surprising array of goods to be had from vending machines, including fresh bouquets. No well-bred Dutchman would visit friends without taking flowers to his hostess, so this particular machine must meet a need. We noticed, passing it early in the evening, that it was full; but an hour or so later all the flowers were gone.

I had the impression that the Dutch, more than other European peoples, still vividly remember the war. In other countries we visited there seems to be a tacit understanding that it happened a long time ago and is best forgotten, or at least not talked about. But to the Dutch the memory of those days is still green, and linked with a justifiable pride in their country's magnificent recovery from its wounds—a recovery symbolized in Rotterdam by two impressive groups of statuary—one, the famous representation of Rotterdam destroyed at the heart as an agonized man with a hole through his body; the other a monumental group of man, woman and child commemorating the sufferings of the civilian population.

We left Rotterdam in style—with a motor-cycle escort! It was Sunday, and, much to the disapproval of the camping management, who did not like the noise of motor-cycles, Harie and his friends arrived to say good-bye to Gerard. When we were ready to roll, the boys fell in in formation and accompanied us for the first few kilometres on the road to the Hague.

The distance from Rotterdam to Amsterdam by the shortest way is not very great, but we followed a roundabout route

through the Hague and then through Haarlem, because we wanted to see the tulip fields—not that it was the season for tulips, but at least we would see where they grew. There was really nothing much to see; just bare fields, thousands of glass-houses, and once or twice fields of yellow and purple pansies, or the big, bright-coloured scentless freesias, which to me seemed so inferior to the exquisite little sweet-smelling ones. On every side was country as flat as a plate, here and there a windmill, a group of houses or a clump of trees to break the monotony, and always, canals. Once we saw a quite large ship steaming through the countryside, and once we had to wait at a bridge which had opened to let boats through.

We did not often lose our way during our travels, but each time we did the mistake occurred in a town. In the open country roads are signposted, and it is not difficult to follow a map, but in towns where there are many streets and intersections it is easy to take a wrong turning, and get on to the wrong road. It was while passing through a small town that this happened to us; we found ourselves on a dyke, a road raised above the land and going straight on for miles in the wrong direction, with no place to turn. On and on and on, till we began to think we would run right out of the Netherlands, and never reach Amsterdam at all; but at last we saw petrol pumps ahead, and pulled in and around them to turn. We didn't need petrol, but I did feel some sympathy for the woman who ran out to serve us with a beaming smile which turned to a scowl as she saw us careering back the way we had come.

The camping at Amsterdam was reached by a little drawbridge over a ditch. To Godfrey and Nicky this was the height of romance. They saw the camping as a beleaguered castle, and waited impatiently for sunset, convinced there would be a ceremonial parade when the drawbridge would be raised and the flag flying from a mast in the grounds lowered: but in this they were disappointed. Nothing happened. My pleasure in the Amsterdam camping was a more mundane one—there was a washing machine, so my usual chore was lightened.

When we registered at the office we were handed the printed camp rules, and were rather dismayed at their restrictiveness—no radios, no dogs, no playing ball, no traffic to drive in after 10.30 p.m.—"It couldn't, the drawbridge would be up," said Godfrey. It all sounded a little grim; but as the day wore on we saw all the rules broken. No dogs—but several people proudly walked huge animals about; no radios—but while we obediently kept our transistor switched off we could hear three others, all on different stations. No ball games—but a party of German tourists played a perpetual game of football which was far more entertaining to watch than any Test match.

Most of the players were middle-aged, and all were extremely stout, especially the women, who wore abbreviated sun-suits displaying vast expanses of thigh and upper arm. They bounced about after the ball surprisingly lightly, but one woman, a jolly, laughing blonde of enormous proportions, could not kick the ball without falling flat on her back. Each time this happened she lay there shrieking with mirth, unable to rise, amid the good-natured banter and jeers of her team-mates, until two of them helped her up. Even when the ball shot into their tent and upset a pot cooking on a stove, nobody seemed to care—it was only an occasion for more laughter.

The ten-thirty rule was not observed either, for cars drove in and out all night.

The chief impression I had of Amsterdam was of cleanliness. Along the tree-lined canals the tall narrow houses with their stepped or twirled gables had a well-scrubbed look: even the air felt clean, in spite of the heavy flow of traffic in the streets.

The canal system of Amsterdam is shaped like a giant spider's web: three concentric circular canals, and other straight canals crossing them. With streets superimposed on this the result is innumerable bridges, how many it would be difficult to say. I have been told various numbers, ranging from three hundred to eight hundred, and should not care to estimate which is correct. Land in Holland is precious: not too much can be wasted on urban sprawl, so houses are narrow and high, and thousands of people live in house-boats on the canals. There is even a house-boat church, where we were amused to see a mother duck and her brood waddling up the gangway to the door, for all the world like a respectable Dutch family going to church. Flower-sellers' barges were laden with pink and red carnations, their spicy scent filling the air.

John had picked up a few Dutch words and phrases, and he mixed them with English in a queer, macaronic jargon. "Let oop," he would say, crossing the road, "Let oop, or bussen mashen", or "Let oop—weilrijders!" One must always watch out for weilrijders. There must be more cyclists per head of population in Holland than in any other country in the world, and they manage to carry fantastic loads. Workmen pedal along wearing wooden shoes, and balancing ladders, sheets of glass and bags of tools; mothers with as many as two children in front and a third behind, as well as a couple of laden shopping baskets; sometimes whole families, the older children on small cycles, father with a couple of toddlers, mother with a baby. We began to think the roads were meant for cyclists and motor transport was there on sufferance. Here and there among the crowds of shoppers we glimpsed women and girls wearing picturesque Dutch costume, or passed the old-fashioned barrel-organs, quaintly ornate, with jerky little mechanical figures that struck bells and gongs while the organ-grinder turned the handle and the music tinkled out.

Tired and hungry after walking about the city, we went to a restaurant near the Royal Palace, where we had huge plates of nasi goreng topped with fried eggs, piled so high even my ravenous sons could not eat it all, followed by enormous cream puffs, coffee for the adults and orange juice for the children, and costing less than a pound for the six of us.

"When we get back to the camp," said John, driving out of the city, "the Smiths will be in that space where a caravan pulled out this morning."

And sure enough, his premonition was correct, for, as we drove over the drawbridge we saw a Dormobile and three figures beside it laughing and waving.

"We saw your caravan," called Mrs Smith, "so we knew you were here."

That is part of the fun of caravan touring—one meets people, makes friends with them, parts from them, then meets them again in another place. Later, we were to meet an Australian couple, Mr and Mrs B., six times in different parts of Austria and Italy. There is a camaraderie among campers which makes for a great deal of friendliness and helpfulness to others. If one party finds a good camping, or a place where there is beautiful scenery or something of particular interest they will tell others about it, or they will warn them of bad roads or unsatisfactory camping sites. Several times we benefited from information given us in this way by other caravanners, and I hope we too were sometimes helpful in our turn. Apart from tourists like us making long trips through Europe, many caravanners in summer are people from the various European countries spending a couple of weeks' annual holiday, either abroad or in their homeland; and Caravan Clubs hold rallies for their members when they all gather at a particular place.

That summer the British Caravan Club held a rally in Germany, and in Koblenz we met some of them on their way home. As we were club members, and flew the pennant, they came over and made themselves known. They had thoroughly enjoyed the rally, they said; each year they went and met friends made at previous rallies. When John rather mildly remarked that Continental campings were better appointed than English ones they laughed. "Why do you think we hold our rallies abroad?"

61

The day before we were to leave Amsterdam was Miriam's fourteenth birthday. For a day or two I had been rather concerned about her, for she seemed very depressed and answered all attempts at conversation in monosyllables. We were puzzled by this, because she was in the country which interested her most; Dutch friends in New Zealand had first aroused her interest in the Netherlands, and travelling on a Dutch ship had intensified it: she had been teaching herself the language and for the last six months had been eagerly talking about "when we go to Holland". Yet here she was, in Amsterdam on her birthday, with a doleful face and a listless manner. In an effort to cheer her up I asked her what she would like to do as a birthday treat, and she burst out, "Do we *have* to go tomorrow? All my life I've wanted to see Amsterdam, and now we're leaving, and I might never be here again!"

So that was it. I looked at John.

"I don't see why we shouldn't stay longer," he said. "We're in no hurry, and I'd like a rest from driving anyway."

It was true there was no hurry. Five glorious months stretched ahead before we must return to England: no trains to catch, no appointments to keep; we were free as air. So we stayed a little longer in Amsterdam, which delighted Miriam and gave us time for so much we might have missed.

On a sunny afternoon we took a boat trip on the canals, drifting beneath trees and graceful bridges past tall Dutch houses and churches and out into the Zuyder Zee, past the big graving docks full of ships under repair, around the port among big ships from all over the world; and back on the canals again. Throughout the trip four stout Dutch matrons in bright floral dresses, bent on a day's pleasure, shrieked at every little dip of the boat, then roared with laughter. Afterwards we drank iced lemonade on a terrace where red and purple and deep blue flowers spilled over the balustrade and dipped into the canal.

We spent a wonderful day at the Rijksmuseum, seeing the Dutch paintings; Vermeers, Rembrandts and Hals; where I delighted in the calm, quiet Dutch faces and the minutely observed costumes, and thrilled to the boisterous life and movement of the incomparable "Night Watch". Here Miriam disappeared, and we all went in different directions looking for her, losing two more children in the process. When we were almost in a state of panic she sauntered up, innocently surprised at such excitement. She had only been looking at the antique dolls' houses. She though we'd know.

Most moving of all was the Anne Frank house, now an International Youth Centre. We joined the queue of visitors to climb the steep stairs till we came to a room with a large bookcase which slid forward to reveal a door: up more stairs and we were in the secret place where the two Jewish families hid from the Gestapo, and where the young Anne kept her famous diary. It would be impossible not to be deeply touched by the pitiful little domestic relics that remain—the pencil marks on the wall where Mr Frank recorded the children's heights, the tiny primitive stove which could have given precious little heat in the bitter northern winter, the pictures Anne had pinned to the wall of the British Princesses Elizabeth and Margaret, film stars and fashions of the day. It was not difficult to imagine the plight of those eight people, huddled in darkness behind blacked-out windows, afraid to make a sound, in constant danger of discovery; and there was heart-ache in the thought of the misery, the suffering, the waste of it all.

But we could not stay in Amsterdam for ever. Miriam had had her wish, and must now be content with her souvenirs—a pair of wooden shoes and a doll in Dutch costume.

From Amsterdam we were going to Germany. It was a long drive, so we planned an early start. We were all up at the crack of dawn, and, breakfast over, had soon finished the usual routine of breaking camp—china carefully packed; folding table dismantled, polythene bags tied over the treacherous gas-lights, windows locked, everything put away in its proper cupboard, and all cupboard doors checked to be sure they would not fly open. (This was important. Once a carelessly-shut cupboard had swung open with the jolting en route and spilled its contents. On arrival, hot and tired, we had a gooey mess of flour, sugar and jam to clean from the floor.) The ice-box and waste-bucket were brought in from their places under the caravan, and finally, the gas-cylinder disconnected and placed carefully on the floor, exactly in the centre to keep the weight evenly distributed; then the legs were raised, the door locked, the caravan hitched to the car, and we were ready.

We said good-bye to the Smiths, and, since our routes now diverged and we were unlikely to meet again, exchanged addresses. Then we piled into the car in our usual formation;

Nicky, the smallest, in front between John and me, the other three in the back; and we all waved cheerily out the windows.

"Good-bye, good-bye. Look us up some time in New Zealand!"

John pressed the starter. Nothing happened. It seemed our early start was not to be—the car refused to budge. We all got out again.

"The car doesn't want to leave Amsterdam either," said Miriam.

John, Gerard, and Mr Smith got to work on the engine, trying to find out what was wrong, and time kept passing; we had lost the cool morning and now must travel in the heat of the day. At last they concluded the trouble was dirty plugs, cleaned them to the best of their ability, and got the car to go. And so, much later than we had intended, off on the road to Germany.

The flat polderland gave way to forest. Once we passed a family party sitting under the trees by the side of the road—the men in baggy trousers, the women with wide lace caps, full skirts and aprons, tiny children dressed like their mothers, with little wooden shoes. It was a charming picture, just momentarily glimpsed as we flashed past, then gone. Through Soestdijke, past the Royal Palace, with soldiers on guard at the gates, and on through the forest.

It became very hot in the car, and we were glad to stop and take the picnic lunch I had prepared into the forest. In the cool green shade we ate sandwiches and drank Thermos coffee, then John and I sat and rested while Gerard and Miriam explored and Godfrey and Nicky ran about playing Robin Hood. An hour or so went by. It was blissful to lie back, looking at green leaves and dappled sunlight and listening to the voices of the boys playing deeper in the woods. Not a soul about but ourselves: but we must push on, there was still a long way to go. We gathered up our lunch wrappings, called the children, and headed back towards the road. Then I saw a notice-board, and out of curiosity tried to read it.

"Is your Dutch dictionary handy, Miriam?"

She fished it out of her handbag, and with its help I laboriously deciphered the sign.

"No admittance to the forest between May and September."

It was July. Oh, well, too late to worry: and at least, as good Kiwis, we had been careful not to start a bushfire!

At Hengelo we stopped at a garage, had the plugs properly cleaned, and got oil and water; and the car seemed to appreciate the attention, for it leaped along.

And so on to the German frontier.

Chapter VIII

IT never ceased to surprise me that, with each frontier crossed, we found ourselves in a new country. What, after all, is a frontier but a thin line drawn on a map, a fence, perhaps, and a candy-striped barrier across a road? And yet, what worlds of difference. It is not just that there is a new language: the architecture, the people, the whole atmosphere changes. As if to emphasize this, almost the first person we saw in Germany was a young girl in dirndl and little apron, her long plaits of golden hair coiled round her head. She might have posed for a travel poster, so exactly did she resemble the popular image of a German mädchen.

We had come one hundred and thirty-six miles in the middle of a sunny July day: we were hot and sticky, tired and thirsty, so the sight of the camping at Lingen-on-Ems was coolly inviting—beside a tree-shaded river a sandy beach with crowds of people swimming, playing ball, eating ice-cream. It was a popular holiday place, but we were the only foreigners and nobody spoke English. However, John's few words of German and sign language were sufficient to register at the camping and to order bread and milk for the next morning. It took the children no time at all to be splashing about in the water, but John and I had first to buy food, so set out for the shops. Lingen-on-Ems proved to be a modern town except for a few old, fairy-tale houses carved and painted like the gingerbread house in *Hansel and Gretel,* which I found enchanting.

I was as nervous as an aspiring actor on a first night—my first attempt at marketing in a really foreign language. In Belgium I had had at least school French, in Holland English was understood, but in Germany—*why* hadn't I learned German? We walked up and down the street a couple of times while I plucked up courage, and studied the shop-windows, memorizing the names of those commodities that were labelled.

"Well, come on," urged John. "What do you want? We have to make a start sometime."

Taking my courage in both hands, I plunged into a butcher's

66

and shopped by the simple expedient of pointing at what I wanted. In the fruit-shop I carefully repeated what I had seen on the labels—tomaten, äpfel, kartoffeln—eine kilo of everything, that made it simple. In the window of the delicatessen were some delicious-looking filled rolls, conveniently ticketed "belagte Brötchen". Simple. "That will save cooking a meal tonight," I said, and went into the shop.

"Sechs belagte Brötchen, bitte."

The man smiled a little at my pronunciation, but he understood, corrected me gently, and, as he put the rolls in a bag asked, "Englisch?" "Ja," I said, because it was too difficult to explain, and anyway, I speak English. This was going well. Who said it was difficult to shop in German? But I hadn't finished yet. As we carried our parcels back to the car John remarked that the children might like cool drinks.

"Why not get them a bottle of orange cordial?" he suggested. He would.

There was nothing about orange cordial in the phrase-book—I did not know then that that peculiarly British drink is unknown on the Continent—but I did find orangeade, so I went into another shop and asked for that, giving it the English pronunciation. The girl did not understand. I tried again, this time pronouncing it the German way.

"Oranyard, bitte."

This time she understood, but was regretful.

"Nein. Limonade?"

"Ja, Limonade."

But what she produced was a small bottle of fizzy lemonade. I wanted cordial, to be diluted with water.

"Nein, mit Wasser."

She looked astounded, and turned to a second girl behind the counter. They both shrugged, then stood regarding me hopefully, wondering what other eccentric suggestions I might make.

"Orangeade mit Wasser," I began again, feverishly searching the shelves, trying to see what I wanted. I couldn't. Desperately, I tried pantomine. I pretended to pour a little from a bottle, shaped with my hands an imaginary jug, and pretented to pour water from it. I knew what I meant, but no one else did. The girl thought I wanted to drink the lemonade there, and fetched a bottle opener and a glass.

"Nein." I stopped her before she had opened it.

"Bier?" she suggested, holding up a bottle of beer.

"Nein, für Kinder."

"Ah, Kinder."

She disappeared, and in a few minutes returned with a bottle of milk.

"Nein."

It seemed hopeless. We stood gazing at each other helplessly. "When I get home," I resolved mentally, "I will never, never be anything but helpful to people who can't speak English."

I was about to give up in despair when another customer, a man, entered the shop.

"Please," I appealed to him, "do you speak English?"

"A few words," he said.

Thankfully, I began again.

"Please explain for me—I want orange drink, the kind you add water."

He looked puzzled for a moment, then his face cleared, and he spoke rapidly in German. Now all was plain. We beamed delightedly at each other, and the girl with a flourish reached for a shelf. It wasn't what I had asked for, but from the point of view of nutrition it was better. So on my first shopping expedition in Germany I bought a large can of concentrated orange juice, labelled, such are the ironies of history, "product of Israel".

Back to the caravan, and a refreshing dip in the river. The camping was filling up: more and more people kept arriving, a few family parties, in caravans, but for the most part, in twos or threes or bigger groups, sturdy, good-looking young boys and girls with packs on their backs; some on foot, some on bicycles or motor-scooters, many in Scout uniform. Soon all the places were filled, and we were reminded of the story we had been told of campers in Germany being wakened in the middle of the night: "Excuse me, if you will move your tent six millimetres to the right we'll fit in one more."

As evening came on the young people gathered at the camp café, drinking beer or Coca-cola, and singing. And how they sang! We took our drinks to a little table under the pines, and sat in the warm, scented darkness listening as they roared out song after song—including "Pack Up Your Troubles" sung in German. The Allied soldiers sang "Lilli Marlene": the enemy's songs are legitimate prizes of war.

"The Little Man in person," said John, disgustedly.

"I didn't know he was on the Continent," said Nicky.

Except for Lille, we had not met as much trouble on Continental roads as we had in England, and Nicky's theory was that the Little Man's Continental branch was managed by an apprentice who was not very clever at filling the road with obstructions. But here we were, some miles past Bremen, on a country road where extensive repairs were being carried out by

a large gang of workmen. For a considerable distance only one narrow lane was open for traffic travelling both ways, and right in front of us was a primitive farm-cart, drawn by an ancient, drowsy horse, and driven by an even more ancient man, sound asleep with the reins held loosely in his hands. The horse ambled along, stopped now and then to crop the grass by the side of the road, moved on a pace or two, stopped again, the driver completely oblivious: and we, stuck helplessly behind him, were unable to pass. A bit annoyed, John sounded the horn, but the old man's slumbers were too deep to be disturbed, and at last our exasperation turned to laughter. The workmen, in their red-and-white striped caps, leaned on their shovels and laughed, we sat in the car and laughed, and Dobbin continued his meal, moving on a little occasionally as the mood took him. Minutes slipped by. Why hurry, anyway? Perhaps Dobbin and his owner had the right attitude to life. Occasionally we progressed a yard. At least we were not going backwards. A couple of cars, coming the other way, drew up at the far end of the narrow stretch of road and waited. More minutes went by. A little further on. Dobbin was nearing the end of the single lane. Then, just as the road broadened again and we were about to pass him, the old man suddenly awoke, glanced back, and with a look of dismay, whipped up his horse. As we drove on we could still hear the laughter of the workmen behind us.

Otterstetter Lake camping was not listed in the official tourist guides, so, except for us, there were no foreigners there. At first glance it looked inviting—soft, fawn-coloured sand beneath pines, with tents and caravans dotted about, children playing, and through the trees a glimpse of the lake; but as we bumped slowly in over the sandy track my pleasure in it took a nose-dive, for a gang of loutish youths, and surprisingly, one old woman, surrounded and followed us. They stood in a rather menacing circle around us, gaping, as we made camp, and then, apparently deciding to enjoy the show in comfort, fetched chairs and sat drinking beer and staring intently. When, after we were settled, I went over to the camp store, they fell in behind me and followed; and as, stumbling over my few German words, I tried to do my shopping, they stood around guffawing and talking in German. I was able to understand enough (particularly from the frequent occurrence of the word "Englischer") to know that they were talking about me. It was not a very pleasant experience, but I told myself that every country has its "teddy boys", "bodgies", or whatever else they are called, and I did not let it prejudice me against Germany too much.

The proprietor of the camping, a big, elderly man with a great shock of upstanding white hair and wearing rather grubby shirtsleeves, addressed us in an odd mixture of German, French and Italian. When John replied in French he was overcome with astonishment. "An Englishman who speaks French! Wunderbar!" So much for the reputation of the English as linguists! He was, he told us, a Latvian, and he spoke seven languages, but English was not one of them. "If I could speak English I'd be a millionaire!" Thereafter, whenever he saw us he would boom in French, "The Englishman who speaks French! If I could speak English I'd be a millionaire!"

We never discovered why a knowledge of English would lead to financial success. Whatever the secret is, we have not found it.

Hamburg I did not like—big, bustling, noisy, and smelling unpleasantly of rubber, dust and petrol fumes. "It's the smell of money," John said, when I remarked on this. Certainly we found prices in Hamburg very high, and felt no inclination to shop, although the goods displayed in the stores were attractive. But the camping at Wilhelmsburg was a pleasant, well-equipped one, with a kitchen and coin-in-a-slot stoves, fortunately, since our bottled gas had run out. However, we were able to replenish it in the city.

Bottled gas comes in several different makes, all probably equally effective. We had started out using an English brand, which we found quite satisfactory, but were dismayed to learn, only a few days before crossing the Channel, that it was not on sale in other countries, so could not be replaced on the Continent. Therefore, while in London we took the opportunity to replace it with Gaz, which is readily available in most European countries, and we had the caravan connections altered accordingly. Usually we found a cylinder of Gaz, used for cooking and lighting, lasted two or three weeks, and, except in Austria, we never had any difficulty in replacing it.

We spent one night in Hamburg—a rather restless night, for trains kept passing across the nearby railway bridge over the Elbe—and, after a brief pause at a garage to have new spark plugs fitted to the car, headed north on the autobahn, through Lübeck and up to the Baltic coast.

Pelzenhaken was a place of soft, white sand, blue sea, and hundreds of blue and orange tents in the sunshine. Across the bay was East Germany, and all day long patrol-boats went up and down, but the throngs of holiday makers did not seem unduly perturbed about ideological differences. One man sat for hours with field-glasses trained on the hills opposite, but for the most part they seemed carefree as they swam, sunbathed, played battledore and shuttlecock, and carried out the usual German beach ritual of making sandpits. Each party digs a shallow circular pit, several feet across, piles up the sand about it to make a wall, which they decorate in elaborate patterns with shells and seaweed, including the name of their home-town written in pebbles, and then they sit or lie inside it to sunbathe, secluded from the world. Godfrey and Nicky flung themselves enthusiastically into the task of digging a pit for themselves. Like a couple of puppies excavating for bones they dug and scrabbled in the sand; inevitably their pit always collapsed, but when this happened they simply abandoned it, and moved on to try again elsewhere. Before long they had managed to churn up a considerable stretch of beach.

I was finding myself more and more irritated by my ignorance of German, and determined to learn as much as I could. I had bought a dictionary, and with its help tried to read every notice and sign that I saw: which was how I found out about the festival. While John was registering at the camp office I laboriously deciphered a poster on the wall. It advertised a European Festival of Folk-lore at Neustadt, lasting a week and

71

opening that very afternoon, and Neustadt was only a couple of miles away. We dashed back to the beach, collected the children, and drove up to see what promised to be an unusual spectacle.

Crowds thronged the little town, and there was an atmosphere of excitement and anticipation. In the cobbled square stands had been erected forming a kind of arena with a platform in the centre. A band was playing, and overhead the flags of the thirteen participating countries flapped in the bright sunshine. We took up a strategic position just by the opening between the stands where the performers would march into the arena, and waited for the procession to begin. We could not have had a better place. They passed within inches of us, each group led by its flag-bearer, all wearing national costume, some singing and dancing or playing musical instruments as they came—the Swiss team, the men shouldering their huge mountain horns and the women looking very fetching in lace caps shaped like butterflies or fans; the Norwegians with their striking embroideries; Bavarians and Austrians, Dutch and French; it was a brilliant and spectacular parade. Among the other countries the Hungarians stood out for the beauty of the girls and for their strangely oriental-looking costumes and elaborate head-dresses of flowers and ribbons; and quite the gayest party was the French—Provençal, almost all middle-aged, but singing and shouting as they came, and obviously enjoying every minute of it. Among this kaleidoscopic parade of colourful dress, we were curious to see what the British would wear. Scots or Welsh could have made a picturesque show, but we knew it was an English team, and in that company a country without a national costume of its own was at a disadvantage. However, when they came into view, marching behind the Union Jack, we saw that the English team had made a brave try—the girls in white blouses and full skirts of various brilliant colours, the men in white shirts, scarlet sleeveless waistcoats with brass buttons, and black trousers. As each team entered the band struck up an appropriate tune and the mayor welcomed them in their own language—quite a feat with so many languages! Then the performance began—and what a show it was! Swiss yodelling, Bavarian slapping dances, English folk-songs, flag-tossing; each item greeted with rapturous applause. It would not have been possible anywhere else in the world to see all these in one place.

Neustadt and Pelzenhaken (it was hard to tell where one

72

ended and the other began) were very friendly to us. The woman in the stationery shop where I bought a German-English dictionary and some exercise-books for the children, insisted on giving us rulers, rubbers, and some prints of modern paintings; and a man camping near us spoke not a word of English, but was eager to become acquainted, and spent a whole evening talking to John with the aid of dictionary, phrase-book and maps. Each pointed out his home-town on the map, and our German friend expressed great surprise at the distance we had come. Once he pointed across the bay at the green hills opposite and said, "East—West" and clapped his hands loudly together. It was a chillingly effective gesture. He kept repeating something we could not understand except for the words—in German— "seven thousand dead—bad", and pointing towards the beach. Discussing it afterwards we were puzzled as to what he had meant. John was inclined to think there might have been a big naval battle off the coast.

"I've never heard of a naval battle where there would be seven thousand dead," I said.

"We'd better not swim," said Miriam. "We'll be treading on skeletons." But five minutes afterwards she was happily splashing about in the water with our friend's daughter, a pretty little girl of thirteen.

Another much smaller girl attached herself to us, and when John and I went swimming insisted on coming with us, demanding that we race her. "Eins, zwei, drei," and off she went, splashing madly. Then we had to let her dive through our legs, or push her around on a lilo, or watch her dive, until we were quite exhausted; when we retired to the beach to sunbathe she came too, and, chattering endlessly in German, curled up on the sand beside us.

In the evening, as we strolled on the beach by starlight, we came on a family party who had strung up some Chinese lanterns and were sitting in deck-chairs listening to two tiny children, each holding a lantern, singing in piping little voices. The lanterns threw a rosy glow on angelic little faces and blonde curls—they might have been Berta Hummel cherubs.

Altogether, I had fallen in love with Pelzenhaken and these cheerful, friendly people, so the shock, when it came, was all the greater.

One evening we strolled along the beach further north than we had been before. Among the sand-dunes we came on a large gravelled space enclosed by a low stone wall and a gate, and in the middle a monument bearing two crosses and a Star of David and the inscription:

K-Z 7,000

Americans
Belgians
Canadians (and alphabetically more than a dozen
nationalities)
1933-45

A few vases of fresh flowers were before it.

Here were the seven thousand dead—not from the sea, but, we realized with horror, victims of Hitler's Reich. It was a mass grave, and this pleasant, friendly place had been a concentration camp. As we stood there an old woman shuffled up, pushed open the gate and stood before the monument with bowed head. She had the air of doing something she had done many times before, and I wondered were her family among the seven thousand.

Silent and subdued we continued our walk. Some of the brightness had gone from sea and sky. On the beach the sun-tanned youngsters still played with balls or shuttlecocks, their cries coming up to us softened in the evening air; family parties still strolled about or relaxed in deck-chairs. It was all the same, but it was changed. I found myself looking speculatively at anyone of middle-age or more. What were you doing then? Hitherto I had felt nothing but affection for these likeable people, seeing in the ugly war memorials in every town, the traces of bomb damage, the many pitiful maimed and disabled in the streets only the evidence of another country that had suffered in war; a fundamentally humane, decent people led astray by a few vicious leaders. Now my feelings became ambivalent. I still liked those about me, but where, I wondered, were the war criminals, the Gestapo, the sadistic concentration camp guards? They hadn't all died. No doubt they were still in Germany, living ordinary lives—and yet, remembering the crowded congregation who had sung so gloriously at Mass in the Neustadt church, and the soft-voiced priest whose sermon, we had picked up just enough German to know, was about love; looking at the jolly fathers playing with their children and good-naturedly letting themselves be buried in sand, it was hard to believe. I returned to the caravan confused and unhappy. We were to learn more of this place.

74

One more night at Hamburg did not endear the city to me any more than the first visit had done, but at least it was restful to arrive at a camping we already knew, and not to have to ask our way about it.

Always, approaching a new place, we had a slight feeling of apprehension as to whether the camping would be a pleasant one, and sometimes, at the sight of it, a sinking of heart; but no such disappointment marred our arrival at Blauer See. It had almost a calendar-picture prettiness—white swans glided about on a round blue lake, surrounded by white sand and pine-trees. Campers swam in the lake or paddled about in canoes, and the air was filled with the delicious mingled scents of new-mown grass and pines. Our spirits rose at the sight of it. But now we found ourselves in financial difficulties. After paying for the camping site and lunch we checked our money and found our total resources were one German mark, one Dutch guilder and twelve and sixpence in English money. This certainly would not go very far, but we had arranged for money to be remitted to Cook's in Hanover, about twenty miles away, so, after checking that we had enough petrol to get there, John and I set off, leaving the children to amuse themselves at the lake. We had no idea where to find Cook's, and not even enough German money to buy a street-map, so we were in a worried mood as we walked up and down the streets of Hanover.

"We'll have to ask the way," I said.

"The trouble with asking the way," said John, "is that it's so difficult to understand the answer, even if they understand our question."

"Look! An American flag on a building over there! There's bound to be someone who speaks English."

The building was Amerika Haus, and an English-speaking receptionist gave us clear instructions to get to Cook's; but when we arrived there at two o'clock we learned it did not open till three. Then, when we did get in, it was to be told they had no knowledge of any remittance, but they were holding some mail for us. Desperately worried, we sat down to read it, and found it included a letter from our bank saying that the money had been remitted, not to Cook's but to the Deutsche Bank in Hanover—and banks closed at three! Truly, Continental business hours are mysterious! Everything seemed to be conspiring against us: the children were twenty miles away with very little food in the caravan; we were not sure we had enough petrol to get back to them, no money, we knew very little German, and the bank had already closed! However, we walked around to the very impressive Deutsche Bank building and found that though the main doors were closed there was a smaller door still open, guarded by a uniformed commissionaire. He did not want to let us in, but we showed him the letter from our bank, which he could not read except for the words, Deutsche Bank, and reluctantly he admitted us. At last our troubles were over. We were treated very courteously, received our money, and returned to the street feeling lightheaded and giddy with relief.

"Come on," said John, "let's celebrate. We deserve it after that fright."

We made for a large bookshop we had seen earlier and bought several books in English, then to the railway station to buy a pile of English and American newspapers and periodicals. For a while, at any rate, we would not be short of reading in our own language. Next to a café—Kropke—where we had coffee and rich cakes full of whipped cream and chocolate sauce, and doubtless ruinously fattening—but who could worry about weight at a time like this?

Back to Blauer See—in the evening light the blue lake was pink, the swans' plumage had taken on a rosy tinge, and among the black pine-branches bats flitted and darted with faint squeaks.

The next day I felt really ill—arms, neck and shoulders were very painful and difficult to move, and a sore throat made it difficult to swallow. Most of the time I lay drowsily outdoors, and the warm sun seemed to help; then, after a day or two, as I began to improve, aches and pains attacked John. Probably it was some kind of 'flu. Whatever it was, we soon recovered, and none of the children was affected.

Once we felt better we enjoyed life at Blauer See. We made several trips to Hanover, where we were struck by the frequent occurrence of Georg in place-names—Georgplatz, Georgstrasse— and were reminded that King George of Hanover was also King George I of Britain. We visited Herrenhausen, the former Royal Palace, with its magnificent baroque gardens—formal gardening at its best, gracious, dignified, musical with the tinkle and splash of many fountains; and we walked by the Marsch See, a huge artificial lake in the heart of the city, created out of a swamp during the thirties to provide work for the unemployed. Here at a restaurant on the shore we lunched on cream of cauliflower soup, veal smothered in mushrooms, and a coffee mousse, with an excellent Moselle wine; looking out as we ate through big windows across beds of bright pink petunias to the lake, dotted with the white sails of little boats.

Hanover is a well laid out, attractive city; but we saw several bombed-out buildings, and were struck here, as in other German cities, by the large numbers of maimed and disabled people in the streets, tragic evidence of war.

One thing which made our stay at Blauer See so enjoyable was the fact that here for the first time we made German friends. Camping near us was a German Protestant minister with his wife, son and daughter. They all spoke English, the young people very well indeed, for they had both spent some months in England as exchange students. They were very kind, friendly people, and it was a great pleasure for us to have the adult conversation from which our ignorance of the language had cut us off. One evening over coffee in our caravan we mentioned that we had been at Pelzenhaken, and Mr W. said gravely that he knew the place well, for the best of reasons—he had himself been imprisoned there, not under Hitler, but later when the British had taken it over and turned it into a prisoner-of-war camp. He added that during the thirties all along that coast there had been a chain of concentration camps. This brought home to me anew the magnitude of Nazi oppression. All the world knows of Dachau, Ravensbrück and other places; few have heard of Pelzenhaken—and yet—"K-Z, 7,000 dead" and this only one of a chain of camps on the Baltic coast. How many millions must have perished!

Chapter IX

BOWLING along the autobahn, all lanes well marked, signposts all the way, it should—theoretically anyway—have been impossible to get lost, but we achieved it.

As usual, while John drove and Gerard read the map, I sat with my indispensable German dictionary, looking up all the words on signposts. Of course, by the time I had interpreted a notice we were always too far ahead for it to be of much help, but at least I had learned the words for future reference. Once an inscription it took me a couple of miles to decipher proved to be "Last pump before autobahn"—and by the time I had worked that out we were on the autobahn! Fortunately, we were well supplied with petrol, but it might have been disastrous.

From Hanover we had planned to go to Hamm, spend one night there, then on to Cologne. The autobahn was magnificent; although we were going up into the mountains there was no sense of climbing: but as the day wore on the weather became very dark and blustery, and the caravan, offering a big surface to the wind, tended to weave, putting a strain on the driver. John had not long recovered from the chill we had had at Blauer See, and soon found his arms and back aching, so he was eager to get to the end of the day's drive. Since we were going to Hamm it seemed reasonable to turn off the autobahn at the Hamm ausfahrt, but we soon found ourselves completely lost. After driving up roads and down roads and obviously getting nowhere, we asked a policeman, who, fortunately, spoke English, and was extremely helpful. We should, it seemed, have left the autobahn well before the Hamm turn-off, but how were we to know that? The policeman gave us very complete instructions for getting back to Hamm, but John thought, seeing we had come so far, we might as well go on to Hagen. So we never got to Hamm, and, as it turned out, we never got to Hagen either.

We returned to the autobahn by way of an intricate arabesque of clover-leaf flyovers across the eight-lane highway, and on we went. Soon we saw the big wheel of a mine, and then another, and another, and we realized we were in the mining district of the Ruhr Valley. We crossed the River Ruhr, flowing between steep dark hills covered with forest which looked—at a distance—very like New Zealand bush. High on a peak we saw what appeared to be a monument, and then a huge dam, or rather, series of dams. Suddenly, John exclaimed:

"Dams! They must be the ones the dam-busters broke!"

The more we surveyed the scenery the more certain we were he was right. Not that there was any trace of damage. As a matter of fact, there is surprisingly little war damage apparent in any part of Western Germany, when one considers the pounding her cities received. But what havoc must have been wrought in the Ruhr! The dams are high on the hills, and far below in the valley runs the river, along its banks railways with a constant stream of trains passing mines and wheatfields. The inundation of the valley must have been crippling. One is awed, both at the courage and determination of the airmen who carried out such a project in this place of terrific winds funnelled between high hills and at the complete recovery of the land.

By now we had come about a hundred and forty miles. In a high wind, with the caravan fighting all the way, it was a struggle to keep on the road, and John said the pain in his arms and back was excruciating; so when we saw a sign "Zeltplatz" (camping place) we decided to go no further. We turned off the autobahn, pulled up at the camp gates, and Gerard and I went in to investigate. We had not gone far before we felt sure it would not do.

"No caravans," I remarked, surveying the hundreds of tents.

"No," said Gerard, "and look at the people; they're not holiday campers—they look more like gipsies."

Dark-skinned for the most part, and strangely dressed, they had a settled look, as though they had been there a very long time. Women sat by their tents working at sewing-machines, and numerous children played about. We stopped a man to ask him the way, but he did not speak English, and I was pretty sure he did not speak German either. When I said, "Büro?" he said, "Da", and beckoned us to follow him. The small grey-haired woman in the office understood my stumbling request to stay one night, "camping wagen und zelt", but she shook her head: "Nicht camping wagen", and she pointed across the river to the precipitous hills beyond. The terrain looked alarming; from where we stood no road was visible, only steep, forest-covered hills, and among the trees a couple of pastel-coloured dots that

79

might have been either caravans or cottages. However, there was a bridge across the river which must lead somewhere, and if, as the woman insisted, that was the way to a "camping wagen platz", it must be negotiable for caravans. We returned to the car still speculating about the camp we had just left. We did not think the people there were holiday makers—there was a total absence of the usual carefree atmosphere. Were they "displaced persons"? Our smattering of German was not sufficient to enquire, so it remained a mystery.

Gerard and I reported the result of our reconnaissance, and John, rather reluctantly, drove over the bridge in the direction the woman had indicated. Over the river and up, up and up, over high bridges across deep ravines, with, as far as we could see, nothing ahead but forest. This certainly didn't seem a suitable caravan route, but, apprehensive though we were, we had to keep on, for there was nowhere to turn. Then the road took a sharp bend, so that it almost went back in the direction it had come, and went down abruptly, a drop that from the top looked almost perpendicular.

"God," exclaimed John, "how on earth will I get up this again?"

"Perhaps there's another way out at the bottom," I suggested optimistically.

"There'd better be," he muttered, cautiously riding the brake down the hill.

We dropped for a considerable distance, past, to our surprise, an open-air theatre, and then we found ourselves in rural Germany; an old-world scene that might have been a setting for musical comedy—an old half-timbered farmhouse-restaurant with window-boxes full of pink petunias and several little tables and chairs set out before it. To one side of the building a rutted track led past an old open barn full of hay and a rickety-looking hay-cart to a farmyard which several caravans and tents shared with about half a dozen black-and-white cows. The road continued on steeply downhill past the farmhouse and curved away among trees. We bumped over the ruts into the yard, and I asked two young women working in the garden near the house where I should register. I had the impression they spoke a rural dialect, for though I had so little German my ear had grown attuned to the sound of the language, and their speech seemed different from what I had hitherto heard. However, they pointed to the house, and I went in and explained to the young girl serving in the restaurant that we wanted to stay one night, "drei Person, drei Kinder, eine Camping-wagen, eine Zelt". She held a consultation with an older woman and finally told me two and a half marks, which I paid. Back to the caravan, where John told me he had paid the farmer three marks! But this slight discrepancy was not really surprising considering the level of efficiency of the farm. There seemed to be a tremendous amount of effort expended to do very little work. For instance, it took two men to push one almost empty wheelbarrow. One man pushed, and a wizened, gnome-like little man in a corduroy jacket capered along behind retrieving the first man's hat and clapping it back on his head each time the wind blew it off, which happened every few seconds.

It was blowing fiercely, and the sky becoming more and more lowering. Struggling against the gale we fought to get the tent up, and had only just succeeded when down came the rain in torrents, and we all hastily leaped to shelter in the caravan. But John was restless and fidgety, and wanted to set off again immediately in the car to go shopping. I was not happy about his driving again in such bad weather, after the long exhausting trip we had already had, and tried to dissuade him, but he insisted, and I realized he could not rest till he had driven up the hill in the car and gauged how difficult it would be the next day towing the caravan. So, leaving the others, he and I set off again, up the hill in the pelting rain, John exclaiming that the gradient must be one in five, or even four. We bought food at a village and returned, but the expedition had not been reassuring, for John was now more worried than ever about the hill. Accordingly, after a meal, the rain—though not the wind— having eased, we set off on foot to explore in the hope of finding another way out of what we were beginning to fear was a cul-de-sac. The hope was vain.

The hill on which the farm was situated sloped steeply down and ended at the river far below. Beneath the heavy grey clouds the Ruhr was not attractive. Evidence of the industrial importance of the valley was everywhere. Notices along the banks warned against swimming because the water was polluted with sewage and trade waste, and along the railway lines beside the river goods-trains rumbled by in a never-ending stream. For some distance we followed a footpath beside the tracks. The rain had stopped, but the trees still dripped dankly, puddles spattered the ground, and wet weeds slapped and soaked our legs as we passed. Creeping on the soggy path we noticed dozens of curious slugs of a kind we had never seen before—about five or six inches long, amber-coloured, jelly-like and repulsive. Altogether, we were not sorry to return to shelter, but we had a sleepless night, for the wind whistled and rocked the caravan till I began to fear it would blow right over and crush the boys in the tent. Every now and then there was a loud detonation, as the gale forced in the aluminium wall, which then sprang out again with a terrifying crack. (The dents blown in the metal that night never quite came out.)

Morning came grey and overcast. Breakfast was a gloomy affair, only a little lightened by the comic relief provided by the two farmhands. They tried to drive the cows through a gate, but seemed as inept at cowherding as they had been at barrow-pushing the evening before. A great deal of shouting and waving and slapping of black-and-white rumps had no effect whatever; like affronted dowagers the cows looked at them coldly, then turned their backs and ignored them; when the men continued insistent the herd, like one animal, made off in the opposite direction and into a sugar-beet field, where half a dozen heads went down to browse. The two men became positively frenzied, shouting imprecations, leaping about, waving their arms, flinging clods; the cows continued their meal. More leaping, shouting and slapping, till at last the animals moved off, by which time the field was a scene of devastation caused, not by the cows, but the men.

Breakfast over, all packed and ready, we had no excuse to linger. The moment had come: the hill must be faced: there was nowhere to go but back the way we had come. Seeing John looking apprehensive I tried to cheer him with bright, and no doubt irritating, remarks to the effect that if this was a caravan site others must have done it before, to which he snapped back that they probably had smaller vans and stronger cars, so I subsided. We all agreed it would lighten the load if John drove up alone and the rest of us walked, but even so it was difficult. In the early morning the car was starting cold; there was no impetus after bumping slowly over the cart-track for the sharp right-angled turn straight up the steepest part of the hill. We all held our breath and prayed. At first it seemed all would be well. Car and caravan moved slowly upward, but just as our hopes were raised the engine died and they began to slide back. We all rushed to get behind the caravan and push. We stopped it rolling down any further, but that was all. John started the car again: it edged forward an inch or two, then stopped. He told me afterwards he was shaking so much that he could scarcely keep his foot on the accelerator—he had fearful visions of car and caravan rolling over us all and down to the river. But a family camping at the farm, the farmer and some of his work people came running out to help. This time, with more than a dozen people pushing, it was successful. The engine caught and car and caravan sailed safely up to the top. Before running on to catch up I turned and called back to the group still standing in the road, "Danke schön" and a man's voice came floating up—in English—"A safe trip to England." At the top of the hill John stopped for us all to scramble in, and, the danger past and the sun just then coming out, we all felt elated and happy, and we sang all the way to Cologne.

At Cologne—or Köln—we had our first sight of the Rhine. We were at the municipal camping, right on the river-bank and almost in the heart of the city. Above us a fine modern bridge carried a constant stream of traffic across the river, and under it an equally constant stream of long black barges chugged ceaselessly up and down with never a break in the procession. Yet oddly enough, in spite of all this busy commercial activity, the land along the river-bank under the bridge approaches had a surprisingly rural air—a small wheatfield with a harvester being worked, the grain pouring from the funnel in a golden stream; trees and flowers, one or two houses in pleasant gardens, and, running off at right angles to the river, what might have been a country lane, bordered by high hedges. The camping was a particularly well-equipped one. A large communal kitchen-dining-room contained laundry tubs, tables and chairs for meals, and coin-in-the-slot stoves. So it was fortunate for us that our bottled gas ran out here, and not at a less well-appointed place, for we were able to cook, and a lamp-post near our caravan gave us some light in the evening—not enough to read by, but bright enough for us to play Scrabble.

In the morning I woke very early, and crept out without disturbing my sleeping family. I found Nicky sitting in the car: he too had found it impossible to stay in bed on such a beautiful morning, and had crept out of the tent without disturbing Godfrey. It was bright and sunny, with already a promise of heat to come; the light sparkled on the water, and even at that early hour the procession of barges moved up and down. We stood watching the endless pageant of the river—sometimes a steamer trailing a long line of barges, occasionally a pleasure-boat, once a strange, square-bowed craft which looked like nothing so much as a detached ship's bridge, chugging along without any ship below it. Even the black barges, uniform in shape and colour though they were, were not without individuality. Each barge flew the flag of its country at its stern—German, Belgian, Dutch—sometimes lines of washing fluttered from the masts; once we saw several children playing surefootedly on the sloping black top. This was the Rhine, one of the world's greatest waterways, celebrated in song and story, a river brimful of history. It seemed incredible that we were really there.

The combination of bright sunshine and copious hot water brought out all my domestic instincts. After breakfast John took table, chair and typewriter to a shady place under a tree and set to work, while I organized a spring-cleaning of our mobile home. I set Miriam, Godfrey and Nicky to work washing walls and ceilings, cleaning windows, and tidying cupboards, then Gerard and I gathered up all the laundry and took it across to the tubs in the kitchen. There was a great deal of it, for the weather had been rainy and the last few campings had not been convenient, so it had been allowed to pile up, and, I washing by hand, Gerard wringing and hanging it out, it took us two and a half hours. Campers who, when we started, were eating breakfast, had returned to the kitchen to cook lunch before we finished, and we got some rather odd looks, but nobody complained at our monopolizing two tubs for so long, and it was very satisfying to see all our clean linen blowing in the breeze. Washing hung out to dry is a common enough sight in most Continental campings—only in England is it frowned upon—but very seldom would one see as much as I had that day.

Dominating the skyline of Cologne are the twin spires of the Cathedral, stone-lace against the sky, huge, yet giving an impression of lightness and delicacy. Providentially, in the heavy wartime bombing of Cologne the Cathedral escaped with very little damage, but other buildings were not so fortunate. John was very anxious to see the church of St Ursula, which was described in a letter by Thomas Hood, but when we found it it was a ruin, the new church to replace it partly built, and a long roll of honour listed the many names of parishioners who had been killed. Indeed, it was obvious the whole district must have been almost completely razed. Some buildings were still battered and smashed, old churches with scaffolding about them were in the process of being restored, and many new blocks of flats, some already complete and occupied, others still being built, were replacing ruined homes.

There are some fascinating shops near the Cathedral, some selling old books and prints, others beautiful church plate and embroidered vestments, for this is a Catholic city. One shop sold only wood-carvings from Oberammergau, and how I should have loved to buy some—but where could they go in a caravan? Our shopping must be strictly utilitarian—a new gas-cylinder, for instance. But I had to have some small souvenir of the city, so I went into a shop and asked for "eau-de-cologne". I realized I had been less than tactful when the proprietor coldly corrected me, "Kölnwasser", and I resolved thereafter to be very careful to pronounce the name of the town in the German way.

Late on our last night there, three tourist coaches arrived at the camp, two from Finland and one from England. This sudden influx of people put a strain on the camp facilities, and long queues formed at toilets and showers. Here the English tourist abroad scarcely showed in a good light, for the rattling of doors, and the Cockney voices shouting, "Hurry up in there—you Germans take all night", cannot have endeared them to their hosts!

Out of Köln camping on a sunny morning, and on to the traffic bridge, which hitherto we had seen only from below.

"Here we go, over the Rhine," I said.

"The Reid family crossed the Rhine," sang John, and we all joined in, "danke schön."

Past a big oil refinery, its great tangle of pipes topped by flames, past houses and wheatfields, and very soon we were in Bonn. Here we had intended to stay a day or two, but once again our plans were changed. There were no campings listed in Bonn, and when we enquired at an information office we were told the only one was on an island in the middle of the river, and there was no way to take vehicles across to it; it was suitable only for trampers. So we had to push on.

"Can't we stop here at all?" asked Godfrey.

"I'm afraid not. We can't park a caravan in the street."

"Well, I think it's pretty poor," said Gerard. "I was looking forward to seeing the capital."

"What's special about a capital?"

"It's the capital of West Germany. It's interesting and important."

"And now I can't see Beethoven's house," pouted Miriam.

"It's no good grumbling—we can't help it," said John, "and I'm having trouble enough in these streets, so be quiet."

It was true; narrow cobbled streets and tram-tracks were not making it easy for the driver, so the family fell silent, and had to content themselves with tantalizing glimpses as we drove through—a number of new government buildings, some of them not quite finished; a street of elegant houses, most of them embassies, and that was Bonn.

On along the banks of the Rhine, as wildly, romantically beautiful as one could wish, with forest-covered hills and rocks, great castles on the pinnacles, and always, the ceaseless stream of barges. The little towns we passed through—Bad Godesberg, Andernach and others—were straight out of Grimm's fairy-tales, the fronts of the houses and the shutters painted in floral designs. Sometimes we passed chair-lifts, taking people up to the heights above the river; once a ridiculously toy-like train chugging along the opposite bank.

"Oh well, not staying in Bonn will mean a little longer in Koblenz," remarked John.

Koblenz was important to him for reasons other than mere sight-seeing. At the time he was working on a book on Thomas Hood, the poet, who had lived there with his family for a couple of years.

"Perhaps we could stay in Koblenz and take a day trip to Bonn," suggested Miriam, hopefully, "just to see it, and go to Beethoven's house."

"Yes, we'll probably do that—it isn't far," replied John.

But we didn't. Koblenz had too much to offer.

At first sight the town looked very old and quaint. It was not until later that we learned that it had been practically razed in the war, and much of it rebuilt in the original style; the streets still narrow and cobbled, the buildings, for the most part, with a Disneyish prettiness. This style extended even to the fire brigade station—the only one I have ever seen with ornate shutters and window-boxes full of pink petunias.

The camping, just where the Moselle meets the Rhine, was very large and very full—tents so close together that the guy-ropes overlapped. New campers kept pouring in, till there was scarcely room for another pup-tent, and motorists who wanted to

86

take their cars out were in danger of finding their place occupied on their return. Most staked out a claim by erecting a little fence of posts and strings of small flags. At last a "Camping Full" sign in four languages went up on the gate—and still new people kept arriving, and, unable to get in, stood around outside, anxiously consulting maps. It was obvious something was happening in Koblenz.

John was to be disappointed in his Hood pilgrimage. After more than a century and two world wars, no trace remained. We found the place where the poet had lived, but war had taken its toll. The house had been in the Castorhof, a large cobbled square, one side of which was taken up by the ancient church of St Castor, dating back to A.D. 836, and having associations with Charlemagne. Now only the church remained—it was partly burned in World War II, but had been restored—the other three sides of the square were merely rubble overgrown with weeds and even young trees, with just one house left, sticking up alone, like a single tooth in the mouth of a crone.

We explored the town, enjoying its atmosphere, and were interested to learn, from the bright posters everywhere, that we had arrived in time for the annual festival of "The Rhine in Flames". So that was why there were so many visitors to the town! We were glad we hadn't stayed in Bonn.

High on the hills on the opposite side of the Rhine from the town stands the Ehrenbreitstein fortress. A generation before Norman William conquered England it stood there, commanding the Rhine and Moselle and all the spreading country beyond. Through all the centuries between it has seen war and strife; it was taken by Napoleon's forces and taken back again by the Germans; it has withstood air raids in two world wars, and now, battle-scarred but as solid as ever, it is no longer garrisoned, but is kept as a show-place; it contains a chapel and a museum, and visitors may admire the view from its battlements or have meals in its restaurant. The day we crossed the river to visit the fortress was extremely hot. John had business in the town in the morning, and, as it was quite stifling in the caravan, I took a chair outside and sat reading in the shade. Three English Boy Scouts approached me, and one said politely:

"Excuse me, are you British?"

I admitted I was, and he produced a large bottle.

"I wonder," he said, "if you would accept this bottle of

methylated spirits? It hasn't been opened, and we are not allowed to keep it."

I explained I would have no use for it, and preferred not to carry anything inflammable in the caravan.

"It's very useful," he said persuasively, "very good for cleaning paint brushes."

I told them I just happened to be right out of paint brushes in need of cleaning, and they wandered off with their bottle, looking for someone else to give it to. By the time John returned it was nearing midday, and hotter than ever. The weather was not very conducive to activity, but we very much wanted to see the fortress, and perhaps up there above the valley there might be a cool breeze. We collected the children and set off.

It was not a particularly easy place to reach. First into caves, cut through the living rock of the hill, deliciously cool after the heat outside. The caves are very extensive, and indeed during the war served as an air-raid shelter for the whole town. It was not possible to become lost in them, for arrows and coloured lights showed the way; we came out again to daylight and the foot of the chair-lift. Rather apprehensively we gazed at the frail-looking little seats, swaying precariously up the mountain, a hundred and eighty metres to the top, we were told. The children were quite thrilled at this exciting method of travelling, but John and I both felt there could be pleasanter ways of climbing a mountain. However, we could hardly turn back now, and anyway, it would be ridiculous to visit the Rhine and not go up at least one chair-lift to a castle; so, inwardly quaking but trying to appear nonchalant, we took our places, taking care to separate Godfrey and Nicky. The seats were arranged in pairs, and I felt I would be much happier if those two had each an older person with him to quell any mischievous impulses.

It was a little frightening, but pleasant too, in a chair in the sunshine, swaying over rocks and trees, one's feet dangling in space. The most alarming moment came quite near the top, when I glanced down and saw, far below, a motor-road, and cars moving along it like beetles. However, we all arrived safely at the fortress, and the magnificent views made it all worth while.

There below us the two great rivers met at the Deutsches Eck, a pointed promontory crowned by a massive and exceedingly ugly monument. Once it was topped with a colossal equestrian statue of Kaiser Wilhelm; but this was destroyed in the war and has never been replaced. Traffic moved like ants over roads and bridges; on the opposite shore of the Rhine brilliant orange, blue and red tents in the camping made a gay frieze of colour, with behind it the silvery-grey town, and beyond that the spreading valley and far-away encircling hills. From the other side of the fortress, away from the river, there was an equally impressive vista of hills and vineyards.

I wanted to stay there a very long time—partly because the view was too beautiful to leave in a hurry, partly to put off as long as possible the descent. But we could not linger for ever, so it was back to the chair-lift and down. I had expected it would be more frightening going down, facing out instead of towards the hill, but it was not, it was quite delightful, drifting slowly downwards, gazing at the wide-spreading panorama. We passed over houses, and a garden with a child nonchalantly playing on a swing directly below the moving chairs, and then, near the bottom, over glass-houses. I wondered if chair-lift passengers ever dropped things through them. It could happen. I noticed some girls removed their shoes before taking their seats, I suppose for fear they might drop off en route.

That evening we made haste to finish dinner early, and hurried to the river-bank with our folding chairs, for this was the night of "The Rhine in Flames", the culmination of the week-long festivities, and we wanted to be sure of a good place. Every vantage point along both banks of the river gradually filled with people; some, like us, with chairs or lilos, others standing or promenading up and down. We had still some hours to wait, but there was so much of interest to see and hear that time did not hang heavily. There was the endless passing pageant of the Rhine traffic on the river, and there were the people, Germans and tourists from all over the world, of every race and colour and speaking every language. Once we were amused to hear behind us a girl's unmistakably American voice—"I have just washed my *whole* face in warm *water*." Here and there were police in their green uniforms, ready to keep order—not that they were needed in that cheerful, good-humoured crowd. At intervals along the banks soldiers waited atop specially erected towers, ready to play their part in the display. Gradually the sunset colours faded from the sky, it grew darker, and a great full moon came out. A stream of traffic poured along the motor-road on the opposite bank, below the fortress, the headlights making an endless belt of light. The evening was warm, and a great number of young people were swimming in the river, shouting and splashing noisily. A boat full of press photographers had anchored a little way out from the shore, and three young men, bent on showing off, swam out and pretended to overturn it. "Eins, zwei, drei," they shouted, and seized the prow; at which the occupants, worried no doubt about their cameras, cried out in alarm, and tried to drive them off. A ripple of laughter along the crowded banks encouraged the swimmers to further and noisier antics.

Suddenly, the flood-lighting of the fortress went out, and simultaneously, flares were lit around the Deutsches Eck. The anticipation mounted. Then around the point, coming down the Rhine, appeared a flotilla of pleasure-boats, about forty of them, all illuminated with red lights. At the same time, at various points along the tops of the mountains red smoke-pots appeared—not flame-coloured, but truly red, the red of Bengal fire; and the fortress became visible, dimly lighted by the red fire and smoke. With the cliffs below it in darkness, its arches seemed to hang in the sky like some mysterious cloud-palace, and the occasional monstrous human shadow cast on its walls as someone moved across the smoke-pots added to the other-worldly effect. It was awe-inspiring like Gotterdämmerung and the burning of Valhalla. The red fires and the red boats were reflected in the water, so that the Rhine seemed literally a river in flames.

Among all that vast crowd along the river-banks and on the boats not a sound could be heard. Even the exhibitionist swimmers were silent. A pause, and then the fireworks began. Up from the fortress went showers and twirls of light; great flowers of every colour and combination of colours opened in the sky. From the towers along the river-banks shot up flares and rockets too bright to look at, before they exploded loudly in showers of stars, while the detonations echoed and re-echoed along the valley of the Rhine like thunder. For nearly an hour it lasted, the red mysterious castle in the sky seen through the drifting smoke, and high above in the zenith fountains and cascades of brilliant light, until finally the climax, when great flowers filled the sky, and from the centre of each sprang another, and from the centre of that another, and another—and another, until it seemed they would never stop, while the thunderous echoes rumbled and roared as if all the gods in Valhalla were beating drums. Three tremendous crashes, and the display was over.

The crowd gathered up rugs, cushions and chairs, and began to move away.

"You know," John remarked, as we strolled back to the caravan, "we really are lucky. Some of these people have come across the world to see this, but the slap-happy Reids just happened to be here."

The next day was Sunday. It was still very hot, and there was a lazy, "after the party" atmosphere: nobody seemed to have the energy to do anything much, and throughout the camping people lay about in relaxed attitudes. As we walked along the river-bank to Mass in the little onion-towered church we noticed a few people rolled in rugs still sleeping on the grass. Evidently after the fireworks they had just curled up where they were for the night. The weather continued to be hot. Two or three times a day a water-truck drove through the camping ground to lay the dust on the roadway, and all the children came from far and near to caper along delightedly behind it, running in and out of the spray.

We stayed several more days in Koblenz. We took boat trips on the Rhine, shopped, explored historic buildings, had coffee and enormous rich cream cakes at open-air cafés, or drank Moselle in a beer-garden under chestnut-trees hung with little red lanterns, while a band played "oom-pah oom-pah" music. One evening we saw an outdoor screening of documentary films.

Our last evening in Koblenz was hotter than ever—far too hot to stay in the caravan, and much too hot to sleep. The children had made friends with some young German boys camping in a tent, and went off to visit them. From the laughter which floated over to us occasionally they seemed to be enjoying themselves and to be having no difficulty in communication. John and I took our chairs outside and read three-day-old English newspapers till it got too dark, and then just sat. Suddenly there was lightning and thunder reverberating from the hills, and then came the rain; great heavy drops followed by a violent downpour. All over the camping people who had been sprawled about outside trying to get cool made a mad dash for shelter. John and I snatched up our chairs and rushed to the caravan, the children leaped into their friends' tent. The heavy downpour continued for some time, and then, as suddenly as it began, it stopped. Before going to bed John and I went for a walk. Everything was transformed. The moon had come out, the air was pleasantly cool, and all the trees and grass which had been dusty and wilted stood up fresh and shining, while the roadways, which had been thick with dust, were now muddy, and every pothole was a deep puddle, so that it was necessary to walk with care.

The change was quite dramatic, but drama seemed part of the atmosphere in Koblenz. In quite ordinary moments the unexpected and surprising suddenly occurred—as on one evening when we were walking near the river and heard a bell toll three times—a pause—one more stroke, and immediately all the barges on the river stopped dead. One moment, the chugging of engines, so constant on the Rhine that one ceases to hear it: the next, dead silence, and the long procession still. It was eerie. Or the occasion in the main shopping street when a man rushed up to John and asked if he spoke English, then, very emotionally and almost in tears, began to pour out a confused story in an accent so strong we could not understand it except for the words "telephone" and "children". John said, "Parlez-vous français?" and the man replied, "Je suis Belge", which should have made it easy, but he still insisted on his incomprehensible English, and seemed in despair not to be understood, flinging his arms about, beating his forehead, and finally he rushed off. He seemed in need of help, but we could not give it, and never learned what it was all about. Even Godfrey, of all people, added his little touch of drama by fainting in church and having to be carried out in the middle of the sermon!

The first mile or so of our drive up the Rhine to Frankfurt-am-Main was taken up with one of those fruitless, aimless family arguments that get nowhere and convince no one. Two said we were going *up* the Rhine, and two said we were going *down*. However, it was not long before the spell of the scenery took over, and nobody cared which was correct. We drove on beside the river on a sunny, hazy day, with the vineyard-covered hills above us and every peak crowned with a castle. I had a guide-book open, and identified each one as we came to it, and read its history aloud—Katz, Maus, Enemy Brothers. Each one was built a thousand years ago "for the purpose of exacting river tolls". A trip up the Rhine in the Middle Ages must have been a costly business, with every mile or so some rapacious baron levying payment. Apparently anyone who could afford it set himself up in a castle and demanded his share of the loot—the original racketeers collecting "protection money". Even the Church got into the act, for one castle was built by a bishop, like all the rest, "to exact river tolls". He must have made a very nice profit, too, for he had the most advantageous position of all—not up on a peak, but on an island in the river. When Sooneck Castle was frankly described as "a brigands' stronghold" I felt the guide-book was telling the truth for the first time. We stopped to photograph the Lorelei rock, so much bigger and more massive than I had expected, where, according to legend, a siren lured ships to their doom; then on through Bingen, where the wicked Bishop Hatto had his tower, to Frankfurt.

I don't know why I disliked Frankfurt. It seemed a pleasant enough city, and the few people we spoke to were friendly, but for some reason we were not happy there, and were quite pleased to leave again the next morning.

Chapter X

IT was 15th August, the Feast of the Assumption, and in Catholic Bavaria a public holiday. When we arrived in the little village of Estenfeld the shops were shut, and, save for a group of youths and girls leaning on bicycles talking and giggling, the streets were empty: but when Godfrey and Nicky spotted a large red ball in a shop-window—their football had been left behind somewhere on the way—the shopkeeper very obligingly opened her door and sold it to them. Every house had window-boxes full of flowers and a little shrine on the wall—either a statue in a niche or a painted or ceramic mural.

The camping ground was quite a small one, but well-equipped, in an apple orchard behind a gasthaus, with roses in full bloom. The proprietor, a very fat, jolly man who spoke only German, asked where we had come from that day, and when I said Frankfurt, asked what the weather had been like there. The previous night there had been an electrical storm, so, dredging up my few German words, I said "Donner und Blitzen", which seemed to amuse him inordinately, for he shook with laughter and repeated it several times. I was not sure whether Frankfurt weather was a local joke or whether I had said something funny, but he was an amiable soul.

In the evening the bells sounded sweetly from the church calling the people to devotions for the feast day, and from every house they came, dressed in their best and carrying prayer-books, till it was a procession streaming down the village street. Some of the women wore the pretty costume of the region—long dark green or black dress, white apron, black silk fringed shawl embroidered with huge red roses, no hat, and hair drawn tightly back into a bun. The church, we found, was quite large, but it was crowded, and, as always in Germany, the congregational singing was superb. After the service, we noticed posters advertising films in the village hall, so we joined the queue. The main feature was an American Western with German voices, and it was odd, to say the least, to hear James Stewart speaking in a deep rumble, and the beautiful Indian squaw, having saved the hero from her people, breathe "Ich liebe dich" in a throaty, Marlene Dietrich voice. But to me, more interesting than the film was the audience.

It was like a country picture-show anywhere. There were mothers and fathers with small children; there were young girls in giggling groups pretending not to notice the boys, who sat together in the back row, guffawing and pushing each other, licking ice-creams and shouting across the intervening seats to the girls. Except that their language was German they might have been Peter Cape's New Zealand farm boys

> " . . . givin' cheek to the sheilas
> Down the hall on Saturday night."

Afterwards we walked home to the caravan through wheat-fields under a big harvest moon.

In the twilight the following evening we walked several miles along a gently undulating road, past wheatfields and apple orchards and once or twice, fields of roses in full bloom. There was not a house in sight—we might have been miles from any habitation, and it was hard to realize that all that day there had been many harvesters busy among the wheat. We walked on till it was nearly dark, and then, at the top of a rise, came to a large crucifix, and below it in a valley, the lights of the next village. The scene seemed to me to typify rural Bavaria, a land of farming people with strong religious faith. Walking back to the camping we all sang lustily, till Nicky broke off to say, "Are all the stories finished?"

There was a guilty silence.

Just before we left England Nicky had had a bright idea. He had suggested that we should each write a story, and then some evenings in the caravan when we had nothing to do we could entertain ourselves by reading them aloud. Everybody had agreed to have a story written in a month, and now the time was up, but travel and sight-seeing, lessons and reading, keeping diaries and sketch books and playing Scrabble had kept us all so busy that none of them were done except Nicky's.

John said, "It's too bad of us, Nicky. We really should have done something about it, because it was a very good idea. Just give us a little longer and I promise you I'll write one."

"So will I," said Miriam and I together, and Gerard added, "I've a good idea for one already."

95

Like so many German cities, Würzburg was heavily bombed in the war but is now so completely rebuilt that there is little damage to be seen. No attempt has been made to restore it exactly as it was; the new buildings are modern in style, but designed in such good taste that the new harmonizes perfectly with the old. Typical is the Mariakapelle, an old church which was completely destroyed by bombing. In its place has risen a new church in pink and grey stone, completely modern, but the few relics that could be salvaged from the old have been incorporated into the new structure with what seems a charming inconsequence. Halfway up a smooth new pillar will appear the elaborately-carved capital of one of the ancient ones; a couple of the Stations of the Cross are the original ones, quite different from the new; and there is a Crucifixion which seems to be very old.

We spent a couple of hours in the gardens of the Residency, a graceful baroque palace, in the ballroom of which a symphony orchestra was rehearsing; the sound of the music came to us now near, now distant, as we sauntered along arcades of hedges, up and down flights of steps adorned with little stone Bavarian shepherds, and through pergolas of roses. For a while we sat and rested near a fountain encircled by trees cut in candle-snuffer shapes with a statue sheltering under each tree as if under an umbrella; then we left the gardens and went to a café for coffee and luscious kirschentorte piled high with whipped cream. No wonder there are so many plump people in Germany!

Next we explored the shops, and were pleased to find one specializing in imported foods, with a sign in the window "English spoken". The German woman who served us spoke English very well, but with an American accent, so John really should have asked for "canned", not "tinned" peaches. As it was, she looked surprised, and said, "Oh, no, sir, not in all Germany will you get ginned peaches—we have them in brandy."

For me, Nuremberg was haunted. A pretty town in the sunshine, with the old and quaint mingling harmoniously with the very new; with flower-filled window-boxes everywhere, even on the towers set in the city walls; but too overlaid with baleful associations to inspire liking or affection. At every turn were reminders of Hitler. We passed the building where the Nuremberg trials were held, and when we reached the municipal camping ground it proved to be in the stadium—that vast stadium, familiar to everyone from news pictures, which was built in the thirties for the huge Nazi rallies. Now, the camping occupies part of the grounds, including the original toilet and shower blocks. As for the stadium itself, the American Army uses half of it as a sports field; the rest is completely neglected. The terraces all around have become overgrown with grass, and the great colonnade, crowned at each end with enormous bowls where symbolic fires used to burn, from which Hitler used to deliver his speeches, is a sorry sight—chipped, broken and battered stonework, gaping spaces where swastikas have been wrenched away, large pieces fallen from the mosaic ceilings; and right across the front the words "Soldiers' Field" roughly painted by the Americans in huge black letters.

It is perhaps not difficult to understand how the Nazi idea at first captured the imagination of the Germans; a beaten and humiliated people saw in it the hope of a national resurgence and a glory as of Imperial Rome. It was surely in an attempt to imitate and outdo Rome that this place was built: a vast stadium and colonnade, an artificial lake, and beyond it a building in obvious imitation of the Colosseum. Now the stadium is fallen into disrepair; on the lake cheeky little pedal-boats flit about, and all along its shore are American Army vehicles, ice-cream stalls, hot-dog stands and young American wives pushing prams. For me, the whole Third Reich seemed symbolized by a huge rubbish-dump beyond the trees, with a truck toiling up its side to dump still more rubbish. As a further melancholy reminder of the terrible past history of this place I noticed among the holiday makers in the camping a woman with a concentration camp number tattooed on her arm, and I wondered what her emotions must be among such evocative surroundings.

For some reason, our fellow-campers in Nuremberg were among the most varied and colourful we had encountered. There was a very large family party of Italians, occupying three big caravans, each with a statue of the Madonna in the window. All day the men sat, fat and comfortably unbuttoned, around a table in the shade playing cards and drinking wine, while the women toiled hour after hour boiling up big tubs on the electric stoves in the communal kitchen and hanging out lines of snowy washing that made me envious. (After weeks of camping-ground washing my linen was distinctly grey.) There were two pretty young German girls, camping with their

97

parents, who made friends with Miriam and Gerard, and the four of them played battledore and shuttlecock and held long, giggling conversations in a mixture of languages. There was a willowy young Englishman, in whose speech the original Midlands warred with an overlay of B.B.C., whose exotic cooking seemed to involve a great many utensils on a great many stoves in the kitchen, while other hungry campers had to wait. He was accompanied by a blonde whose entire function in life seemed to be to appear decorative, for she was never seen to do anything but sit about in attractive poses, or to wear anything but a pale blue bikini, sun-glasses and a spectacular hat. And there were Johnny and his father.

We had only just arrived when a man came over to us, and, looking at the K I W I on our caravan, said, "Hullo there, New Zealanders. I'm from Sydney myself." His accent was distinctly American. He went on to tell us that he had not been back to Australia for many years, and that he and his son were in show business. The son was a plump, precocious nine-year-old, and his father's, "Here, Johnny, come and play with the boys", had an unfortunate effect on all three children. Godfrey and Nicky on the one side and Johnny on the other stood hostilely sizing each other up, like dogs about to fight; then Godfrey, essentially a kind child, said, "Let's have a game" and fetched the big red ball from the caravan. But it was not a success. Johnny, who had obviously lived more with adults than children, had little idea of how to play, and, naturally enough, finding himself at a disadvantage, became boastful, which did not please the other two. In the end they went off for a walk, Johnny trailing rather wistfully behind, and when later they came in to lessons he hung about the caravan door emphatically repeating nobody made *him* do any old lessons, but all the same, I felt, envying them. Poor Johnny, a lonely, not very happy child, I think, but he had his moment of glory. In the evening all the campers gathered round while father and son sang and danced and played guitars, to vociferous applause.

Later, John and I took a walk, out the stadium gates and along a broad tree-lined avenue to a small airstrip where Hitler used to keep his private plane—all overgrown now with weeds and entangled with rusty barbed wire. There we sat for a while in the afterglow, admiring black pines against pale sky, and shadowy undergrowth; but in my mind I could see Brownshirt ranks, and hear the tramp of marching feet and ghostly "Sieg Heils" echoing in the air. I was not sorry to leave Nuremberg.

The scenery in the Jura must be some of the most beautiful in Germany. From Nuremberg to Regensburg it was enchantment all the way. The day was bright and sunny, and the ripe wheatfields gleamed golden, dotted here and there with scarlet poppies and bright blue cornflowers. Occasionally we saw women driving tractors in the fields, but for the most part farm-carts were used, drawn by cows. It seemed to us expecting a great deal of the poor cow, if she must work and give milk as well! It was harvest time, and every little village we passed through was decorated for the Volkfest, or harvest festival, with garlands and arches of greenery mingled with banners. In one village all the banners were yellow and white, in another blue. In one village square we were delighted by the picture—glimpsed in passing and then gone—made by an old bearded Franciscan friar, standing in contemplation by a fountain where water spurted from two bronze fish.

Gradually, as we climbed higher the wheatfields gave way to pine forests and hayfields, the hay stacked in European fashion about a post.

The only blemish on this lovely day was the fact that the car was not pulling well. We were climbing all the way, up a rutted and not very well engineered road. Our progress upward became a crawl, and the engine was obviously overheating.

We went through a little town with on its outskirts a large house which appeared to be a children's home, for about twenty toddlers played with toys in the garden, while a nun washed clothes in a tub under a tree. A long, long pull, up and up, slowly and seeming in imminent danger of stopping, and at last we were at the top. Here we rested, to let the engine cool and to admire the scene.

We were on a plateau. Beside the road stood a large, weather-beaten crucifix. Fields of barley and wheat stretched away on all sides, making patterns of squares and strips of differing colour, and cornflowers and poppies spangled the fields. Away to our left the little town through which we had just passed seemed in the bright, clear air to be made up of squares and triangles of red and white, like those pictures kindergarten children make by pasting coloured paper shapes on to card. The sun was shining, and a fairly strong breeze made a delicate, silvery singing in the grain. It was pleasant to sit there and rest, and pleasant, too, to move on, for we were over the top of the range, and now the road ran downhill.

"Daddy," Nicky asked, looking at the people working in the fields, "these people are peasants, aren't they?"

"Yes, I suppose so."

"Well, why when people want to be rude to anyone do they call them peasants?"

"I don't, and your mother doesn't."

"I know *you* don't, but some people do."

"Yes, they do," chimed in Miriam, "and I think it's awful. Peasants are as good as anyone else."

"Of course they are."

"Well, why do people mean it to be insulting?"

"Well," said John, carefully negotiating a tricky bend, "it's not meant to be insulting to *peasants,* but to the person it's used to describe. And it doesn't refer to an occupation so much as to a state of mind. When somebody describes someone else as a peasant he means he has no culture and doesn't know how to behave."

"That's awful. Peasants have *so* got culture and they do so know how to behave."

"Yes, but as I said it doesn't mean real peasants. Just as when someone is described as a Bohemian it doesn't mean he comes from the country that used to be called Bohemia, but is now part of Czechoslovakia."

"Dad," put in Gerard, who was reading the map, "I'm not sure which way we turn here. Would you pull up for a minute and look at the map?"

John pulled up. A little hamlet dozing in the sun, and not a soul in sight save a very old woman, toothless and bent, with a kerchief over her head, scrubbing her steps with a bucket and broom. While John was studying the map we sat idly watching her at work. All at once she raised her voluminous skirts, relieved herself in the bucket, and went on scrubbing. In the car there was a gasp, and a shocked silence.

"Well," said John, handing back the map and switching on the ignition, "now you know what people mean by 'peasant'."

In Regensburg our timing could not have been worse. To begin with, we arrived about noon on a Saturday. The camping was pleasant enough—an orchard behind a gasthaus, right on the banks of the Danube—but there was no camp store, and as it was a long way to the shops and we were hot and thirsty we decided to have a cup of tea first. And that was our first mistake, for it turned out to be early closing day in Regensburg, and by the time we got to the shops they were all shut. We had very little food and a week-end before us; so we spent the rest of the afternoon cruising about looking for a shop—any kind of food shop—that might be open. But they were all closed. In the Cathedral Square the market people were packing up for the

day, but one or two women still lingered at their stalls, selling fruit and vegetables, including the special giant radishes of the region: here I bought plums, tomatoes and a cucumber. Further on I came on a slot-machine selling packaged food, and bought all it contained—two tins of herrings, a wedge of processed cheese and a packet of cocktail straws! Obviously the machine was intended for the spur-of-the-moment party-giver, not the mother of a family doing week-end marketing. However, I had a few emergency tins and some potatoes, so I thought we could get by, if we had some meals at restaurants. I could not buy bread, but at a café managed to get a packet of zwieback. As he handed me my change, the proprietor, who spoke English, said, "Wait a moment." Mystified, I waited while he went away and returned with a parcel, which he handed me, saying, "With my compliments." It proved to be a box of Regensburg bon-bons— large chocolate biscuits, each with a different historic Regensburg building on it in marzipan. This was not the only kind gesture I received in Regensburg. Later a German woman came to the door of the caravan and said something I could not understand. She spoke again, slowly, and I tried hard, but could not make it out. I tried English and French and my few words of German, but in spite of efforts on both sides we could not communicate. At last she threw her arms around me and hugged me, and with "Auf Wiedersehn" was gone. I felt both warmed and saddened by the incident. She wanted so much to be friends and I wanted so much to get to know people, but the language barrier was just too great.

Having settled the matter of marketing to the best of our ability, the next matter for attention was a visit to a garage to find out why the car was so sluggish. This took a long time, for the mechanics checked the engine thoroughly, and then gave their verdict—dirty spark plugs. Since new ones had been fitted at Hamburg this seemed unlikely; however, they were cleaned. By that time the day was gone.

Regensburg, once Ratisbon, is steeped in history. It was a fortified Roman outpost, and later an independent Imperial city; from it the Crusaders, under Godfrey de Bouillon, set out for the Holy Land; in the Middle Ages it was the most important city in southern Germany; from 1663 to 1806 seat of the German Imperial Diet; in the Napoleonic Wars it was besieged. It is probably one of the most fascinating cities in Germany, but we had been too busy to see it. However, the next day— Sunday—we planned a full day of exploration. But again we miscalculated and timed things badly.

After Mass at St Magnus's Church we bought a map of the city and worked out an itinerary. Posters everywhere proclaimed an exhibition to commemorate two thousand years of Regensburg's history, which sounded interesting, so we decided to see it in the afternoon, visiting the Schloss before lunch: but when we reached the Schloss we learned there was a guided tour in the morning—for which we were too late—and it was not possible to visit it at other times. Instead, we went to the crypt of a nearby monastery—very old, with the indescribable, chill smell of ancient stone buildings, and rich with baroque decoration. Glass coffins contained skeletons opulently dressed in lace and gauze and cloth of gold. But even here we were late, and a young, bearded priest waited politely for us to go, so that he could lock up behind us.

We lunched at the railway station—rather apprehensively, remembering British railway food. But any fears were groundless. The meal was excellent—a rich soup with meatballs, followed by chicken and salad, with oil, not the nasty "salad cream" of England; fruit, and a Moselle wine. Then on we went to the Museum to see the Two Thousand Years exhibition; but we found that on Sunday it was open from ten o'clock to one, and by now it was one-thirty, so once again we were too late.

"Let's go to the Rathaus—there's a medieval torture chamber there," said Godfrey with relish.

"I think I'd prefer the Cathedral," said John.

"Oh, no," protested Miriam. "We've seen lots of cathedrals, but we've never seen a real torture chamber."

"Madame Tussaud's was enough for me," I said.

"But that was only waxworks. This is real. Please, can't we see the torture chamber?"

The rights of parents must be asserted, even if only temporarily —we visited the Cathedral before going to the Rathaus. But we couldn't see the torture chamber—it was not open on Sunday.

"Well, can we stay another day and see it tomorrow, Daddy? Please. We've never seen a real torture chamber."

However, laboriously deciphering the notice outside the building, we learned it was not open on Monday either.

"Stay two days and see it on Tuesday?" asked Godfrey hesitantly. But there was no conviction in his voice. He knew it was a lost cause.

We returned to the caravan in a mood of frustration. A whole week-end in Regensburg and we had seen so little. Remembering a couple of Sundays the previous winter when we had had to wait in cold, sleety weather for London museums to open at two-thirty, I wondered why in England, where, according to statistics, less than a quarter of the population go to church, all art galleries and museums are closed on Sunday mornings and open in the afternoons, while in Catholic Bavaria, where almost all the people go to Mass, they are open on Sunday morning but closed in the afternoon. It is one of those mysteries of life to which I'll never know the answer.

103

H

But at least we had seen St Magnus's, and that alone made our visit worth while. This church is rococo at its most exuberant. As we went in Godfrey and Nicky ran on ahead. When they reached the door they suddenly stopped dead, and I heard a gasp of surprise. On entering I was startled myself. Everything was ablaze and aglitter with gold and brilliant colour against white, all looking as fresh and bright as if it were newly built— a wealth of twisted pillars, white statues picked out with gold; St Michael in shining gold armour surmounting the pulpit; cherubs peeping over cornices, painted ceiling; artificial windows opening on painted vistas; false balconies trailing plaster draperies in vivid colours fringed with gold. It was a style we had seen before and were to see many times again, but never in such lavish profusion. It burst on us like a thunderclap.

Chapter XI

DRIVING along through the Danube valley on a summer morning with the caravan behind us and the car pulling well, life seemed very good. We passed Valhalla, a mountain topped with a marble copy of the Parthenon, which is Germany's Hall of Fame; we crossed the Iser, and John and I loudly declaimed "Hohenlinden", much to the disgust of the young.

"They talk about us being silly and noisy," said Miriam. "Listen to them!"

"You know," said John, "I think the Little Man has lost his touch. He's left us alone for a long time—I think he's decided we're too good for him."

"I wouldn't be too sure," said Miriam. "He may be saving it up and planning a real whopper."

How right she was.

At first everything went swimmingly. We went through flat fields with hills far on the horizon, then along the banks of the Danube, here with a peaceful prettiness, willows, swans and houses all reflected in the dark green water. The houses in this country were of the chalet type, with wide eaves and a great deal of wood-carving, and from their inevitable window-boxes flowers tumbled down in long, luxuriant sprays of brilliant colour. Sometimes in villages decorated for the harvest festival we passed maypoles crowned with wreaths of wheat and dangling long coloured streamers.

It was gradually borne in upon us that we were off the usual tourist route. The people we passed watched us with a great deal of curiosity, and once a little boy in lederhosen ran out of a house shouting, "Mama, Wohnwagen!" and his mother too ran out to look. Quite evidently they did not see many caravans. However, this did not worry us at first, for the camping guide listed a camp and Youth Hostel at Passau, so we felt reasonably sure of having somewhere to stay that night. But the nearer we approached to Passau the greater the attention the caravan attracted. We began to think this was an ominous sign; and we did not see on the outskirts of the town the usual signposts pointing the way to a camping. In the central square nobody we asked could direct us; then a taxi drew up, and the driver said, yes, there was a camping, but—and he looked dubiously at the caravan. However, he told us how to get there, and off we went. It was a nightmare drive, through cobbled streets so narrow there seemed barely inches to spare on each side of us, and we were in dread of meeting something coming the other way, particularly at the right-angled turns, which were difficult enough to negotiate without that added hazard. We drove over a bridge across the Danube, and there loomed ahead of us the sheer rock face of a mountain, crowned on the summit by a castle. We seemed to be driving straight for the cliff, but as we approached nearer we saw a tunnel was cut through the rock, so we went under the mountain to emerge on the other side and see a "Camping" sign—pointing up a precipitous zig-zag footpath to the castle, which was used as a Youth Hostel. No wonder caravans were rare in this region—that path would have been impossible for a bicycle! We could not stop there in the narrow road, we had to keep on across another bridge, and found ourselves on a quay, ending nowhere. There was no way to go forward, we had to go back. Under the enthralled gaze of a gaggle of small boys, who, in the fashion of boys everywhere, just suddenly appeared where something was happening, we had to swivel the caravan round by hand, turn the car—not at all easy on the narrow quay with a drop into the water all too possible—rehitch and go back the way we had come. We ran the gauntlet of the traffic again, and parked on a quiet street just outside the town to think about what we could do.

Obviously we could not stay in Passau; the only camping was impossible and we could not park car and caravan overnight in the street. The nearest place listed in *Camping in Germany,* the official tourist publication, was at Munich; but that was a hundred miles away. We had already come a long way, and it was very hot; the idea of another long drive was not appealing.

"The only thing I can think of is to push on into Austria," said John.

"Austria? Today?"

It was obviously the only solution; the border was much nearer than Munich. But I have never left one country for another, however delightful the second, without a pang of regret.

"The only thing is," John went on, "we'll have to buy a new gas-cylinder first."

Austria is the only European country where Gaz is unobtainable, so we had to be sure, before we crossed the frontier, that we were well supplied if we did not want to find ourselves unable to cook.

"You'd better wait here," he continued, "and Gerard and I will go and find a shop."

They were gone nearly an hour. It was very hot. The sun beat on the car, and even with all the windows open it was stifling. I began to feel faint, and walked up and down for a while to try to get some air. Miriam joined me, but Godfrey and Nicky preferred to stay where they were, getting more tired and irritable every minute. A quarrel seemed inevitable, so I created a diversion by reading aloud the first book which came to hand—as it happened, W. W. Jacobs. At last the men of the party returned, and we were ready for Austria.

"Passports ready?" asked John.

"Here's mine," I said, for I always carried it with me.

"Mine's in the caravan," said Gerard, who was the only one of the children old enough to have his own passport. "I'll get it."

He was a long time in the caravan and we began to get impatient. At last I went to see what he was doing.

"I can't find it."

Consternation! We let down the legs of the caravan, and all six of us started a search, going over every possible place—and every impossible one—but not a trace of the missing passport could we find. Scolding could do no good, but it was difficult to be patient.

"Gerard, think! Where did you put it?"

"I've always kept it in that cupboard over my bunk."

"Well, it isn't there now. When did you see it last?"

"I had it in Hanover, I know."

"Hanover! But that's nearly three weeks ago. It could be anywhere!"

107

"I was sure it was in the cupboard."

"Look, Gerard, several times since then I asked you if it was safe and you said it was."

"I know. I thought it was safe in the cupboard."

The afternoon was wearing on. Passers-by were looking at us curiously. It must have seemed very eccentric behaviour on our part to park in a suburban street and toss about everything in the caravan. Clearly the missing document was not to be found. To be in a foreign country without a passport—it is the nightmare of every traveller, and it had really happened to us! Sick with worry, we sat in the car, considering what to do. We were certain there would be no British Consul in so remote a place.

"Should we go to the police?" I asked, but John said, "No, I'm for pushing on to Austria and telling the frontier guards."

"But we'll never get into the country without a passport."

"Let's try it, anyway, and see what happens." He started the car.

All too soon, it seemed, we were at the frontier, and the guard was approaching us.

"Let me do the talking," said John in a low tone, and jumped out of the car to meet him.

"Good afternoon. Passports. Here are my wife's and mine. The children are included on mine."

"Ja. Three children." The guard read aloud their names and ages, and moved towards the car to see them.

"Oh, I suppose you'll want to see this," said John, producing the green carnet that British motorists carry on the Continent, "and this", and out came further documents. The guard turned back to him, while in the car we all held our breath.

"Ja. They are in order, sir."

He turned again towards the car to check that the three children on the passport tallied with the children in the car. Discovery seemed imminent, and I was sure guilt was written all over my face. In the back seat Gerard tried to be invisible. John, however, had not given up.

"Do you want to see this?—and this?—and this?" Various wholly irrelevant documents were appearing from his pockets.

"No, sir, I do not require that. I have seen all I need", and apparently deciding this was a fussily over-conscientious traveller, the guard stepped back and waved us on. John drove on, and five of us breathed again.

Just across the border was a camping, but we did not dare to stop—our instinct was to put as much distance between us and the frontier as possible.

So there we were, in Austria, but minus a passport, and with only German money, for we had not risked staying at the frontier post to change it.

"Well," I said, when I dared speak again, "we're in Austria. But how do we get out again without a passport?"

"We'll go to the British Consul at the first town where there is one," said John.

"And how do we explain coming in without it?"

"We'll leap that hurdle when we come to it. Anyway, we're here."

The road went up and down, and on every hill the car coughed and spluttered alarmingly. At last, on a slope that in happier circumstances would have been no trouble at all the engine died, and we came to a halt. At first we thought it had been overheated by the long drive, aggravated by standing so long in the hot sun in Passau, and to a couple of passing motorists who offered help we explained in bad German that the engine was hot, and we were waiting for it to cool; but after a long wait it still would not start. There was nothing for it but to push to the top of the hill and hope it would go on the downgrade. Even with our combined exertions the weight of car and caravan made it very hard work, and after an hour we had moved only about twenty yards. By then the sun was low; we had to get somewhere for the night and quickly. Inch by inch upwards. Surely a quarter of an hour ago that tree was level with the tow-bar? Now it is about a foot lower down. There's a lot more hill. It will take all night. Two young men appeared and lent a hand pushing, and their strength made all the difference. We gained the top of the hill. One of them spoke English, and when we told him we were making for Linz he shook his head, and said he was sure we would never make it, because there were much worse hills ahead than this one. John asked if it would be permitted to park for the night, and he said, "On the road, no. In the forest, yes."

All we needed was to find a forest.

But now the road went downhill, and on we went, hoping for the best, till deep in the valley we came to the little town of Taufkirchen. Ahead of us, at the end of the village street, we could see the road continuing on sharply uphill. By now it was beginning to get dark. It had been a long, worrying, exhausting

109

day, and we were all tired, hungry and thirsty, for there had been no time for lunch.

"I think what we all need is a meal," said John. "Come on", and he stopped the car and led the way to a gasthaus.

"But we've no Austrian money," I protested.

"We'll see what German will do."

The proprietress, a pleasantly smiling woman, said she would accept German money. She did not serve hot meals at this hour, but could find us some cold food. Her deprecating manner did less than justice to the generous meal which appeared—plate after plate of cold sausage, gherkins, hard-boiled eggs, tomatoes, delicious rolls and ices. We fell to with a will, and after several cups of strong coffee felt fortified to tackle whatever might come on the road to Linz. But it happened again. Once on the hill, a dead stop, and we had to get out and push. Up the slope in the twilight came a man and two children, a boy and a girl of perhaps nine and ten, all three of them barefoot.

"Englisch Kinder," the father said, pointing to our children, and all the youngsters stood self-consciously smiling and eyeing each other. Then they too joined us in pushing, and the top of another hill was reached. We thanked them, and they disappeared in the darkness.

It seemed hopeless. It was night and Linz was still thirty miles away, on a road that went up and down like a switchback. There was nothing to do but camp for the night.

"No forest," I murmured.

We were surrounded by wheatfields. We could not stay on the road, and we could not ruin some farmer's wheat by driving over it. However, we saw a rough cart-track leading into a field and drove on to it, resolving to be up very early in the morning and on the road before the people came to work in the fields, for the track we were on would be used for the harvest carts.

We had a troubled, worried night, and I don't think any of us slept much. Once, waking from a restless sleep, I sat up and looked out the window. The moon had risen and all about us the wheat glinted and shone golden in its light—a truly beautiful sight.

Before sunrise we were all awake and anxious to go on. It promised to be a splendid day. The sky was opalescent pink and blue above the golden wheat, and far down below us the valleys were filled with mist, so that they appeared to be lakes. Here and there on the hills opposite, looking very tiny in the distance, were farmhouses, with lights still showing. By the time we had washed somewhat sketchily—we had very little water—and had a breakfast of sorts, with black coffee because the milk was sour, men and women were already hard at work in the fields. It was nearly six o'clock, and the morning mist had begun to roll away.

At first the car seemed to perform a bit better than it had the day before, but we were not taking any chances. When we saw a hill ahead the children and I scrambled out and walked, and we found that without the weight of five passengers it could pull up hills, though still with difficulty. We had decided to push on in the direction of Linz, walking up all the hills if necessary, but if we came to a camping before we got there, the children and I would stay in the caravan while John went on in the car to a garage in Linz where, according to the A A Guide, English was spoken. Without the weight of the caravan he should be able to negotiate the hills.

Before long we came to a sign "Camping 2 Kilometres", pointing down a side-road which was little more than a cart-track. We stopped to consider. Two kilometres is not far, but the road looked very rough, and the car was misbehaving. If we broke down we would be off the main road and less likely to get help. On the other hand, if we kept straight on we might not find another camping place. In the end we despatched Gerard and Miriam on foot to see what it was like, while the rest of us waited where we were. In a few moments a police car pulled up, and two gendarmes, resplendent in their grey, red and silver uniforms, told us we must not park on the highway. John tried to explain that we had sent two children to see if we could take the caravan to the camping; but the gendarmes looked very puzzled, as well they might, for what he actually said was that we had sent zwei kinder to put the caravan in the bath. In the end we got it straightened out, and they left. In a few minutes another policeman appeared, this time on a motor-cycle, and asked what we were doing there. Again explanations; but this one was more helpful. Pointing along the main road towards Linz, he said, "Camping eine Kilometre—wunderbar camping." This was encouraging, and so, as soon as Gerard and Miriam returned—with the news that the side-road would be impossible—we went on. Sure enough, in exactly a kilometre, we came to a farmhouse with the word "Camping" painted in big white letters on the steep-pitched roof, and a driveway which continued past the house and through an open gate to disappear into a wood. There was no sign of life in the house—it was still only about seven o'clock—but we sent Gerard in to reconnoitre, and he came out all smiles.

"It's the most delightfully picturesque little place you ever saw," he said. "Honestly, it's like fairyland."

Truly, he did not exaggerate. We were to spend a few days here, but we never learned its name or even if it had a name. For us it was the "fairy grotto", which seemed to us quite apt. It was circular, except for the entrance entirely surrounded by perpendicular rock cliffs crowned by trees and overgrown by plants and creepers. In the centre of the grotto, which was perhaps a hundred yards across, was a pool so deep that the local people claimed it was bottomless, and the water appeared almost black. Bright peacock-coloured dragonflies skimmed the surface, and all around was a loud twittering of birds and the occasional call of a cuckoo. Probably a century ago it had been a quarry, later abandoned, and time and nature had transformed it. Another party left soon after we arrived, so for most of the time we had this enchanting spot to ourselves.

John went on to Linz, saying he did not know how serious the car trouble was, and if it took long to fix he might have to stay overnight; while the children and I at the grotto busied ourselves by turning the caravan out thoroughly, in the faint hope that the missing passport might still be found. Many lost treasures came to light—pencils, books, souvenirs and a long-vanished sandal—but no passport. However, we had at least achieved something—the caravan was now like a new pin.

We swam in the pool, and I passed a lazy afternoon sunbathing while the boys scrambled around the cliff-tops gathering black-berries, until we heard a triumphant tooting of the horn, and all rushed to meet John, back from Linz with the seat beside him piled high with parcels—cheese and jam, frankfurters, Viennese pastries, Coca-cola—and the cheering news that the car was fixed. There had been nothing basically wrong except that the spark plugs, fitted in Germany, had been meant for a different model car.

After all the strain of the previous couple of days we felt a rest was needed, and what place could be better than the "fairy grotto"? We decided to stay for a while.

Later in the evening, as if to make the magic complete, a group of young men came to swim in the pool by moonlight, and then they yodelled, the sound echoing around and back and forth from the rock walls of the grotto. It was the true sound of Austria.

It was a delightful interlude in our travels, resting, swimming in the pool, going for walks or driving in the car to the nearest village, St Willibald, which was a few miles away. There were no houses near our grotto apart from the one on whose property it was, and an inn. All around stretched fields, and at a crossroad was a wayside shrine—a big crucifix and beside it a tiny chapel, scarcely bigger than a child's playhouse. One day Nicky and I went in and found ourselves in a church in miniature, with four chairs, wooden statues and fresh flowers, and above the little altar a quaintly primitive painting of St George. It was a very moving thing to find, out in the fields, a place like this where passers-by could, if they wished, slip in for a few minutes' prayer and meditation.

In the early morning the grotto had a strange, mysterious beauty, with the dim light filtering down through the leaves, and a kind of mist, like steam, above the surface of the water. I almost expected to see emerge from it an arm "clothed in white samite, mystic, wonderful".

Up to midday we were alone, but in the afternoons there were usually people coming to swim in the pool, which was probably the only bathing place in the district. When they tired of running about and swimming Miriam and Nicky spent a good deal of time sketching the scenery.

It was quite idyllic, but we could not stay for ever. So early one morning we set out for Linz, en route to Vienna, sure now that all was well with the car. But it did not take us long to discover that our confidence was misplaced, and the Little Man still had a few tricks up his sleeve.

All went well till we came to a village called Feuerbach. The road twisted through the town and then turned steeply uphill. Halfway up the car stopped. "Everybody out!" said John, and with the alacrity of long practice we all scrambled out and began to push. A woman in the pretty dirndl and apron of the country came riding down the hill on a bicycle. She stopped and watched us for a minute, then pedalled off furiously down into the village. From our vantage point halfway up the hill we could see her running excitedly from house to house; we could not hear her, but we could see her talking and pointing up at us. At each house somebody joined her, till at last she had gathered

113

a quite large group of people, and they all advanced up the hill and joined us behind the caravan, helping to push. But it was a very steep slope, and even with so much assistance we did not advance much. Then a well-dressed man with an authoritative air appeared on the scene. "Tractor! tractor!" he said. He called a little girl to him and spoke rapidly to her in German. She nodded and ran off, apparently to fetch a tractor. We all went on pushing. Some time went by. Then the authoritative man sent off a boy on a bicycle. Just as we had reached the crest of the hill, and John had at last managed to start the car, *three* tractors converged on us from different directions, no longer needed. Now it was going we did not dare stop the car for fear it would not start again; we merely waved our thanks to them as we sped off and they waved cheerfully back. A little further on we stopped in the shade of some pines to let the engine cool. Inevitably a police car drew up, but went on again when we explained the engine was hot. After a suitable interval, John pressed the starter. All that happened was a strange and very ominous noise.

"That's it," he said with resignation. "We've had it this time."

"One thing you can be sure of in this country," I said. "There's always another policeman along in a minute."

Sure enough there was. With the help of my invaluable German dictionary we explained we needed a tow-truck and a mechanic, and he promised to send them from the next village. Within an astonishingly short time they arrived. It appeared the clutch-plate had broken; the tow-truck could take the car to the garage, but not the caravan. What to do? The helpful mechanic soon organized matters. He went to a nearby farmhouse and obtained permission to leave the caravan in the driveway. This was a very generous gesture on the part of the farmer, for it was haymaking time and the presence of our caravan caused him some inconvenience. Dozens of men and women were in the fields mowing with scythes, and then piling the hay into heaps to be picked up by carts, which then had to edge very cautiously around us with very little room to spare. But this was typical of the Austrians. Everywhere we found them generous and helpful to the visitor, even at the cost of their own comfort. For a couple of hours I supervised the children's lessons, and then about midday John and I walked the half-mile or so to the village, Prambachkirchen, to see how the car was progressing. All the business places, including the garage, had closed for the lunch-hour, so we could do nothing but walk up and down the street enjoying the quiet, rural atmosphere of the place. We paid a visit to the little church—as usual in Austrian country churches, the simple, unadorned exterior belied the riotous rococo decoration within—and then went to the gasthaus for coffee. The dining room was large, white-walled, with a low ceiling of dark, carved wood, and deep window embrasures. Walls in Austria are thick, for the winters can be bitter, but now it was high summer, and the windows were open. Hunting horns and antlers hung in profusion about the walls. The people eating their midday meal and drinking beer at the tables, it was obvious from the way the proprietor and his wife greeted them,

were all regular customers. From time to time a small boy with bare feet and the inevitable leather shorts wandered over to the bar and filled himself a glass from a large, unlabelled bottle. I hoped this was something little boys were allowed to drink, but could not help noticing it always happened while his mother was bustling back and forth to the kitchen serving the customers!

Back at the caravan we whiled away the long afternoon watching the haymakers at work, playing Scrabble, sketching the scene, until at about five o'clock John set off again to the village to see how work was progressing on the car, while Miriam and I started preparing dinner. We had just opened various cans and put food in saucepans on the stove when, suddenly, the car was there and John was calling, "Come on, everybody! Ready to move!"

What a moment! How could we pack saucepans in use, and how on earth prevent opened food from spilling en route?

"Come on—five minutes!" John was saying, and somehow it

was done, everything in place, gas disconnected, legs raised, caravan hitched. The mechanic had driven the car back to us, and he wanted to drive it towing the caravan to see how it performed—hence the rush. So off we went at a breakneck pace which made us half-terrified, half-elated that the car was capable of it. Later we wondered if he had been misled by a speedometer in miles, not kilometres, and had not realized the speed he was doing. Anyway, all was well now with our car, and after paying the bill—surprisingly low for a whole day's work—we continued on our way.

We went through Linz just at the evening rush hour, and we passed the entrance to the municipal camping without stopping, for we had decided to stay that night at Amstetten, some miles further on; but we had not reckoned on the Austrian helpfulness to strangers. Several people in the street, seeing a car and caravan run past the camping, assumed we had inadvertently missed the entrance and ran after us, shouting, "Camping—camping," and pointing back. With cars and trams coming in all directions we could not stop to explain and thank them—all we could do was lean out the windows shouting, "Amstetten! Amstetten!"

And so at last to our camp and our long-delayed meal. It was one of the few occasions when we arrived at a destination by night, for we usually tried to time each stage of our journey so that we had daylight while we made camp.

Chapter XII

AFTER our recent set-backs it was a pleasure to find the road from Amstetten to Vienna much better than we had expected. The map we were using showed a not-very-good road and a "projected autobahn". We were relieved to find it was already out of date, and the autobahn was completed, save for a very short stretch still under construction, where, something we had certainly not expected to see in Western Europe, the gangs working with pick and shovel included as many women as men. It brought home to us the fact that Austria, for all its superficial appearance of prosperity, is far from being a rich country. On either side were mountains and woods; in the valleys fields patterned in strips and squares of green and gold and brown, little villages clustered about onion-spired churches, and everywhere harvesters and haymakers at work.

Our first concern in Vienna, of course, was to rectify the passport situation, and we lost no time in making our way to the British Consulate. The official who saw us listened very courteously to our story, examined the passports of the family, and asked, "Have you any idea where it was lost?"

"Somewhere in Germany, he doesn't know exactly where," said John.

"In Germany? Then how did you cross the frontier?"

"Oh, the guard let us through," said John casually, as if it were the most natural thing in the world.

I expected this to cause consternation—the date and time to be demanded, the unfortunate guard reported and dismissed in ignominy; but all the imperturable Englishman said was, "Yes, the Austrians are very eager to help tourists. Of course, you would probably find it a different matter if you tried to leave the country without a passport." We had received ample demonstration of Austrian helpfulness. "Well, young man," he went on, turning to Gerard, "in all the years I have been here this has never happened before. You have the distinction of being the first New Zealander I have known to lose his passport." Gerard looked suitably abashed. "Frankly, I don't quite know

117

what to do. I'll have to write to London and get in touch with the New Zealand High Commissioner, and see what we can do about issuing a duplicate. In the meantime, of course, it goes without saying you must not leave Vienna."

"And how long will it take?"

"That's difficult to say. The last time we had to issue a new passport it took a month, but the circumstances were different—an English girl who had married an Austrian."

A month! No time, then, to visit Switzerland and see the friend we had hoped to meet there!

"In this case," he went on, "I think it might be about a fortnight."

"Well, there's this about it," I remarked to John as we came out into the sunshine. "If we had to be held up somewhere it couldn't have happened in a nicer place."

It was true. In the two weeks we were there I came to love Vienna, the dignified grace of its buildings and gardens, the friendly charm of its people, the pretty girls in their picturesque Austrian dress. And, above all, we had time—time to relax and enjoy it. John had a rest from constant driving, we had no longer the worry of being without a passport, for the matter was in hand; or the anxiety of an undependable car. It was two weeks of sheer delight. We visited the enormous fun-fair of the Prater, and rode up in the big wheel, with its memories of *The Third Man* and Harry Lime; walked in the Vienna Woods; sampled new wine in a heuriger where an accordion played czardas; had coffee and rich cream cakes in a restaurant where a string orchestra played Strauss waltzes; we visited the fabulous palaces of Schönbrunn and Neue Hofburg; we window-shopped in the fashionable Kärntnerstrasse, where the prices were daunting, and shopped in Mariahilferstrasse, where they were more reasonable; we visited St Stephen's Cathedral and the wonderful baroque Karlskirche, spent hours in art galleries, took a trip to Baden Summer Theatre to see Viennese operetta still performed in the style of an earlier generation. We visited Mayerling of tragic memory, where a convent now stands on the site of the hunting lodge where Prince Rudolph and Countess Vetser died; and Seegrotte, an abandoned mine used by the Nazis as a subterranean aeroplane factory, later destroyed by the Russians, and now an underground lake where visitors can drift in little boats through dimly-lit arches and pillars of rock. Sometimes we just loafed in the camping, or walked a short distance down a tree-shaded street of big, elegant houses to a little open-air café with grapevines trained to form a thick green roof, where we had coffee or delicious Italian ice-cream. There Gerard, Miriam and a little French girl with whom they had made friends became so well-known that as soon as they appeared the waiter put their favourite record on the turntable.

As we were to stay in one place longer than usual it seemed a good idea to send my washing to a laundry and have it done properly for once. It took me a while to find one, but I tracked it down at last, and arrived triumphantly at the establishment with suitcases crammed with clothes and linen. Yes, they could do it for me. Would I make out a laundry list? And I was handed a printed form in German, very little of which I could read. The woman did not speak English, so she had to make out the list herself. She obligingly tipped out my suitcases all over counter and floor, and held up each separate article for consideration before entering it on the list. The laundry, right in the heart of the city, was obviously a popular one, and soon a long line of customers with duffel-bags and suitcases—all of them, I am sure, with their laundry lists properly made out—had formed behind me, waiting for attention. I felt uncomfortable at being such a nuisance, and embarrassed at the public display of my dirty linen, but nobody objected or became impatient—in fact, all were very friendly and sympathetic to the foreigner who couldn't even fill in her own laundry list. Once again, I was to be grateful for the Austrians' attitude to the stranger in their midst. In part, this springs from an innate courtesy, in part from the fact that tourism is the country's chief industry, and it is important for them that visitors should be satisfied. But that does not make their kindness any less genuine, and always there is dignity, and never the slightest trace of servility. At last the job was done, and amid smiles and bows all round, I was ushered out with the words, "Friday—five days". It was only when we had returned to the caravan that we discovered, in my eagerness to be rid of the "tell-tale grey" of three months' washing by hand, usually in cold water, I had over-reached myself and had taken to the laundry every single towel we possessed. Nothing for it but to buy some new ones. So off I went to the Konsum (co-operative) shop in the nearby shopping centre.

The camping was situated in a residential suburb of Vienna, with shops right opposite where all the local housewives did their marketing, and I greatly enjoyed joining them. It gave me

I

a tremendous sense of belonging, of being part of the life of the place. In the short time that I had been doing my daily shopping there, I had become quite well-known, and the women behind the Konsum counter always gave me a friendly greeting when I came in. Another, smaller shop in the same block I did not visit quite so often, though I did go there occasionally. Once I wanted matches, and thought that that was what I asked for in German, but the proprietress could not understand me. Probably because she was used to visitors from the camping, she kept dictionaries of various languages on a shelf, but for some reason she assumed I was French, and handed me the French-German one. I did not disillusion her, but merely looked up "alumette" in the dictionary, pointed to it, and received my matches.

"Merci, madame, au revoir," she said, to which I replied, "Merci, au 'voir." But I was almost afraid to go to that shop again—I was sure I couldn't keep it up!

However, on this occasion at the Konsum I knew the German for every article I wanted, so felt confident enough. While I waited to be served I heard three other women also waiting having an animated conversation—and suddenly to my astonishment I realized I could understand what they were saying. One of them had just become a grandmother and was receiving the congratulations of the others. It was a beautiful child, she told them proudly, but her daughter had had a hard time because it was so big—fünf kilo! Mentally I translated that into pounds—a very big baby indeed! Then it was my turn to be served and, feeling excited and confident at the realization of how much I had learned in the weeks in Germany and Austria, briskly rattled off my requirements. Another customer turned to me and asked, "Englisch?" "Nein," I replied, "Neuseeland." I did not expect her to know where that was, but she nodded, shaped an imaginary globe with her hands and pointed to the bottom of it. "Pacific Ocean," she said in German. "A very long way." By this time all the shop was listening and exclaiming at the great distance I had come.

"You speak German well," said one, and I said, "Nein", deprecatingly, but all nodded and insisted in chorus, "Ja, ja, gut." It wasn't true, of course; it was Viennese politeness: but I left the shop walking on air. After my experience at the laundry it did a great deal to restore my amour-propre.

At last we received a letter from the British Consulate. Would we call? When we arrived there we were told that a temporary

United Kingdom passport would be issued to Gerard for six months, but at the first opportunity he must report to a New Zealand authority. In the meantime, he would need new passport photographs, and we were given the address of a photographer.

The studio was on the fifth floor, and the single antiquated lift was out of order. As we puffed upwards, John and I consoled ourselves with the thought that this bit of exercise might help to counteract the effects of all the rich cream cakes we had been consuming in Vienna. The old-fashioned studio was presided over by an elderly couple; while the husband took the pictures, the wife acted as receptionist. The walls of the waiting-room were covered with photographs, some going back very many years, and they included an amazing number of famous people—three Popes, cardinals, royalty of every country in Europe, musicians, opera singers, statesmen. I was quite fascinated, and the old lady was pleased by my interest. While the photograph was being taken she took me around the room showing them to me, and we talked together in a mixture of German and French. Was the young man my son? Had I other children? Yes, I had six others. Seven children! Wunderbar! She too was a mother; and she beckoned me to an inner room, leaving John in the waiting-room. I found myself in her private portrait gallery, and she stood proudly watching for my reaction. It was a charming record, covering nearly sixty years; the whole life of my hostess told in photographs of her taken by her husband, from the blonde, pig-tailed seventeen-year-old gazing shyly over an armful of flowers—"fiançailles", she told me—through annual studies, in one of which, called "Madonna", she held her first child, to a Golden Wedding picture, a few later, and, finally, a study called "Muttertag", in which she sat in an armchair, leaning forward smiling to receive flowers from a group of grandchildren. It was fascinating to see the young girl year by year growing older, yet remaining recognizably the same person; and it was, too, an interesting record of changing fashions, from the early years of the century up to the sixties. On the opposite wall were companion pictures: she and her husband together from their wedding day on each successive anniversary to the Golden Wedding. I felt I had been greatly privileged to be shown these records of their lives, and tried to convey this in my halting way—I think she understood.

We took the photographs to the Consulate, and four days later received a message that the passport could be collected.

Once Gerard had it—and was repeatedly warned not to lose this one—John was all for leaving immediately. I protested.

"The day's half gone already, and it's ninety miles over the Alps. Can't we stay till tomorrow?"

No, we couldn't. He had made up his mind and nothing would change it. Sadly we packed, hitched caravan to car, and rolled out of the city, craning our necks for one last glimpse of lovely Schönbrunn Palace as we passed. Good-bye, Vienna. I hope some day I may see you again!

We passed a Russian war cemetery, with hammer and sickle on every headstone, and a flat plain with the mountains a hazy outline ahead. Gradually they became more clearly defined and resolved themselves into folds and layers; then through a forest of fir-trees tapped for turpentine, its strong oily scent filling the air. It was very hot, and we became thirsty. As we came to a little town an outdoor café with a large sign "Limonade" looked inviting, so we stopped.

"Kaffee?" asked the waiter, brightly.

"Nein, Limonade, bitte."

"Coca-cola," he said.

"Nein, Limonade", and we pointed to the sign.

"Coca-cola," he said firmly, and Coca-cola it was. We spoke English, therefore we were Americans. Americans drink Coca-cola. Ergo, we drank Coca-cola.

Almost before we knew it we had reached the mountains and were starting up the Semmering Pass. As we zig-zagged up into the Alps the scenery was breath-taking—fir-covered mountains, wide-eaved chalets, castles hanging on apparently inaccessible peaks, and far below fields with round haystacks lined up like soldiers. Up and up and up. In the rarefied air the radiator bubbled and boiled, and we had to stop. This being Austria, it was not long before two policemen appeared, and also an A.A. patrolman, who came over and looked at the engine. He spoke German slowly and clearly so that we could understand. It was vapour lock, he said; we had an English car, and English cars were not really suitable for high altitudes, but in half an hour it should be able to go. It was a bright day, the scenery wonderful and the air like wine. I suggested to the boys that we should walk on, and John could pick us up higher up the pass. So straight up we went, waist-deep in purple clover, penny royal and other alpine flowers, past dark fir-trees and clumps of mountain ash brilliant with scarlet berries, across the road a couple of times where it zig-zagged up, until we stood at the top of the pass, directly above the car and caravan, which looked like tiny toys so far below. We shouted and waved and saw John and Miriam wave back. At the very top of the pass was a gasthaus with shutters gaily painted in floral patterns and window-boxes full of flowers. Here, when John came up in the car, we had coffee on a terrace overlooking the wide panorama of mountains and valleys. Nearby was a chalet built of logs, and there was a lazy tinkling of cow-bells from a few creamy-fawn cows.

"It's not everyone," said Gerard, "who can say he's walked over an Alpine pass."

"You didn't," said John. "You only walked a little way up one side."

"It was not a little way," said Godfrey, indignantly. "It was a long walk."

"Well, anyway, it sounds good to say I walked on an Alpine pass," said Gerard.

We began the long descent down the other side. Down and down and down—it seemed it would never end. Darkness was coming on, and we had given up hope of getting to our intended destination—Brücke—before nightfall. We must find a nearer campingplatz. And so we came to Langenwang, deep in a valley between two mountain passes, to receive a welcome from the proprietor so warm it was overwhelming.

He ran back and forth as excitedly as if we were his dearest, long-lost friends, begging us to use all the camping had to offer, and promising anything else we could possibly want.

"New Zealand? You're from New Zealand? Look, I'll show you", and he hurried away, to return with a file of letters of commendation from former guests, flipping them over till he found one from a New Zealander. His wife, he told us, kept the nearby store; off he went and brought her back to meet us. She too was just as eagerly welcoming—we must come to see her shop, she sold everything. I went with her to buy bread, and came back loaded down, having bought a great many more goods, and spent a great deal more money than I had intended, she was so persuasive and hard to resist.

"Sardines? Won't you need sardines? They're very good camping food. Now, you've no fresh milk tonight. What about wine? Or beer? Yoghurt's very good. Have some yoghurt? And of course you must have some fresh fruit."

All this bubbling goodwill was infectious. In the camping

dining room we pushed two tables together and we were in a party mood as we sat down to a meal of cold food and rather warm white wine we had brought from Vienna. An Australian couple, Mr and Mrs B., were also camped there, and I paused to chat to Mrs B. While we talked, her husband came back from the store, his arms full of beer, wine, Coca-cola, eggs, cheese, sardines and fruit. He had, he said ruefully, just gone up there for a bottle of beer! We all agreed, amid laughter, it would be rather expensive to stay here too long!

The next day we awoke to rain. John wanted toilet soap, and went off to the store to buy some.

"Take care she doesn't sell you the shop," I warned.

"I'm a pretty tough nut," he replied. "You can't sell me anything I don't want."

He came back with a rather shamefaced air, and deposited on the table soap, tea, coffee, some fresh rolls and a box of coloured pencils for the children.

"Oh well," he said. "They're all things we can use."

She must have been the world's champion saleswoman!

Even in the rain, the scenery as we drove on was magnificent. We passed through several little villages. One, called Kindberg, was enchanting, and we stopped to film it, in spite of the rain. All the houses were carved and painted, and the village pump was surmounted by a group of wooden dancing figures in national dress, painted in natural colours. The harvest pole, which was to be seen in many villages, was in this case a particularly high and elaborate one, with carved figures all the way down it representing different occupations—a blacksmith, a butcher, a baker making pretzels. At the other end of the village was a statue of a naked child sitting on a mountain peak and an inscription "Der Kind am Berg". No doubt there was some legend to account for the name of the place.

The rain kept coming down harder and harder. Just as we came to a railway crossing the gates closed, and we had to wait. It seemed a very long time before the train appeared, and even then the gates did not open. Perhaps ten more minutes went by before a second train passed, and at last we could cross. But immediately past the railway line the road went steeply uphill. We had been stationary for well over twenty minutes in the pouring rain, and the engine was cold; starting straight up that hill without impetus was too much. The car ground to a halt. Once more, it was everybody out and push. In a minute or two we were all drenched to the skin, rain running in streams off our hair and down our necks, and the water, flowing like a river down the road, poured over our feet up to the ankles as we all stood at the back of the caravan, straining with all our strength, but quite unable to move it. A good deal of traffic passed us, each vehicle, as if we were not wet enough, showering us with muddy water. Some other cars laboured and crawled up that steep hill, too; but nobody else was towing a great heavy caravan! There comes a moment when you are so wet and miserable you suddenly decide things couldn't possibly be worse and you couldn't be wetter; and from that moment you begin to feel better, and even, in a wry way, to enjoy it. We had long passed that point, and had settled down resignedly to a long, long, wet push, when help came. A large Mercedes-Benz pulled up, and the driver jumped out, a good-looking young man in Austrian costume, an elegant knickerbocker suit of grey with green facings. In excellent English he asked if he could help, and added that he had a tow-rope. We thanked him, but pointed out that we had a caravan and to tow both car and caravan was asking a great deal. Not at all, he said, his car was quite powerful enough; but the only problem was that the tow-rope was meant to tow him, not for him to pull other vehicles, so though there was a bracket to fix it on the front of his car there was none on the back. All this time the rain was coming down heavily, and I was quite distressed to see his beautiful clothes getting wetter and wetter, but he seemed to regard that as a matter of no importance.

"I have it," he said. "I'll go to the top of the hill, turn, and come down facing you. Then I can back up towing."

This seemed quite overwhelming kindness—in such weather most motorists would have hesitated about getting out of their cars; let alone driving backwards up such a hill towing another car and a caravan weighing a ton. But our good Samaritan brushed aside all protests and expressions of thanks. Off he went up the hill, and came back facing us. Gerard, so wet and muddy a little more did not matter, crawled under the cars to fix the tow-line, and off we went. It must have been a couple of miles up a steep, winding road in blinding rain, our friend backing all the way. When finally we had reached the top, and he stopped and got out to disconnect the tow-line, we tried again to thank him, but he cut us short.

"I saw N Z on your car," he said, "and K I W I on your caravan. For three years I was with United Nations and my closest friend was a New Zealander. I couldn't see Kiwis in trouble and not help."

Blessings on our unknown countryman!

"Look at this," said Gerard proudly, when we were back in the car, and he flexed his arm. From the elbow of his sodden jersey ran a rivulet of dirty water.

"We're all wet—you're not the only one," I snapped rather testily. Water was dripping from the hem of my skirt, and forming a pool at my feet.

"I hope you don't all catch cold," said John anxiously. "Do you feel chilled? I'm sorry that had to happen in the rain."

"It wasn't your fault," I answered, "but the sooner we can find a camping place and change our clothes the better."

But when we came to Judenberg and a camping John was rather dubious. As is so often the case, it was in the orchard of a gasthaus. No doubt in spring with the trees in blossom it would have been delightful. Now it was unattractive. The grass was high and the ground soggy; rain dripped heavily from the trees. John was afraid the wheels might get bogged down, and the heavy branches hung so low he was not at all sure that the caravan would fit under them.

"Perhaps we'd better push on and see if we can find something better," he said doubtfully.

"But we don't know how far we might have to go," I answered, "and even if we do find another, there's no guarantee it will be any better."

"Yes, we'd better not waste time looking for one. We can't afford to have everyone down with pneumonia."

So we stayed. It was wonderful to get into clean, dry clothes and have a meal and hot coffee; though, looking ruefully at the pile of muddy, discarded garments, I wondered what on earth I could do with them. I couldn't hang them out in the rain; and the caravan, comfortable and cosy little home though it was, had no room for drying them. In the end I bundled them all up, tossed them in the toilet and shut the door. As a matter of fact, the toilet had scarcely been used since England, as there were usually all necessary conveniences at campings, so it tended to become a dumping place for what was not needed.

Judenberg, when the rain had eased and we ventured out to look at it, proved to be quite a large place. All the townspeople without exception wore Austrian dress—the men in particular looked very smart—and I was interested to notice that

126

these were the only clothes on display in the shops; even when dress lengths were shown draped on to figures they were draped in such a way as to form the characteristic bodice, dirndl and apron.

In spite of our experience, the next day we had not so much as a sniffle.

Wörthersee is known as the Riviera of Austria. Along the shores of the lake casinos, luxury hotels, pensions and campings crowd each other. Lawns of hotels slope down, dotted with gay umbrellas, to private beaches; white sails of yachts dip and swoop on the blue water, water-skiers whoosh along, and beyond, in the distance, the snow-capped mountains of Yugoslavia pierce the sky. It was summer, and everywhere were crowds of holiday makers, clustering around souvenir shops, eating cream cakes in open-air cafés, swimming and sunbathing; dancing at tea-dances in hotel ballrooms, losing money in the casino, or playing with gambling machines. But very few of them were Austrians, who are not rich people. For most this place is beyond their means, so it is the more prosperous Germans who flock here to enjoy a holiday abroad, yet where their own language is spoken. John and I, strolling one day along the main street in Velden, one of the little towns on the shore of the lake, noticed that every car parked along its length, except ours, had a German number-plate.

Chapter XIII

WÖRTHERSEE was our last stopping place in Austria. We spent a few days there, then on into Italy—on a Saturday, which, we found, was not a good idea. Hundreds of cars were headed in the same direction, many of them making for Venice and a weekend at the Lido, and we soon found ourselves packed in a queue stretching for miles, halted at the customs barrier. Then it was a matter of moving a few yards, stopping, waiting, moving on a little more, and so on for an hour and a half. However, all things end eventually; at last we passed the frontier and were in Italy. For the next three hours we travelled through the fantastically magnificent scenery of the Dolomites.

Both the Austrian Alps and the Dolomites are beautiful, but in entirely different ways. The Alps are very high, but—in summer at least—have a gentle, smiling aspect, a certain softness and sweetness. In the Dolomites all is rugged, craggy grandeur— great jagged peaks of white rock, so sharp against the pale blue sky they seem to be pasted there; innumerable waterfalls plashing down to the river rushing and roaring below; a railway crossing and recrossing the motor-road over viaducts of stone arches, as romantic against the green trees as a backdrop for a Victorian melodrama.

In a village called Ospedaletto we camped on a smooth lawn dotted with fruit-trees and surrounded by a high stone wall. The only other campers were a German couple who were examining a fig-tree with rather puzzled expressions. The woman came over to us and said in excellent English:

"Excuse me, could you tell me what are the fruit on this tree?"

"Figs," I said, "but I'm sorry I don't know the German word."

"Figs!" she exclaimed. "I know what figs are!" With sparkling eyes she ran back to her husband, spoke to him, and together they stood contemplating the tree with almost reverent attention.

"Never did I think I would see figs grow!" she said. Her husband spoke, and she translated.

"My husband says always before they are dry, brown things in a little box."

"Don't eat them," I warned. "They are not ripe."

"Oh, I understand that. But I have seen a fig-tree!"

I smiled a little at her excitement, but I understood the thrill of exotic fruit. I have always had an ambition to taste a date fresh from the palm—perhaps some day I shall.

Near the camping was a store, and as I went towards it a bicycle appeared weaving drunkenly along the road, ridden by an elderly man in leather jacket and Tyrolean hat. He was singing loudly and tipsily, and as he came nearer we were rather surprised to hear the words of his song: "Parlo italiano, Mussolini, spaghetti" repeated over and over again. He dismounted, or rather fell off his bicycle, and followed me into the shop, shouting, "Scusi, scusi, scusi." Addressing me, he asked:

"Deutsch?"

"Nein," I answered.

"Hollandisch?"

"Nein."

"Französisch? Italienisch?"

"Nein."

Whereupon he looked at me with bleary gravity, spread his arms wide, and said:

"Nicht Deutsch; nicht Französisch; nicht Hollandisch— misérable!"

He was apparently known to the shopkeeper and regarded as a pest, for he was brusquely ordered out.

The next day would be Sunday, so I asked the storekeeper the way to the church and the time of Mass, and I was secretly delighted that my Italian was understood. She pointed out the shortest road, and told me Mass would be at half-past six next morning, and I would be sure to get there in time, because—she made a gesture of pulling a rope and added, "Ding dong."

Being forewarned had not prepared us for the reality. At five o'clock we were awakened by the clattering and reverberating of bells, echoing back from the mountains and filling the whole air with such a clamour it seemed the very earth was shaking. We thought at first our watches had stopped, but they hadn't. The insistent bells kept on and on, making sleep impossible, so we rose and went out. It was a bright morning, some mountain peaks just tipped by the sun, others veiled in wisps of mist, the sky clear and cloudless. The village street was quiet, all the houses shuttered; except for ourselves no one in sight save an old woman filling a jug at the village pump. We were obviously far too early. It seemed the custom to waken the villagers with a noise of bells in very good time. We passed the church, still quite deserted, and continued our walk along the narrow, crooked canyon of the village street, between the closed houses, and out into open fields, around in a circle and back again another way; by which time Ospedaletto was stirring and all its inhabitants, in twos and threes and family groups, were on their way to Mass. In the church we found ourselves surrounded by women; John and the boys, slightly embarrassed, thought they were the sole representatives of their sex till we rose to go, and realized it was women in front, men at the back. This must have been a purely local custom, for we never saw it anywhere else.

And so we took the road again, on a sunny Sunday morning; through vineyards and fields of corn and sunflowers; past little stone cottages with grapevines trained over them; through small towns where groups of men stood talking in the sunshine or gathered in clusters at cafés. Here and there we passed a wedding procession—in Italy Sunday is a favourite day for weddings —the bonnets of the cars covered with flowers. Once we stopped at a café for ice-cream—the wonderful Italian gelato cassata, so much better than ice-cream anywhere else, full of fruit and candied peel. Perhaps it was the fault of the Little Man that, approaching Venice we took a wrong turning, and found ourselves on the long causeway leading to the city, in the traffic lane for the Lido vehicular ferry, where we had not intended to go. There were thousands of cars moving in each direction, and our error meant some awkwardness in backing and turning, and for a few minutes held up the flow of traffic, but soon we were again on the causeway, headed back the way we had come, to our camping place at Fusina, in a district with the ominous and wholly unwarranted name of Malcontento. The camping, right on the shore, had everything we could possibly require—service station, bottled gas depot, the best-stocked camp shop I had known, café; sun and shade in just the right proportions, and frequent water-buses across the lagoon to Venice, which rose opposite, seeming to float, like a city in a dream, above the surface of the water. The only drawback was the mosquitoes, which were large, numerous and ferocious. The store did a roaring trade in insect repellent.

The next day, bright and early, with an English family camping nearby, we walked down to the water-bus landing, eagerly looking forward to a day in Venice. The water-bus, when it came, proved to be a funny, antiquated little launch, carrying about thirty or forty passengers. She gave a comical little toot, and moved off. I was about to take a seat when I realized it was very hot, and to my horror saw the wooden seat was smouldering and smoking. We all jumped up, very alarmed, and John and the children pushed me forward, saying "Quick! You know Italian. Tell the captain! Quick, it might blow up." I dashed through the cabin, trying to remember how to say, "The ship's on fire" in Italian, rushed to the man at the wheel and shouted at him, frantically pointing to the stern. All he did was nod imperturbably and continue steering. Excitedly, I repeated it, urging him to do something. He merely sighed, and nodded to another member of the crew, who sauntered back, glanced casually at the charred and smoking woodwork, flicked a damp cloth at it, and returned to his place. Obviously, no one was going to do anything, so I went back to the others, who had all moved as far from the fire as they could, and were still looking at it apprehensively. It just didn't seem according to the rules— here were the phlegmatic Anglo-Saxons getting excited, and the

131

excitable Latins remaining quite unmoved! We concluded that this was something that happened every trip and they were quite used to it; in all probability we would stay afloat till we reached Venice. Having reached that comfortable conclusion, we settled down to enjoy gliding across the silky pale-turquoise water, till we reached the pink Palace of the Doges and Piazza di S. Marco.

The only word that really describes Venice is dreamlike. It is unreal, like an artist's caprice, with buildings and houses rising from the water, and much more lovely than any artist could paint it. But there is nothing dreamy about the Venetians—when it comes to business they are very much on the ball. I soon learned it was dangerous to stop and admire goods in shop-windows. Invariably the shopkeeper was lurking like a spider in wait for just such a moment, and one would find oneself being hustled inside with promises of much better goods than those on display.

At Cook's we found piles of mail, and, very excited, scooped it all up and made for Florian's, on the shady side of Piazza di S. Marco, to sit sipping coffee and reading it. Travelling about gipsy fashion as we were doing, receiving letters from home was a rare enough event to make a truly red letter day.

There is always an atmosphere of excitement and high holiday in Piazza di S. Marco, because of course, most of the people there are out to enjoy themselves. Tourists are everywhere. More American than Italian is spoken, and, with the vendors of corn for the pigeons, the eager young men offering their services as guides to see the glass-blowers or lace-makers at work, the cafés, the string quartettes playing the more obvious Italian melodies, the general impression is one of gaiety. But the visitor of limited means is safer on the Rialto, where prices are lower. It was while Miriam and I were choosing Venetian glass neck-laces on the Rialto that we heard a cheery voice call, "Hullo, Kiwis" and turned to greet Mr and Mrs B., the Australians we had last met at Langenwang.

Each day we started out with a sight-seeing plan, but each day Venice itself lured us from it. The narrow streets and passages, the people, the cafés, were all so fascinating that just sauntering and looking was sight-seeing enough. To stand on a bridge on the Grand Canal looking at the Oriental-seeming buildings with their colourful sun-blinds and watching the gondolas and fussy motor-boats go by, was bliss; and, when the sun became too hot, it was a joy to plunge into the cool darkness of narrow streets and alleys. There was always something unexpected to be savoured and enjoyed—a tenor voice suddenly heard from a window singing a snatch of opera; a sign on a café "English Fish and Chips"; the Venetian faces, so familiar from Italian paintings; the thrill of coming suddenly on an inscription "In this house John Ruskin lived and worked"; the glimpse through a barred window of a furnace and glass-blowers at work. Nevertheless, we did visit St Mark's, all a dark golden glitter; and the Accademia, with its wonderful Tintorettos, Tiepolos and Veroneses. We went to the Palace of the Doges, took photos of the Bridge of Sighs, and saw glass-blowers at work, afterwards being conducted through showroom after showroom of Venetian glassware—some beautiful, some hideous. I was on tenterhooks lest Godfrey or Nicky blunder into some costly and fragile piece, but fortunately, there were no mishaps. We lunched at a very reasonably priced café where the food was delicious—spaghetti alla Napoli, wiener schnitzel, hugh piles of grapes and pears, and white wine. When the children sprinkled grated cheese on the spaghetti sparingly, as if it were salt, the waiter was quite distressed. "No, no, no," he cried, and seizing the cheese bowl proceeded to smother their plates. The first time my children had ever been reproved for being too dainty!

In the evenings we went back to Fusina by water-bus. We never again saw the boat which had caught fire the first morning; all our other trips were made on very smart modern craft with fibreglass seats; but all the same the trip was not without incident. One evening we were halfway across when we saw a large, cumbersome barge, laden with barrels and boxes, making straight for us, its crew of two obviously quite unaware of what was happening. The passengers on that side of the boat cried out and leaped from their seats a moment before the barge struck us amidships. It had been an alarming moment, although the damage was negligible, but then it turned to farce. The bargeman, although it was undoubtedly his own fault, flew into a rage. He shouted and danced with fury, shaking his fist and screaming abuse at the captain of the ferry, who simply ignored him. Then he dived below, to appear a moment later brandishing a large book. Still shouting he thumbed through it, found what he wanted, slapped the open page triumphantly, read aloud a passage in a shout, took out a pen, made some notes, and danced in his bare feet up and down the length of his barge again, still bellowing and yelling. Meanwhile, the sprucelydressed ferry captain continued to act as if the bargeman were not there, still holding to a steady course, while the barge followed on. When we disembarked at Fusina landing stage the captain was still being completely unconcerned and the bargeman, the sunset gleaming on his bright red hair, was still gesticulating and shouting. We did not wait to see what happened when he too reached the landing. But nobody could say trips across the Laguna were dull!

We left Venice on a bright, very hot day, for Bologna. A couple of wrong turnings at the beginning sent us around in a circle, and we had covered nine miles before we had progressed at all on our way. Not long after leaving Venice we saw ahead of us on the road a crowd of small children, all dressed in white. As we approached we saw they were forming into line, and we slowed down. It was the funeral of a child. The little mourners made a guard of honour outside the church as the hearse moved away, the whole of its bodywork covered with white flowers, and long white ribbon streamers hanging from the roof and fluttering out behind as it moved. The white coffin glimpsed through the glass looked very tiny.

On through Padua, St Anthony's city, of which we saw little save the rose-coloured basilica; through Ferrara, and Monselice, where Petrarch lived.

We stopped at a pleasant restaurant where, on a wide, cool verandah, we lunched on spaghetti, gelato and coffee. The waiter spoke English, and seemed very interested in our caravan and our trip. Where were we going? John said, Bologna today and tomorrow on to Florence.

"Oh no," he said. "Why not Florence today? You could be there by half-past three on the autostrada."

We laughed, but after he had gone John said, "You know, I think he's got something. The idea attracts me. After all, we wouldn't really see much of Bologna. We'd arrive in the afternoon, spend most of the time cooking a meal and resting, and then be off in the morning. I think we'll push on."

So that was what we did. A brief rest at Bologna, where Nicky, inevitably, made friends with a cat, and did not want to leave it—and on to the Autostrada del Sole.

We had been impressed by the German autobahn—but that was before we saw the Italian autostrada, which as a piece of engineering is unsurpassed. We climbed and climbed, gently at first, over hills which looked dry and brown, for there had been a long drought. Here and there in the distance of this sepia landscape churches and villages recalled the backgrounds of old paintings. Then, suddenly it seemed, we were high in the mountains. A series of huge viaducts carried us up and up, until the valley was hundreds of feet below. Through a couple of tunnels, and still on and up. It was a blazing hot day, and we were not really surprised when the radiator boiled, and we had to pull over into the emergency lane and stop. We were not really sorry, either, for it was a pleasant relief to get out of the car and walk about in the cool breeze. The inevitable traffic police appeared, and when we explained the trouble said, exactly as their Austrian counterparts had said in the Alps, "Half an hour."

The Apennine Range rises far above the surrounding country in a series of jagged peaks and folds; and the autostrada draws a straight line across them. Tremendously high viaducts across valleys and tunnels through peaks alternate for miles. Sometimes there is a considerable distance of daylight before plunging into another tunnel, sometimes it is extremely short. Once we shot out of a tunnel to find ourselves in the smoke and flames of a forest fire, but only a couple of hundred yards across a viaduct and we were in darkness again, to emerge on the opposite side of the mountain where there was not the slightest sign of fire. Sometimes an "artificial tunnel", as they call it, instead of cutting through a mountain, skims its surface, and has on the outer side no wall, but a colonnade of pillars, giving picturesque glimpses of the countryside. We stopped again to rest in what looked like completely deserted country, and were astonished when an old woman appeared selling orangeade. Very welcome it was indeed. Clearly this was a regular stopping place for motorists to cool off. Then in the dusk came the long, gentle descent to Florence. Through the toll booth, to an information office for a map of the city, and then we ran the gauntlet of the Florentine traffic, where, as far as we could see, it was a case of every man for himself and the devil take the hindmost. On that first mad drive there seemed to be no lights, no traffic officers and no rules. Road courtesy didn't seem to apply—it was push your way through or get left.

"Wasn't Venice lovely?" said Miriam, wistfully. "No traffic." And indeed a city without vehicles or horns or petrol fumes is a delicious oasis in the modern world.

Camping Michelangelo in Florence is one of the dozen or so camping places I remember with particular affection. Sloping down from the road in a series of terraces, with tents and caravans dotted about among the olive-trees, when we were there it was crowded, gay and rather noisy. Some of the camping places we stayed at were used by the people of the country, enjoying an annual holiday in the open air; others catered largely for tourists and the campers were cosmopolitan. The latter was the case in Florence. There was the American family with elaborate tent and camping equipment, and a smaller tent for their coloured maid. There was the English colonel, bringing his wife on a sentimental journey to show her the roads he had travelled in the war. There were forty lively French schoolboys, travelling in a bus, in the care of two priests, returning from a pilgrimage to Rome—I did not envy the priests their task, but they seemed to take it in their stride. There was the cheery group of girls, three Australians, one Canadian and one New Zealander, touring Europe in an ancient and battered London taxi; and the young Belgian couple with a fat, adorable baby, whose daily open-air bath always drew a circle of cooing admirers. It all added up to a quite exciting atmosphere.

This is one of the really well-equipped campings, with excellent showers and toilets, shops, post office, service station, laundry, and the café on a terrace with a wrought-iron railing, open save for a translucent green roof, has a superb view across the proud towers and cupolas and tawny-gold houses of the city to the hills beyond. It was very pleasant to sit here, drinking Chianti or orange juice, or eating ice-cream, enjoying the panorama spread before us; but Florence has too much to offer to spend all one's time just sitting.

First, to the Cathedral. I had been thrilled by cathedrals before—the lacy stone tracery of Cologne, the Oriental splendour of San Marco in Venice; the grandeur of Lincoln, Canterbury and Brussels—but Florence has a different kind of beauty—colour. The exterior of pink, green, black and white marble, and Giotto's wonderful tower, look brand-new, as fresh and as clean as if they had been built yesterday, instead of centuries ago. Inside, cool and dark after the outdoor heat, it is much more austere than the brilliant exterior would lead one to expect; but the mosaics in the Baptistry are splendid indeed, and the golden door a living Bible. While we were there, a troop of little boys in pale blue shorts and shirts poured off a bus labelled "Villaggio dei Raguzzi", and into the Cathedral —Boys' Town in Italy as well as America.

We spent an afternoon in the Boboli Gardens, not at the time looking their best, for drought had dried and turned the lawns to brown, and formal gardens need to be green. We passed many happy hours exploring the Straw Market, where fine articles of Florentine tooled leather can be bought very cheaply, or walking on the bridges over the Arno—the Ponte Vecchio with its goldsmiths' shops, and the inevitable men in the doorways waiting to lure tourists in; or the Ponte di S. Trinità, startlingly familiar from the picture of Dante and Beatrice reproduced on so many walls. Sometimes we took a short stroll uphill from the camp to Piazzale Michelangelo, where the noble young marble David, sling-shot in hand, looks gravely out over the city, and where Florentines and visitors stroll in the cool of the evening, or stop at little booths to buy ice-cream, a toy, or a slice of watermelon, which they eat on the spot, spitting the seeds into the bins provided for the purpose.

We were delighted to meet again Mr and Mrs B., who seemed to be following a similar route to ours, and parked next to us in the camping.

The terrific heat made the thought of exertion distasteful; it was tempting just to lie in the shade; but if one bestirred oneself, and kept moving about, somehow it seemed cooler. One very hot evening we were sitting quietly after dinner, looking out over the lights spread below, when I suddenly said:

"Here we are in Florence, and we sit and read. Let's go and see how the city looks by night."

"That's a good idea," said John. "Come on, everybody, let's go."

"Do we *have* to?" asked Miriam plaintively, making no move.

"I can't be bothered," said Gerard. "I like it here."

We called the two younger ones, who were playing with a little English boy.

"Oh, *hang*. We're just having a good game."

"Can't you play tomorrow?"

"No, that boy will be gone tomorrow."

In the end, with instructions to Gerard to keep an eye on the others, John and I went alone. We went by bus—an exhilarating experience to say the least. Although the road twisted and wound like a tortured snake down to the city, the bus went at a breakneck speed all the way. As in all Italian buses, there

137

were few seats, most of the passengers standing, and at every turn all were flung about on top of each other alarmingly, but nobody seemed to mind; they just laughed, picked themselves up and braced themselves for the next corner and the next tumble. Even when we got into the town and were running through narrow crowded streets the pace did not slacken. The driver must have had nerves of steel. We walked about the streets, looking at hotels and restaurants, and window-shopping at department stores, which were all still open, and we wandered through the market, which was just closing. It was fascinating to see the practised efficiency with which the market people packed together their wares, closed their stalls and left order where only a few minutes before had been chaos, without pausing for a moment in their gossip and chat. We stopped for a while at a confectioner's shop to admire the baskets of flowers and fruit all made of marzipan, so realistic the peaches really seemed to have downy skins; and we bought for the children some "ghiaia d'Arno" (Arno pebbles), sweets which looked for all the world like smooth rounded pebbles from the river-bed. We sat at a sidewalk café eating ice-cream and watching the people go by—family parties including small children and even babies, although it was late, taking the air after the heat of the day. Then back to the camping, and to bed—far too warm to use our sleeping-bags—with the caravan door wide open, the full moon streaming in, and somewhere nearby a man's voice singing in Italian.

It would take a very long time to see all there is to see and admire in Florence; the wonderful Uffizi Gallery alone would take weeks to see properly: it is quite impossible in one visit.

138

Here I was excited by the classical statues: the Dancing Faun, the Crouching Slave, the exquisite Venus, the Laocoon: but for me the most moving experience of all was a rather unexpected one—the Botticelli "Birth of Venus". I had not thought that this picture, so familiar in reproduction, would appeal to me particularly, but it did, and I found it difficult to tear myself away from it. The stiff little waves and the falling blossoms have a certain humour, a light-hearted playfulness, but the face of the Venus is hauntingly beautiful. The catalogue describes it as a sad face, but I would not call it that. It is a strangely young, unawakened face, innocent, as a baby or a young animal is innocent, the expression that of a new creature with a mind as yet unused. I found it irresistible and quite unforgettable.

On Sunday we went to Mass at San Miniato, a ninth century Romanesque church with a black and white marble façade, and a commanding position high above the golden city in its cup of hills. The ancient frescoes, still well preserved, included a very large one of St Christopher (dear St Christopher, I thought, he's been helping us and has brought us a long way) and the rafters were painted in patterns which reminded us very much of the rafters of a Maori whare. There was a wedding taking place, and the church was crowded. This was our first experience of the Italian custom of solemnizing marriages at the regular Sunday Mass, but we were to be present at several other weddings before we left Italy. On this occasion, between the wedding guests and the regular congregation, the church was not big enough for all the people, and a priest announced that, for those not attending the wedding, there would be another Mass in the crypt. So down we trooped—but it was odd, to say the least, at the most solemn moment of the Mass, to hear bursting forth above us the *Lohengrin* Wedding March, followed by "Ave Maria" sung by a choir with full orchestral accompaniment.

All the time we were in Florence the extreme heat persisted. On our last day the weather was overcast and drizzly, but the temperature higher than ever. Evening brought no relief. As it was far too hot to stay in the caravan we went up to the terrace café, in the hope that there might be some slight breeze. Most of the campers had the same idea, and the place was crowded. We had not been there very long when the storm broke—thunder and lightning, and then a deluge of rain. But there, under the transparent roof, we were dry, and at least the air became a little cooler. Nobody wanted to brave the downpour to return to tent or caravan, so everyone just sat on and on— at first quietly talking, eating, drinking, playing chess or Scrabble; then a group of young people started to sing to a guitar, others joined in and the gathering began to take on the atmosphere of a party.

"I wonder what the girls in the taxi will do tonight?" I remarked to John. These five lasses had a casual attitude to camping—no tent, just sleeping-bags spread on the ground.

"They certainly can't sleep out in this," John replied, "and they'll be cramped in the taxi. We'd better offer them our car."

We did not sleep much, for the thunder kept us awake. The next morning it was still raining, and the camping was a mess. On each of the terraces a great lake had formed, and many tents had collapsed. Everywhere bedraggled campers were wringing out clothes and bedding. As we watched, one girl, who had been sleeping on a lilo, floated right out of her tent; her mattress had become a raft. Fortunately for our boys, they had pitched their tent in a sheltered, well-drained spot at the top of a slope, and they and the stray cat which was Nicky's current Pussy Brigade member had kept perfectly dry.

The taxi girls came over to thank us: three of them had slept in the taxi and two in our car, so they were all quite dry. They intended, they said, to push on.

"Your car run well?" John asked.

"Well, we get there," said the girl who seemed to be the leader, an Australian. "I'm not an expert on cars, but I can generally make it go."

"How is it on hills?"

"Oh, I just shove it in first, hard down on the accelerator and hope for the best. The other day something fell out of it. We didn't know what it was, but it still goes, so I don't suppose it matters."

We hoped they would get safely back to England!

This was the day we had intended to leave Florence, but the weather was so bad we felt it might be wiser to stay. We lingered, John busy at his typewriter, the children doing lessons; then, mid-morning, the rain eased—and suddenly, a shaft of sunlight.

"Sole! Sole!" cried an Italian voice from a nearby tent, and then broke into song, "O Sole Mio!"

The weather was fine again. We put aside our work, packed, and were away.

Chapter XIV

"MUMMY, all the ladies are looking at you. It's your clothes."
Startled, I looked around me. It was perfectly true. Every doorway in the narrow street, every little shop, seemed to have a pair of dark eyes, all fixed on me. And I thought I had been so tactful, too, changing my usual shorts or slacks for a dress before going into the village! But apparently in Tavarnelle sleeveless green and white cotton print is not considered appropriate wear for the middle-aged mother of a family. In the Italian countryside Mamma, whatever her age, wears black, even in the heat of a Tuscan summer.

If all had gone according to plan we would not have been in Tavarnelle at all. It is not a resort. For the average tourist it is just another little village, not particularly beautiful, on the road from Florence to Siena—unless, as happened to us, his car breaks down.

We had left Florence in sunshine after the storm, and driven past a huge American war cemetery where the little white crosses in rows were so close and numerous that at some angles as we moved past the green grass between them disappeared altogether and the ground seemed white, out into the Tuscan countryside, with its olives and cypresses, farmhouses with shutters and curved roof tiles, and, of course, vineyards, vineyards and more vineyards. This is the Chianti district, producing the bulk of Italy's wine. But we could not give ourselves up to wholehearted enjoyment of the scenery, because we were having car problems again. The narrow road twisted and curved, winding up, up and up. Every time we thought we must have reached the top—another bend, and still upward. Inevitably, the radiator boiled, and we had to stop. A wait, on a bit more, and another stoppage. We all got out and pushed.

"When people ask me what I saw of the Alps and Italy," sighed Nicky, "I'll say the back of the caravan."

Hours passed—stopping, pushing, getting on a little way, boiling, stopping again. The sun streamed down; we were all drenched with perspiration, thirsty and thoroughly uncomfortable. Two youths on a motor-cycle stopped and asked if they could help. Italian young men, more than any others, love cars—everywhere we found they enjoyed examining motors. In Italy one has only to open a bonnet to find a group of lads will gather around, peering in and discussing it. These boys were no exception. Having satisfied themselves that there was nothing they could do to fix it, they good-naturedly joined us behind the caravan and helped push, until the motor started again, then said good-bye and went roaring off into the distance. No sooner had they gone than disaster struck. The clutch-plate broke, and we were really stranded. The Little Man had not given up.

There was nothing to be done. I made coffee and we had a meal of rolls and grapes while we waited for help to come. When he had eaten, John went off a little way, and walked up and down by himself, looking white and anxious. He was not feeling well, for he had had another attack of 'flu, and also a painful boil. I felt sorry for him, for I knew in the circumstances trouble with the car must have seemed the last straw, so I was not altogether surprised when he came back and said:

"I can't stand any more of this. Let's chuck the whole thing."

"Yes, but how shall we get back?"

"I've been thinking. . . . When we get to Siena let's sell the caravan—it doesn't matter if we don't get much for it. It'll be worth a loss to be rid of the strain. We can buy another tent."

"We can't possibly carry all our stuff in the car. Perhaps we could send most of it back to England."

"Yes, and I'll buy a roof-rack for the rest. Look, Joyce, I simply can't face any more of this. Every hill means trouble. The car's all right; it's just that this great caravan is putting too much strain on it on the hills. It was madness to try."

"No, it wasn't. We've come through so far. It really has worked. We've come over the Alps, the Dolomites, the Apennines. Heavens, come to think of it, we've been over just about all the mountain ranges there are—don't be too despairing."

"It's all very well being cheerful about it, but I'm the driver. I know how hard it is."

"It certainly would be a lot easier with just the car. Well, let's do it then. We'll sell the caravan."

Suddenly, a look of consternation came over his face.

"But we can't—I've just remembered. We'd be breaking the law if we did. If we take vehicles out of England we have to take them back."

"A caravan doesn't go by itself—is it a vehicle?"

"Of course it is."

So that was that. We were committed to continuing as planned. In the meantime we were stuck—no dwelling in sight, and evening coming on, and since the motor-cyclists a couple of hours ago we had seen no traffic at all. At last a battered little car appeared, and to our great relief three very nice young Englishmen got out. We explained the situation, and they went on, promising to send a mechanic from the next village. After hours of seeing no one, we were suddenly offered more help than we needed, for next a policeman arrived and asked what was the trouble. In my best Italian I explained that un Inglese had gone for a mechanic, and he drove on. Afterwards we wondered if we had been wise to refuse his help, for we had no idea how far it was to the next village, and the Englishmen had said they did not speak Italian, so even if they had found a mechanic, they might not have been able to explain to him. However, we need not have worried, for very soon a small, antiquated-looking tow-truck and two mechanics arrived. They examined the car, and said they would have to tow it. What, I asked, would we do with the caravan? Take it along, of course; their truck was very strong. Was it far? No, only two kilometres to Tavarnelle. Then perhaps if we walked it would make the load lighter? No, no, no—the bambini in the truck with the driver, the parents in the car! And so the little Heath Robinson contraption moved off. It looked frail and shaky, but it pulled both car and caravan with ease behind it, and at dusk we came to Tavarnelle—a whole day to cover twenty miles!

The very first building in the village was the garage, a very spruce, modern building attached to a house, with a little shrine of Our Lady in a niche on the front. The car would be fixed tomorrow, they said. In the meantime, we could leave the caravan in the yard and stay in it overnight.

So there we stayed. As soon as we had unpacked and changed our clothes, Miriam and I went off up the village to buy food. A narrow, cobbled street, in each doorway a woman sitting working at embroidery; several shops, their doorways curtained with gaily-coloured plastic strips to keep out insects; a couple of cafés; about half a dozen cycle repair shops, for obviously the cycle, not the car, is the usual method of transport here; a cobbled town square, one side of which was taken up by the church outside which the priest in his soutane stood chatting—

143

that was Tavarnelle. The grocery smelled deliciously of pasta—so many different kinds of pasta—spaghetti, macaroni, and many, many other shapes and thicknesses on display in glass-fronted bins; and on the shelves, among the packaged goods, a tiny red lamp burned before a little shrine. In the shops they were pleasantly helpful, recommending the best kind of cheese or mortadella, picking out the firmest tomatoes. Cars might roar through from Florence to Siena and Rome, but the people of Tavarnelle just went about their business. Everybody knew everybody else, and the stranger in their midst was unusual enough to be an object of interest, but they were ready to extend to him a helping hand.

After dinner the evening stretched before us with nothing to do.

"What about the stories—are they all finished?" asked Nicky, who had not forgotten his story-writing plan. Some were finished; the procrastinators promised to finish their contributions, and those who had finished read theirs aloud. Nicky's was a humorous tale about the early days of motoring; John's a boys' adventure story set in the New Zealand bush, and mine about the tribulations of a family caravanning through Germany. Each was applauded, and, relaxed, we went to bed.

The next morning I went to the garage to beg a can of water and to ask how soon the car would be done. The proprietor told me he had had to send to Florence for a part, but he would have it done that evening about six, or even five if we were fortunate.

A whole day to fill in. There was no point in sitting all day in the caravan; and we could hardly spend hours just walking up and down the two hundred yards or so of village street. What could we do? John, studying maps to plan the next stage of our journey, looked up to remark that a youth hostel and camping was shown only a kilometre past the village; so we decided to walk along and see it—and perhaps with luck be allowed to use the washrooms and toilets. Once more through the village, past the shops and the church, and the bakery with a great heap of ashes from the oven piled outside it, and out into the country again. We had no difficulty in finding the youth hostel —a large, pleasant-looking white house with all its windows open to the sun. Behind it was the camping, but not a tent or caravan in sight. We thought it must have closed for the season, but obviously the youth hostel was occupied, so I went in search of the proprietor, and found him at the back of the house. He did not speak English, so again I was glad of my small knowledge of Italian. No, he assured me, both hostel and campeggio were open, it just happened nobody was there. I explained that our car had broken down and was being repaired in the village, but would not be done until the evening, and in the meantime we had nowhere to go, and could we please use the camping? He was extremely kind, and insisted that we must spend the day in the hostel—it was all ours.

He led us into a long, cool room; one wall was entirely made up of windows and French doors; in the wall facing it was a huge fireplace, with ingle seats set in it, and down the middle of the room a long table with copper bowls and pieces of pottery arranged down its length. In one corner was a combined office and bar, and the walls were covered with brightly coloured travel posters. Comfortable chairs and piles of magazines in a variety of languages made it very inviting. Here we stayed all day, using the washrooms to make good the deficiencies of our morning toilet, and then settling down to play games and read the magazines, while Nicky sketched the room. It was, I think, one of his best pictures. I have it still, and it always evokes that quiet, restful day, sitting at ease in cool comfort while the sun blazed down outdoors. Nothing could have been better for John just then than a few peaceful hours of relaxation. At noon I went to the village to buy rolls and grapes and the long narrow Italian tomatoes which have a flavour all their own, and we ate them out of doors, sitting at a little table in the shade. At about four o'clock we left, thanking our host, who refused any payment, and returned to the garage. The car, we were told, would be ready in about two hours. We made coffee, and packed ready to leave at the first possible moment; then there was nothing to do but sit in the caravan and wait, idly looking out the window at the activity of the garage and yard.

A rather scrawny-looking fowl was pecking about, occasionally getting in the mechanics' way, when it was chased off, giving indignant clucks. At last, the inevitable happened—it went out into the road and was run over. The woman driving the car stopped, picked up the corpse and ceremoniously presented it to the garage proprietor, who received it with a courtly bow and beaming smile, and as many expressions of thanks as if she had done him a great favour, instead of killing off his livestock. He disappeared with it into the house, and a little

145

later we noticed a small flurry of white feathers drifting out of an open window. Chicken for dinner that night!

The sun was on the horizon, casting a level blinding light, and the trees and hills were sharp black silhouettes against the sky when we were told the car was ready. They had replaced the clutch-plate—when it broke in Austria it had been welded, and had broken again. Now, with a new one, and one or two other minor defects rectified, the car fairly pranced along, and as a matter of fact, never gave us a moment's worry again. The garage men had done a really good job. So, in the evening, we continued on the road to Siena. We had been in Tavarnelle only twenty-four hours, but I felt I had come to know this typical little Tuscan town, and I still remember it with affection.

It was a joy to find we sailed effortlessly up hills far higher and steeper than the one which had previously been our downfall, and so it was in a mood of elation that we reached Siena, and camped beneath vines loaded with purple grapes. I bought salami and Chianti at the camp store, and then we settled down to hear Gerard's story, which was about motor-racing. The next morning, when for the first time we saw the campeggio by daylight, it looked even better than we had hoped. Campers, we learned, could help themselves to the grapes; and when I took some clothes to the ironing-room to press them, I was told it would be free. This was luxury indeed, for every other camping we visited made a small charge for the use of the ironing-room.

We were too late for the Palio, the exciting horse race in medieval costume which every year attracts hundreds of tourists, but some of the decorations and emblems of the competing teams were still in place, and we could imagine how thrilling it must have been on that day to be in the Piazza del Campo, the beautiful cockle-shell shaped piazza where the event is held.

Time in Siena seems to have stood still. In spite of the cinemas, the Fiats parked along every street, the modern goods in the shops, the demonstration by strikers during our visit, one has the curious feeling of being at the same time in the Middle Ages and the twentieth century. Partly, this impression comes from the fresh appearance of even ancient buildings. There is no sign of weathering in the black and white marble of the Cathedral, or the red brick of the city walls and the Basilica of St Dominic; and the use of red brick itself seems modern to

146

anyone coming from England, where ancient buildings are of stone. But Siena might have been built yesterday, and yesterday might have been A.D. 1300. St Catherine, Siena's most famous daughter, is still very much alive here, although she died in 1380. The street in which she lived, Via di S. Caterina, cannot have changed very much. Steep and narrow, with strings of washing hanging everywhere, it has stone arches across it, as if to buttress the houses, which seem in imminent danger of tumbling together; her house, however, has been altered and rebuilt out of all recognition. In the Basilica of St Dominic her head is preserved and displayed in a glass-fronted reliquary (the body is in Rome), also the habit she wore; and there is a pillar against which she is said to have stood frequently in meditation.

There is so much to see in Siena, and we had only one day. The delay in Tavarnelle meant we must push on. So it was a very crowded and exhausting day indeed, and I felt far too tired in the evening to bother cooking. Instead, we had a blissful meal at a café where, in the open air, by the light of the moon and candles, we dined on spaghetti and green salad, followed by gelato, and Chianti, then settled down to hear Godfrey's story —a plane crash in the Australian desert, and the Flying Doctor to the rescue.

The next morning we left very early—before the milkman had arrived, in fact. The day was dark and overcast, and even before we had left the city the rain came pelting down. The road climbed up in a series of loops and swerves and hairpin bends; and the driving rain reduced visibility to a few feet. The downpour was so heavy the windscreen wipers were inadequate, and after a while John gave up trying to peer through them, and drove with his head out the window, and water streaming down his face and dripping off his hair.

The country had changed and become much more rugged than we had yet seen in Italy—steep hills with rocky outcrops, and in the valley stony river-beds. Through Buonconvento, near the famous monastery of Montoliveto, where a long line of monks in white habits with cowls over their heads passed us silently walking through the rain. The road continued to spiral and turn up a mountain, and the wind and rain to lash John's face as he drove with his head out the window, almost hanging over the steep drop on the outer side; and on the very summit a walled town and castle looked wildly romantic as they appeared and disappeared in the shifting clouds. We were not quite sure where we were, till we saw a signpost pointing to Aquapendente, and somebody facetiously remarked that a name with "water" in it seemed very appropriate. We felt as if we, and the whole world, were under a colossal waterfall. The narrow road, the steep drop at the side, the wind, the rain, the poor visibility, made it a nerve-racking experience, and it was with relief we left the mountain behind.

"If only we'd come a year or so later we'd have avoided that," said John. "Look!" and he pointed to where an autostrada was under construction, which would by-pass the mountain. By now the rain had stopped, but there was an autumnal chill in the air, to remind us it was September, and summer was dying.

At the first glimpse Lago di Bolsena, cupped by hills, deep blue, with a couple of small islands floating on it, reminded me surprisingly of Wellington Harbour. Bolsena itself is a lakeside resort which caters largely for tourists. All along the shore are kiosks selling picture-postcards, beach hats, hot pizza, or offering boats for hire; but back from the lake, only a few hundred yards from these twentieth century delights, in complete contrast, the medieval quarter climbs the hill. Here, a maze of cobbled streets, some entirely made up of steps, and all so narrow it is barely possible for two persons to walk abreast, twist and wind between ancient stone houses, and women go by with tubs of laundry on their heads. All the people, we were surprised to notice, stopped what they were doing and turned to stare after us as we passed. We had thought, so close to the big hotels on the shore, they would be used to foreigners; but perhaps most visitors prefer the beach to antiquities.

"Look," said Miriam, pointing through the caravan window. "The Sea of Galilee!"

Framed in trees, we could see the lake, and in the rather chilly apricot sunset fishermen were putting out in little boats to let down their nets, standing up and rowing with a curious sideways motion. The shapes of the boats and the sails, and the attitudes of the men, did indeed make a Biblical picture.

"It's too good an evening to stay here," said John. "Let's go for a walk."

So out we went again, well wrapped up against the cold wind, along the shore in the sunset light and out on to a stone breakwater, to look down into the depths of the lake, murky and stagnant on one side; on the other limpid and deep, with numerous fish swimming about. The fishermen should have had a good catch.

At dawn the next morning the lake was even lovelier; and now the fishermen, helped by women in shawls and headscarves, were drawing in their nets. It looked even more like the Sea of Galilee.

Quite early in the morning we took the road to Rome. Now the country was very different from Tuscany—much harsher in appearance, and the people seemed poorer. At first there was not much traffic except little ass or ox carts; in the fields men were working with primitive-looking ploughs drawn by oxen. Now and again women passed balancing laundry tubs on their heads.

Through the bustling city of Viterbo, dominated by the great crumbling walls of the old Papal Palace, and on along the ancient Via Cascia.

"Look," exclaimed Gerard, "an old Roman viaduct. Doesn't it look modern? It could be a new railway bridge."

"That's funny," said Godfrey, who in the course of our travels had picked up some rudimentary knowledge of architectural styles. "It has pointed Gothic arches. Is it really Roman?"

It took us all a few moments to realize we were seeing an optical illusion. The viaduct stood out in sharp silhouette against the sun, and, approaching it as we were at an angle, the arches did appear narrow and pointed, but as we came nearer and faced it directly, their actual round Romanesque shape became apparent.

It was a sobering shock to all of us to pass many caves, where ragged, ill-fed looking people, including many children, were living. One reads of these things, of course; but it is not until one actually sees it that the full realization comes of how much poverty and misery there still is in Italy, in spite of the prosperity, comfort and progress of the northern part of the country.

On and on we went, all getting more and more excited the nearer we came to Rome. For a panicky moment we thought we had taken the wrong road, but no, we were going the right way. The traffic gradually increased and became very thick. Then we were part of a vast procession, an endless stream of vehicles going to the city. Our excitement increased.

"A hundred lire," said John, "for the first one to see the dome of St Peter's", and a moment later Nicky shouted, "There it is! I see it! St Peter's!"

149

And there it was! Rome!

"We've made it!" exclaimed John exultantly. "We're here!"

For Rome was in a sense our journey's end. This was as far as we would go; from now on we would be travelling back towards England. And who could fail to be stirred by their arrival in the Eternal City? So much to see and do! Ten days would scarcely be enough.

We liked Campeggio Monte Antenne from the moment we saw it. Quite large, and approached by a long winding road through the bright green umbrella pines of Rome, it must surely be set on the very top of one of the Seven Hills. It was warmly welcoming from the very first moment, when we stopped at the office to register, and the beautiful girl in charge, who spoke several languages, took our particulars. Car—caravan. A family party? How many persons? Parents and four children. And the ages of the children? John told her seventeen, fourteen, twelve and ten. Oh no, signor, twelve, ten, seven and four. John, thinking she had not understood, repeated it slowly and clearly, seventeen, fourteen—and with twinkling eyes she nodded. Yes, sir, I understood—twelve, ten, seven, four. And then he remembered children under twelve were free. It was Roman hospitality.

Rome was very hospitable to us in many ways. It was the only occasion on the Continent we were invited to visit a private home, and the evening we spent so warmly and graciously welcomed by an Italian family meant a great deal to us. They lived in a modern apartment building with marble floors throughout, and when I expressed my admiration our host seemed amused at my enthusiasm.

"Marble? It's cheap. There are mountains of it at Carrara!"

On another evening an Italian friend took us to dine in a delightful restaurant in a building over two thousand years old, and later drove us about Rome to show us places we could never have found for ourselves.

Rome is big, beautiful, bustling; a city of contrasts—so very old, so very new; so very hot in the sun, so cool in the shade; so rich in some parts, so poor in others. It would take a lifetime to know and appreciate it, and when, with dozens of other tourists, we tossed coins in the Trevi fountain and wished we might come back, even if we had no belief in the superstition, the wish was real enough.

The terrors of Roman traffic were worse by far than I had expected. Every driver seems to be under the impression he is competing in a race, and it is a point of honour with him not to be passed by anything. We decided from the start it was far less nerve-racking to use public transport than to drive, so each day we drove down the winding road through the pines from the campeggio, parked the car in Piazza Vescovia, and took a bus or a tram wherever we wanted to go. We soon learned that Roman bus manners are different from New Zealand ones. There, the child is privileged. The first time we went into the city Miriam was sitting next to a young woman holding a baby. A very old, bent woman got on, and Miriam automatically arose, only to have the young woman dump the baby in her seat! When later Godfrey and Nicky offered their seats to elderly people, and at once had them snapped up by two boys younger than themselves, I told them, though it was contrary to all previous training, on no account to stand, whoever got on the bus. It went against the grain, but, I told them, when in Rome . . .

When, tired of sight-seeing, we returned to the campeggio, we never lacked company, and it was never dull. Here once again we met our Australian friends, Mr and Mrs B., and a number of New Zealanders, including acquaintances from home. Two Italian schoolboys camping in a pup-tent, Agostino and Franco, made friends with Miriam and Gerard. Neither spoke English, but they learned French at school, and the four of them had long conversations in two varieties of school French, no doubt to the benefit of both pairs. Gerard and Agostino found a common interest in chess, and long evenings were whiled away in the caravan over the chess-board, with the others looking on and giving unwanted advice. Agostino knew one English verb, and delighted in airing it. Suddenly, he would stand up, announce "To sit", and plump down heavily on the cushions, to beam around at all of us proudly. It never failed to produce loud laughter, but I began to wish the youngsters would teach him a few more words!

Sometimes we would go to the open-air restaurant for ice-cream. The children enjoyed it, but John and I were usually driven away by the juke-box—and Angelo. Angelo was a handsome little boy of about nine, with great innocent eyes that suggested he was well named, but the truth was, he was a bit of an imp. Somehow he had learned the trick of playing the juke-box without putting in a coin, and he was very proud of the accomplishment, demonstrating again and again for the benefit

151

of a circle of highly impressed youngsters, and playing their requests. Then his mother would appear, shouting at him to stop it at once, and pointing out the dire things that would happen to people who were so wicked, whereupon the small fry would scatter like sparrows; but soon Angelo would be back, and the air ringing with "Ciao, ciao, bambina" or "Basta, basta".

Hundreds of books have been written about Rome, and no doubt hundreds more will be written—one could spend a lifetime reading them. It would be presumptuous on my part to attempt to describe what has been described so much better many times before. I can only list some of the things that impressed me.

The Catacombs—it is a moving and humbling experience to tread those long subterranean corridors hallowed by the blood of martyrs and to remember the courage and devotion of the early Christians in the face of savage persecution.

The Colosseum—we shamelessly listened to an English-speaking guide taking around a conducted party, and noted his account differed from the generally accepted beliefs—Christians were never killed here, in fact all persecution had ceased before the Colosseum was built; gladiators didn't get hurt, in fact it was not as dangerous as modern boxing. We were not convinced, but we could not fail to admire the superb design of the building—how many modern stadiums or theatres would be so well planned for the quick and efficient handling of crowds?

And then Constantine's Arch, where I spent so long studying the reliefs, fascinated by the picture they give of Roman life and dress, that I quite failed to notice the rest of the family had moved on, and I had to plunge alone through the terrifying traffic to catch them up before they disappeared—they hadn't even noticed my absence!

A place of endless fascination, for me as well as for the children, was the Nativity Scene in the crypt of the Basilica of Sts Cosmas and Damian. This Christmas tableau dates back to the seventeenth century, and gives an absorbing picture of Neapolitan life at that time. As well as the stable, with the Christ Child, the shepherds, the Magi, and Herod leaning from his window to see which way they go, there are hundreds of figures, all exact as to detail and costume, carved in wood, painted in natural colour, and dressed in clothing of various fabrics; and the surprising thing is that life in Italy—in the country, that is— has changed so little. There are men and women doing the same things in the same way as we had seen them in real life— women washing and hanging out linen, or carrying burdens on their heads; men selling meat and fish, using scales exactly like those we had seen in the markets; a child in a walking-frame such as we had seen in use.

It was awe-inspiring to stand in the Pantheon, and to think of all that has happened in that perfectly-proportioned building since the smoke of sacrifices to pagan gods first went up through the opening in the dome two thousand years ago—originally a pagan temple, then a Christian church, and never in all the centuries out of use! And across the Tiber by the famous bridge with Bernini's angels, Castel Sant'Angelo, so redolent of history, and commanding such a magnificent view of Rome from its roof.

In Europe in summer practically every place with any pretensions to historical interest presents "Son et Lumière" performances in the evenings. John and I had several times intended to go to them, but for one reason or another had not done so. Now we were glad we had waited for the Forum. I do not think any other place—except perhaps the Acropolis in Greece—could have been so impressive. There were two sessions, the second, to which we were going, beginning at ten-thirty. Although it was a fine evening there was an autumnal chill in the air, and we wore our warmest clothes; but even so, having arrived rather early, we were very glad to have time for hot coffee first. Then we waited outside, and were interested and amused by the taxi-drivers, waiting to catch the departing audience from the earlier session. They stood in a group on a high piece of ground where they could hear what was going on, smoking and chatting, a picture of sociability; but as soon as they saw the show was coming to an end all friendly feelings vanished. Out went their cigarettes and, like one man, they suddenly sprinted for the gate, pushing and shoving each other away, jockeying for position, and nearly knocking two women over in the rush, each man determined to be first. For all their eagerness, I noticed few of them got fares.

We went in, and sat under the stars, on the tiers of seats overlooking the Forum. Son et Lumière is an ideal way of displaying historic places; combining as it does recorded sound and commentary and imaginative flood-lighting, it is vastly more effective than any acted pageant could be in depicting history. It was thrilling, there in the very place where it all happened, to hear retold the whole story of Rome, from its very beginnings, Romulus and Remus; to hear coming nearer and moving along the Via Sacra the sound of a triumph, clop-clop of horses, jingle and clash of armour, tramp of feet, shouts of the populace; the murder of Julius Caesar; the burning of Rome under Nero, with all bathed in flickering red light; and finally, the triumph of Christianity, with all the churches about the Forum flood-lit, and the air filled with the exultant pealing of bells.

But the most memorable experience of all was the audience with the Pope—John XXIII—in St Peter's. It was to be the last audience before the Cathedral was closed to the public for the first session of the Oecumenical Council, which was to start the following month, and it was also the occasion on which a new organ was to be blessed. We were anxious that on this very special day nothing should go amiss. Suppose we went to the wrong place, or got caught up in the wrong queue? It would be much easier if we already knew the way. So, the day before, we went to the Vatican by way of rehearsal, as it were, to spy out the land.

St Peter's Square, with the great colonnades and the fountains playing, did not at first appear very big, and St Peter's itself seemed no larger than many other buildings; but then, as we walked across the Square to the Cathedral came the realization of how great was the distance. The perfect proportions, everything so exactly scaled to everything else, had at first glance disguised the vastness. Inside the Cathedral we were greeted by a loud noise of hammers, where men were at work erecting great stands of seats in readiness for the Council. Again, a momentary disappointment. Why, it's very beautiful, but not very big! Then Gerard whispered, "Look at that man up there", and pointed. Far above our heads a workman was busy, looking

154

scarcely bigger than a fly. Once again the perfect proportions had concealed the tremendous size. I do not know why, but for some reason I had expected St Peter's to be rather dark—"a dim, religious light". Actually, all is brightness; brilliance of sunshine through great windows, gold and vivid colour in mosaics. It was quite clearly from St Peter's that Sir Christopher Wren got his inspiration for St Paul's.

Gerard was doing a swift mental calculation.

"I suppose you realize," he said, "that Mt Wellington would fit in here easily."

In my mind's eye I called up a picture of that hill near our New Zealand home, and was suitably impressed.

On this first exploratory visit we did not linger, but returned to the caravan planning an early start next morning. The day dawned bright and sunny, and a little cooler. By seven-thirty we were on our way, first by tram then by bus, to the Vatican. At that hour it was a Rome we had not seen before. Streets and trams were crowded with people on their way to work—for us, a special, once-in-a-lifetime occasion; for them, just a normal week-day! It seemed impossible that life in the city was going on just as usual. St Peter's Square looked different too; yesterday it had been almost empty; today it was crowded: groups of pilgrims, parties of schoolchildren, priests, nuns in every imaginable colour and style of habit; Swiss Guards in their picturesque red, yellow and blue uniforms and plumed helmets. Standing in the sun we watched the changing of the guard; then, having learned the door to which our tickets would admit us, made our way there, to find there was already a long queue of people edging up ahead of us. Just behind us was a party of Americans, mostly middle-aged women, smartly dressed, with loud voices. They were accompanied by a priest who had been there before, and who occupied the time of waiting by describing to them the interior of the Cathedral and the form the ceremony would take. After a while we noticed the priest, an exceptionally big and tall man, who had been behind us, was now far ahead in the queue, and at the same time it dawned on his party that he was getting away from them.

"Say, Father," called one of the women, "how come you were in back of us and now you're way up there?"

He looked back laughing over the heads of the crowd.

"It's the 'permesso' and the twist," he said, demonstrating his method of penetrating the crush of people.

155

Then we were inside, in an excellent position to see the whole ceremony, and very near the new organ which was to be blessed. There was still an hour and a half before the beginning of the audience, but I have never known time to pass so quickly. Somewhere across the Cathedral, there was a large party of German pilgrims, and they broke spontaneously into song, one hymn following another, the rich full-bodied sound filling that vast space. Then at last in the distance we could hear clapping and cheering coming nearer, the singing faltered into silence, and the procession entered the Cathedral—Vatican officials, cardinals in scarlet, bishops in purple, Swiss Guards with lances, their helmets gleaming and plumes nodding, and at last —the Holy Father himself, white-robed, carried aloft in a chair. A circuit of the whole Cathedral, so that everybody could see him, turning to right and to left, smiling and blessing the multitude, while tremendous cheers and cries of "Viva il Papa" echoed round and up into the very dome. Opposite us a large group of nuns took off their belts and waved them vigorously over their heads. Then he descended, walking briskly down a railed-off space to the organ to bless it—to our delight passing within a few feet of us. His step was youthful and vigorous, and his voice when he spoke strong and resonant—surprisingly so for a man of over eighty. I don't think anyone in that vast crowd could have guessed that he was already very sick and within a few months would be dead.

After the blessing the Pope returned to his throne, and the various groups of pilgrims present were announced—they came from every corner of the globe. Next followed the Holy Father's address. He spoke first in Italian and then in French, and it was obvious, from the laughter which rocked around the building, that he was making many jokes, but neither my Italian nor my French were adequate to appreciate them. Interpreters took over, and the address was repeated in German, English and Spanish. Next followed a recital by two organs—the new one and the old one—and two choirs, the Pope smiling and leading the applause after each item: then the procession re-formed, His Holiness was carried out again, and the audience was over.

Afterwards we did not hurry away, but passed some time in St Peter's; then along the Viale Vaticano to the Vatican Galleries and up the wonderful double spiral staircase to spend hours there viewing the many treasures, the visit culminating in the incomparable Sistine Chapel itself. A memorable day.

Much as we should have liked to, we could not linger in Rome for ever. One morning quite early we hitched our caravan, and drove around the perimeter of the city, past the stadiums built for the Olympic Games in 1960, with their big statues of athletes, skirted the wall of Vatican City, and away.

Arrivederci, Roma! Arrivederci, the delicious smoky scent of the Monte Antenne pines; arrivederci, the tinkling of innumerable fountains. We headed north.

Chapter XV

We travelled up the Mediterranean coast, sometimes almost along the beach, sometimes turning inland a little, but never far from the sea, till we came to Albinia, where we stayed one night. The grassy campeggio was set among pines, by a beach of fine white sand. The sea was calm and silky-smooth, and the sky heavily overcast. We had scarcely arrived when it started to rain and there was thunder and lightning. It was a curious fact, while we were in Italy we noticed there was never rain without an electrical storm as well.

Later it cleared, and John and I went for a walk in the rosy sunset. On the beach a few people were surf-casting; further along there was a little store, a restaurant called "Il Pescatore" and a bar where several men sat playing cards, a circular open-sided, thatched structure like a large bandstand, and inland, away from the sea, a few houses. That was Albinia, peaceful and quiet: but suddenly the silence was shattered by shots, and startled, we saw a man among the pines, shooting at birds. I remembered again the remark of an Australian at Florence: "Have you noticed you never hear birds singing in Italy? They shoot them all." I had not noticed till it was drawn to my attention. Later, in France too, we noticed there was a great deal of banging away at small birds. Doubtless in wine-producing countries it is important to protect the grapes, but that is not the only reason for the destruction. In Italy on market stalls one can see tiny dressed birds laid out in rows. There seems to be a good sale for them.

We had planned to make an early start next morning, and at sunrise, when the pines were black against a vivid pink sky, we were packed and ready to depart, only to be frustrated by finding the gate locked, and no one to open it. So there we had to sit and wait for several hours, half exasperated, half amused at the ridiculous situation—imprisoned in a camping ground! But eventually the caretaker arrived to release us and off we went, still travelling north, on the old Aurelian Way, through flat country with mountains far to our right. Here and there on their slopes clung picturesque little towns and castles. Occasionally we passed carts drawn by white oxen with huge spreading horns, and once a party of gipsies in two carts, each pulled by a dispirited horse, with another horse being led. The carts were piled so high with goods, pots, pans, people and children we wondered how the poor beasts could keep on their feet, let alone move. We stopped at a small town for ice-cream at an open-air café outside a cinema with posters advertising a Western called "Bill il Sanguinario". Billy the Kid?

Then the road turned to the coast again, and we went on through the loveliest scenery imaginable—bright sunshine; on our left the sparkling turquoise Mediterranean with far out the island of Elba and the smaller one of Capraia; on our right, umbrella pines, little resort towns with shuttered houses coloured pink or blue or white. We skirted the busy city of Livorno (Leghorn), passed a large oil refinery and a big American Army camp, and came at last to Pisa.

"A hundred lire," said John, "for the first to see the Leaning Tower", and as usual it was Nicky who shouted, "There it is! I see it!"

It is not for nothing that the cathedral square of Pisa is called "Piazza dei Miracoli". It is almost miraculous. The great bubble of the Baptistry dome, the perfect white Cathedral, and the famous Leaning Tower—so much further out of perpendicular than I had expected—all snowy white against green lawn, must make up one of the most exquisite groups of buildings in the world.

159

Pisa is not a big city, but it is an important railway junction. To reach the camping it was necessary to cross two lots of tracks, and never once, during our stay there, were we able to go directly through; always the gates seemed to be closed in front of us. Sometimes, having waited a considerable time for the first barrier to be raised we would start confidently across, only to have the second one close in our faces, and there we would be, caught in a No Man's Land in the middle, with trains thundering past fore and aft.

One could not visit Pisa without climbing the Leaning Tower, but it is an experience I have no desire to repeat. I, who pride myself on being a good sailor and am "never, never sick at sea", felt a distinct sensation of mal-de-mer before I had got very far up. It comes from the unexpected feeling of climbing a spiral ascent of a tower—which one expects to be *up*—and then finding oneself apparently going *down,* or at the least horizontally, added to the fact that one is very conscious of the unrailed open galleries all the way up. The younger members of the family, of course, were quite immune to this malaise, and galloped cheerfully and excitedly to the very top and out on the roof; but I did not follow. Instead I crept shamelessly down again, and with trembling knees sat waiting for them on the Cathedral steps. On the whole, I preferred to admire the tower from ground level.

We ran the gauntlet of the souvenir sellers in the Piazza dei Miracoli—the vendors of scarves, china plates, postcards, dolls, leather goods, the ice-cream men with barrows shaped like gondolas—and wandered through the streets as far as the River Arno—here smelling unpleasantly of drains and decaying vegetables—and back again; saw the University, and passed a military barracks just as the guard was changing.

"The British Grenadiers were never like this," I murmured, while John unslung his movie camera to record the deathless moment. The soldiers sauntered up and stood at all angles, one tying his bootlace, another taking off his hat to comb his hair, and another, noticing John, leaned forward from the ranks to waggle a reproving finger.

At a restaurant near the Cathedral a wedding breakfast was in progress. Just as we passed, the bride, her white gown spattered with spaghetti, burst out the door, and started off across the square, the bridegroom, who had apparently been accidentally responsible for the disaster, following expostulating. It was

160

to no avail: she was furious and said so in no uncertain terms. The last glimpse we had of them she was striding in high heels across the cobbles, her veil floating out behind her, still talking loudly and angrily, the bridegroom still trotting behind trying to placate her. Was it, we wondered, a preview of their married life? Certainly the Italian street scene is never short of drama!

An opulent Rolls-Royce with British number plates passed us.

"I suppose they're going to the camping too," remarked Godfrey, and we all burst out laughing.

"I'm sure they're not," said John, but Godfrey was right. When we returned, there it was, parked next to our caravan, and its owners busy erecting a tent.

That evening, when at last Godfrey and Nicky were in bed, our hopes of a quiet evening were shattered by a great deal of noise and giggling from the tent, and I went to investigate. A large white cat was sharing Nicky's bed.

"He's a member of the Pussy Brigade; he's just come to report to me," explained Nicky.

I put the cat out, but it promptly went back in again; we zipped up the tent, and it wriggled in under the fabric; after several more attempts we just had to give up and leave it there, to Nicky's delight. The Pussy Brigade seemed very loyal to its commander!

"After all that," said John, when we had settled down again, "I want to do the town. Come on."

Leaving the others in the caravan, he and I set out on foot. The narrow streets were dark, shops and houses shuttered, and there were few people about. In Piazza Garibaldi a butcher-shop, with several pheasants hanging in the doorway, was open but did not appear to be doing much business. Next to it, in the "Bar Tutte Sport" there was TV and a lot of talk and laughter, but outside on the wide verandah people sat quietly in twos and threes at little tables drinking coffee. Here we sat for a while, watching a man at the next table amusing his friends by making his folded handkerchief appear to be a bird, fluttering in his hands and up on to his shoulder most realistically. Then we turned, and walked home through the quiet streets. And that was Pisa by night.

By now it was October. The summer vacation had ended, and when we left Pisa early on a misty morning we passed several groups of children on their way to school, little boys and girls alike wearing black or white smocks with big, floppy coloured bows at the neck.

Returning to Florence and Campeggio Michelangelo was like a homecoming. As we drove through the city the children excitedly pointed out landmarks to each other, and when we arrived the camp staff remembered us and greeted us as old friends. What was surprising was that it was just as hot as it had been three weeks earlier. Elsewhere we had found the weather much cooler, but in Florence the sun still blazed down, robbing one of all desire to do anything but lie in the shade. John had business to attend to in Florence—which was why we had returned—and we stayed two days until it was completed, two days when we did little sight-seeing, but as it were took stock, and attended to various matters, such as visiting a hairdresser, replenishing the supply of gas, supervising the children's lessons, which had been somewhat neglected of recent weeks, and a hundred and one other little things. Nicky spent some time sitting in the terrace-restaurant sketching the view of Florence, watched with interest by the waiters, and John and I found a shop which sold foreign books. This was a real pleasure, for we all found it very difficult to keep up an adequate supply of reading in English.

One evening Gerard and I were playing Scrabble, when I glanced up and saw reflected in the window the interior of the caravan. I was about to go on with the game, when it occurred to me that, though I could see seats and table clearly, I could not see any image of ourselves seated at them. I looked around to see if there was a mirror which reflected at an odd angle. There was none. It was eerie, and I felt a chill prickle of superstitious dread for a moment—till it dawned on me that what I saw was not a reflection at all. I was looking straight out our window and in the window of an identical caravan parked next to us—another Bluebird, with the same pastel pink walls, red curtains and cushions and pale natural woodwork. It was the only time we ever saw a counterpart of our KIWI.

From Florence, off on the Autostrada del Sole again, going in the opposite direction. This time Gerard and Godfrey kept a careful tally of tunnels and viaducts, and as we approached Bologna they proudly announced that in 15,917 kilometres there had been thirty-eight bridges and twenty-three tunnels. How they arrived at this marvellous accuracy I would not be prepared to say!

162

A month earlier the campeggio at Reggio nell'Emilia must have been a crowded and lively spot. There was a large swimming pool, complete with diving stands, surrounded with a terrace where ornamental shrubs grew in urns, a large and quite elaborate restaurant, a dance floor, table tennis room, fine toilets and showers and a big shop. But now the season had ended. The swimming pool was empty, the restaurant and store closed, and the water turned off except for one cold tap. Everything looked a little forlorn. But it was still very pleasant to camp in the dappled sunlight under the chestnut trees, and later, in the cool of the evening, a group of local people gathered around a table on the terrace near the swimming pool and sat there drinking wine. After a while they began to sing—inevitably, "O Sole Mio".

"You know," John remarked, "if that were in a film about Italy we'd say it was corny—overdoing the local colour." But it was not just local colour; the group on the terrace were quite real and completely unself-conscious.

Reggio nell'Emilia is a not particularly attractive, but prosperous-looking city. Everywhere were beautifully-dressed, well-cared-for-looking children. The whole town was decorated with bunting and plastered with posters for a Communist Youth Congress, which was to be held the following week; and there were also a great many notices giving, for the benefit of visiting delegates, the hours of Mass at the various churches.

"We're in the Don Camillo country," John remarked.

Obviously, Reggio is a Communist town, but Communist Italian style, with religion still playing an important part in the life of the people.

On a sunny, hazy day we went through cities whose names were poems—Parma, Fidenza, Piacenza—and through vineyards where dozens of pickers were gathering the purple grapes into baskets and loading them on ass carts, to Tortona. Here we had intended to stay for a day or two, but we found the entrance to the only campeggio was through a narrow little street we would have no hope of negotiating with a large caravan, so we merely paused in the town for an hour or so. At a restaurant in a charming little square with black and white cobblestones laid to form a pattern and a mossy fountain playing in the centre, we lunched on spaghetti, then on our way again, to Genoa.

That afternoon's drive was, I think, one of the most interesting we had in Europe. We crossed high mountains again, but the slope went up so gently we were at the top and on the way down the other side almost before we knew it. The scenery was picturesque, reminding us very much of Austria with its mountains, onion-towered churches, and occasionally, on inaccessible-seeming peaks, castles or monasteries. Now and again, in the valleys far below, we glimpsed the white gravel beds of rivers which had dried up in the long summer drought. But it was not the natural scenery which caught our attention. An autostrada was under construction, which would, like the one we had taken from Florence to Bologna, be an alternation of viaducts and tunnels. At the moment tunnellers were burrowing through mountains, armies of men were working on vast erections of scaffolding rising from the valley floor to the peaks, and many great complicated machines were operating. Within a year or so the narrow road by which we twisted and turned up and down through the folds of the hills would be superseded; in the meantime, we were fascinated by the spectacle of the activity that would bring about the change, and marvelled at the enormous height of the apparently fragile scaffolds. Then suddenly we plunged into a tunnel, so long and dark there was no glimmer of light at the end, and our headlights made little impression. The darkness seemed tangible, pressing down and around us: at first just blank, dizzying blackness, with, on the near side, the headlights faintly illumining rough-hewn rock walls; then, far, far ahead, a tiny pinpoint of red light, which I took at first to be the tail-light of a car ahead; but it came closer and grew larger, changing from red to orange to white, and resolved itself into the headlights of a car coming towards us. On and on, with the red lights appearing, changing, growing, and then cars passing us, and still the impenetrable blackness; until at last, far ahead, the mouth of the tunnel flamed orange and red, so that we seemed to be shooting straight down into the fires of Hell: but as we came closer the colours faded to ordinary daylight, and at last out into sunlight which seemed blue by contrast.

Now we met the oil-tankers—very large, each one towing a second twin tanker, bumper to bumper, mile after mile, heading south with all the petrol to keep the industry and traffic of Italy moving. We had been passing them for a long time when the children started counting them; but when they reached two hundred and seventy-five they tired of the game—and still the tankers came on. Now we came to their source, the huge oil refinery of Bolsenetta. From the hills above it we seemed to be looking down into the Inferno—labyrinths and twisted coils of pipes, flames shooting from chimneys, and the air heavy with an oily smell.

Pegli is near enough to Genoa to be counted an outer suburb, but it is also a holiday resort. Along the sea front hotels and cinemas, restaurants and souvenir shops face across a green strip of park towards the blue Gulf of Genoa, but behind them steep streets lead up to where, in tall apartment buildings and pleasant homes with gardens, the permanent residents live. Because the mountains fall very abruptly to the sea, a ramble through the streets of the town is full of surprises. There are sudden sharp turns and rises; unexpected flights of steps go up or down; sometimes there are streets like no others I have seen, with houses on one side, but on the other the eighth or ninth storeys of apartment buildings, connected to the pavement by little bridges across a chasm. I could not help feeling it would be nerve-racking to bring up children here, in constant danger of falls; indeed, on one occasion I saw two small boys of perhaps ten scuffling and fighting on one of these bridges, watched by another boy of the same age, seated casually on the wall, his feet dangling in space. Their mother called to them from the window to stop, but they took no notice. Perhaps it was to avoid such perils that so many pretty young mammas sat every day among the palms and flower-beds of the park along the sea front, chatting together and watching their children tearing up and down the paths on scooters and tricycles.

The campeggio, shaded by pines, was high above the town, on the edge of the Parco Villa Doria. Every now and then it was shaken by a muffled shock, and there was a constant, high-pitched whine on one note, maddening at first till one grew used to it. Another camper told us a tunnel was being built under the park for an oil pipeline from the refinery, and the whine was a pump drawing air into the excavation. Later John and I strolled through the park to the mouth of the tunnel, and seeing how huge it was—much bigger than we expected—wondered if our informant had been mistaken. It looked big enough to be a road tunnel. The park at the time was rather depressing. It

165

had been artfully laid out with statues, little ornamental lakes, and winding paths through clumps of woodland, but the tunnelling work had caused a great deal of havoc. We hoped it would later be restored.

One evening I went over to wash my hands before cooking the dinner, and a young girl followed me into the washroom.

"You're New Zealanders, aren't you?" she said. "So am I. I've been watching you and envying you. It must be marvellous to have your family with you travelling."

We talked so long that when I returned my indignant family demanded whether I had forgotten about their dinner. I felt concerned about the girl, and wished I had been in a position to help her. She was about nineteen, lonely, homesick and unhappy. She would have liked to go home, but her companions intended to stay in Europe longer and she had not enough money to travel alone.

I do not think New Zealand and Australian parents who allow their daughters to wander the world like this always realize what they are getting into. It seems a fine idea for a young girl to set off for Britain on a "working holiday", to join up with a group of other young people and tour the Continent in an old car—and so it can be. There can be no finer education than travel and the memories last a lifetime. But—and it is a very big but—the girl must be mature and level-headed enough to stand on her own feet and cope with whatever may arise, and above all, she must be certain she has enough money to get home whenever she wishes, or she may find herself in serious difficulties. Unless she has her return fare before she leaves New Zealand she has little chance of saving it. Salaries in Britain are lower than in New Zealand, always assuming she can find an employer willing to accept someone who will probably not stay very long, and many European countries do not allow foreigners to be employed without permits, which are difficult to get. We had earlier met another, even younger New Zealand girl who had run out of money in Greece. The people with whom she was travelling had gone back to England, leaving her alone and literally penniless in a country where she could not speak the language and where foreigners are not allowed to work, and her situation was desperate till an Australian woman rescued her and took her home.

On Sunday morning we went to Mass in Capella Doria, the chapel in the park, following the sound of the bells, and arrived in good time, to find a small crowd of smartly-dressed people outside the church, and an atmosphere of excitement. A wedding. The white-buttonholed ushers assured me there would be Mass at nine-thirty, and waved us into the church. Here we waited for a very long time, alone save for two elderly women, and had begun to think it was a mistake and there would be no service, when, to the strains of the Wedding March, the bridal party arrived and took their places at the front, and all the congregation poured in behind them. Apparently everybody had lingered outside to see the bride arrive. The Italian custom of solemnizing marriages at the Sunday morning Mass has probably arisen because it is the one day of the week when most people can be present; whatever the reason, I felt it must engender a great deal of community warmth and friendliness that the whole parish should be present to wish the young couple well. Afterwards, many of the people went from the chapel to the little walled cemetery nearby to lay wreaths and flowers and light candles on the graves.

John by now was impatient to be away. I had begun to feel saddened a little each time we moved on—soon we would be leaving Italy. I was sorry to leave every country, but Italy above all had my heart. John on the other hand was becoming more and more anxious to push on into France. The year was advancing, soon we would have cold weather, and camping grounds might close for the season: he did not want to leave it too late. So we set off by autostrada along the Ligurian coast.

It was a spectacular drive. Although there was a slight mist, the diffused sunlight was very strong. On our left was the sea, milky-turquoise near the shore, purple shot with glints of gold further out and the horizon obscured by mist; on our right, rocky mountains and occasional little towns perched precariously on their slopes. We passed several camping grounds, all closed for the season, and began to feel rather dismayed, though none of us put it into words. Had we, like Cinderella, stayed too long? We did not despair, for we had been told of a campeggio at Albenga which remained open all the year. But our information proved wrong—it was closed. However, a woman who was apparently the caretaker assured us we would find another one, called Florida, still open, and pointed out the way.

At the Florida the proprietor—an Austrian with an Italian wife—was apologetic. The campeggio was not at its best; the season was over; most of the staff had already left; the stock in

M

the shop was getting low. But we were so relieved to find it open that we would have been content with much less than Campeggio Florida had to offer. The grounds were pleasant, and the restaurant still open. The cakes were fresh and very good, and the coffee the best I had tasted in Italy. When I told him so he was gratified, and agreed with me that it was hard to get a good cup of coffee in the country. This had been my one disappointment in Italy, for I am fond of good coffee, and had expected better. Once in despair I ordered "caffè americano" in the hope that it might be more to my liking, but it proved to be a cup of the usual Italian coffee and a jug of cold water!

Although it was late in the year there were still campers—English, Germans, Dutch—who no doubt found autumn milder on the Riviera than in their own Northern lands. Like every other campeggio and hotel along this coast, the Florida had its private beach: it was reached by following a narrow path between hutches filled with rabbits and chickens, through a kitchen garden, and then a short subway under a railway line. The beach was deserted and a little chilly. Long pergola-like shelters roofed with straw-matting had been erected on the yellow sand to give shade from the sun, but now they were not needed, and the shore was uninviting, so we changed our minds about swimming, and returned to the caravan.

But there was nothing uninviting about the town of Albenga itself—in fact, its atmosphere was warmly welcoming. Although it was Sunday evening, and all the shops were closed, the streets were crowded with people, the many restaurants and cafés were full, and long queues waited outside the cinemas. When we stopped at a sidewalk café the proprietress, a dark, motherly woman with enormous gold hoop earrings, fussed about us as if we were her own family, insisting on bringing an extra chair for Miriam and me to put our handbags on, and coming back every few minutes with solicitous enquiries—was there enough sugar? Was the coffee to our liking? (It was very good) —and even after we had paid her and left she ran down the street after us to press apples into the children's hands.

The next day we found Albenga was just as attractive by daylight. Hotels and pensions were numerous near the beach, but the older part of the town was made up of little narrow streets of shuttered houses with washing hanging everywhere. We paused on a bridge across the River Centa with ceramic scenes from Red Riding Hood set in its balustrade, to watch women washing clothes in the river, beating them white, then spreading them on the stony ground to dry. From the bridge we looked down at the ruins of a Roman villa submerged in the water. There were other Roman traces in Albenga. We spent an absorbed and happy hour at the Roman Ship Museum. This ship was wrecked just off the coast about two thousand years ago, and expeditions in recent years have raised a great deal of it, including more than a hundred of the amphorae which held its cargo of oil and wine. It is one of the most interesting specialized museums I have visited.

Albenga was to be our last Italian stopping-place, so it was with sadness that I left it, to continue on along the coast road. A pause at Imperia, where I spent the last of my small change on pizza and grapes—the last Italian food I would buy—and where, predictably, a group of youths gathered round to examine the car, and then on to the border. Here the Italian guard took our passports, and, to the amusement of the children, read aloud with relish the full names of the whole family, mispronouncing nearly every word. The French guard seemed totally uninterested, and did not even ask if we had anything to declare.

And so—good-bye to Italy, its sunshine, its glorious scenery and architecture, its beautiful girls, its sense of an ancient and enduring culture, its atmosphere of warmth and vitality. I was very sad to go, and my greatest wish is that someday I might return.

Chapter XVI

AGAIN, as always on crossing a border, that shock of surprise at being immediately in another country. We were now unmistakably in France: the architecture, the atmosphere were all entirely French. We did not make a very auspicious entry. In the first town, Menton, we were a split second too late in seeing that a large parked truck concealed a No Entry sign, and we found ourselves sailing, great caravan and all, the wrong way down a one-way street. The effect was spectacular. All along the pavement were cafés, and people leaped up from their tables to shout and wave to us to go back. As we progressed the wave of agitation rippled along the pavement like the bow wave of a ship; every on-coming vehicle and bus was filled with reproving faces, waggling fingers, indignant gestures. One smartly-dressed woman ran right out into the roadway, apparently with the idea of stopping us. But there was nothing we could do. There was a great deal of traffic; obviously to stop and turn would only make bad worse; it was better just to keep on. At first we were embarrassed and dismayed, but it was a long street, and the further we went, the greater the succession of open-mouthed, horrified, indignant faces, the funnier they looked. In the end we were all helpless with laughter, and John was trying to look contrite as well.

The information office at the border had told us to follow the coast road, as the Haute Corniche and the Moyen Corniche were not suitable for caravans: but when we saw the Inférieure Corniche we began to ask ourselves, how haute must the Haute Corniche be? For the coast road itself was high above the sea, winding abruptly and narrowly around rocky cliffs, and giving magnificent panoramas of the Mediterranean scene. A sharp turn of the cliff road, and there below us, with numerous yachts riding at anchor on its still water, was the bay of Monte Carlo.

Monaco at first glance seems an incongruity on the Riviera. All that coast has a leisurely atmosphere—the leisure of holiday-making at resorts like Nice or Cannes, or the slow tempo of life in small towns where fishing and carnation growing are the chief industries; but Monte Carlo is decidedly a twentieth century city dedicated to business and bustle. Great skyscrapers rear themselves above a bay crowded with shipping; and only the Royal Palace on a headland, or the green-roofed Casino, seems to speak of an earlier, less hectic way of life. This impression, of course, is a superficial one. Monte Carlo is still largely devoted to the leisure of those with time and money to spend: the tourist provides most of its revenue, and the ships in the harbour are mostly luxury yachts. Nevertheless, it is also true that big business has in recent decades found Monaco—with its low taxes—a convenient base for operations.

We had intended to stay one night in Nice, but had difficulty in finding the camping, and when, after several false turns and enquiries, we did find it, it was closed. It was rather a dismal-looking place, and I was not sorry to be unable to stay. I was in fact disappointed with Nice—the buildings were drab and the beach stony—but our pause there was really too brief to make a fair judgment. The road outside the camping was too narrow to turn: nothing else for it, everybody out, unhitch the caravan, turn it by hand, turn the car, rehitch. A couple of small boys appeared, very interested in all this procedure, and full of helpful suggestions. Why were we going? Why didn't we stay at the camping? Because, said John, the camping is closed. But, m'sieur, le patron can open it. At this John cheered up a bit. Perhaps after all we need go no further. Où est le patron? The excited small boys ran off to find him. We waited. Back came the small boys. Le patron says it's closed. All this time we had been in a narrow road which led nowhere but to the camp. Now when we wanted to move we found a large line repair truck parked across the entrance while the men worked on the telegraph lines, and there we had to sit and wait for an hour or so until they were done.

Twice more we went to places listed in the camping guide, each time to find them closed. Each time they were situated down narrow side roads where we could not turn without un-hitching, so the wearisome procedure had to be repeated. By now we were getting worried and depressed. Summer was gone, the camping season over. Would we be unable to find any place to stay? True, the Michelin Camping Guide, which we were using, listed a number of camping grounds which stayed open all the year, but this had already proved to be inaccurate. As we drove on to Cannes the mood in the car was less than cheerful.

171

Through Cannes, too preoccupied to notice it much, and we turned away from the sea and up into the mountains. We were cheered somewhat by being told, on stopping to enquire at an unexpected little antique shop, that there was a camping open all the year, and so, following the shopkeeper's directions, we came to Auberge des Lentisques. It made us glad all the others had been closed, for had they been open we would never have found it, and it was worth finding.

Strictly speaking, it was not a camping, but an inn with a parking place for a few caravans. The inn itself was typically Provençal in architecture—wide-eaved, two-storeyed, but the upper storey merely an open space surrounded by a balustrade and arches supporting the roof, and in each arch, a great pottery jar. The gardens surrounding it were artfully wild, with winding walks through trees and shrubs which half-concealed little summer houses and arbours. Beside a large swimming pool shaded by trees were swings and other play equipment. In this picturesque spot we stayed; in the evening the innkeeper brought over a steaming pot of delicious soup for our dinner, and afterwards John and I sat outside enjoying the evening and watching the antics of Godfrey and the young son of the innkeeper, a boy of about the same age. The French boy stood some distance away, eyeing Godfrey, then edged up, climbed a rope and performed a few acrobatic feats. Godfrey, not to be outdone, without even glancing at him, did the same. The other boy tried something harder, Godfrey followed, and so they went on, each ostentatiously not seeing the other, but contesting all the same. They could not speak each other's language, so they held a boasting match without words. Godfrey was the only one of us brave enough for a pre-breakfast dip in the pool next morning, but he came out blue and with chattering teeth. Summer was over.

If I had not cared for the little we had seen of Nice, I was delighted by Cannes. The sun was shining, and down at sea level it was much warmer than it had been up at the inn. The great sweep of beach, while not crowded, yet had a fair sprinkling of people swimming and sunbathing on the fine white sand. Two American naval vessels were anchored out in the bay, and Godfrey and Nicky became quite absorbed in all the activity going on about them—launches bringing sailors ashore, and helicopters flying around in circles and coming in one at a time to land on deck. Every few minutes as we sat in the sunshine we were approached by Oriental carpet sellers, who seemed to be very numerous, but not, I should say, particularly successful. I did not see any make a sale. Leaving the beach, we found great enjoyment in wandering about the streets to see all there was to see—the elegant and famous hotels, the Festival Palace, venue of the annual Film Festival, with its separate entrances labelled "Jury" and "Vedettes"; the jewellers' and art dealers' shops; the beautiful—and expensive—toys and clothes; the shops selling crystallized fruits with imaginative window displays that tempted one in to buy; the fishmongers' stalls piled high with spiny sea urchins, squid, and brightly coloured fish of various unfamiliar kinds.

Although we knew the famous Matisse chapel at Vence is seldom open to the public, we felt it would be a pity to be so near and not visit it, even if all we could see was the exterior; so we set off to drive the thirty miles or so up to it. As we climbed higher and higher into the stony grey-green mountains we saw spread far below a wide panorama of sunlit blue Mediterranean fringed with white beaches. Here and there perched high on peaks were graceful, tile-roofed Provençal houses; once, across a valley a walled city like a scene from a fairy-tale, and, at last, the little mountain town of Vence. Here we stopped in a small square so shaded by buildings and over-hung by trees that it was quite dark, even in the midday sun, and in a little shop we bought picture-postcards and asked the way to the chapel. The woman said it was closed, but she pointed out the road to us, adding severely, "Ce n'est pas beau." Not for her, modern art!

From the road the chapel is so unassuming that we almost passed it without noticing—a simple white building with a roof of blue and white tiles; but under the eaves are deceptively simple, typically Matisse saints, and above it rises a graceful cross made up of bronze flames. We peered at the stained glass windows, trying very hard to see them, but from the outside, in full sunlight, it was difficult to make out anything except a vague impression of greens and golds. It was tantalizing to be so near and unable to enter, but we were neither surprised nor disappointed. We realized that to have arrived during the viewing hours, without careful planning, would have been too much to expect, and we could appreciate the reason for the restriction. The chapel belongs to a convent. When it was first opened so many people flocked from all over the world to see it that the nuns found it was so crowded every hour of the day

173

with sight-seers they could not use it themselves, and at last they were obliged to limit severely the time it was open to the public. We recognized the justice of this, and even without seeing the interior, found the trip there extremely rewarding.

Quite near Auberge des Lentisques, where we were staying, is the fascinating little town of Mougins. To visit it was to step back into the past. Crowning the top of a mountain, with wide views in every direction, it huddles within its walls just as it must have done from medieval times, to all appearances virtually unchanged. At the entrance to the village there is a large carpark with a sign saying that parking is compulsory, vehicles must not enter the town. And no wonder, for the streets between the antique stone houses are tiny cobbled passages, sometimes so steep they might almost be called ramps. Once there was a large abbey here, on which the town depended for its livelihood. Mougins then was quite important, but in the French Revolution the abbey was destroyed, and most of the villagers, deprived of employment, moved down to the coast to form the new fishing village of Cannes, which later developed into the modern resort. Now Mougins dozes on its hilltop, quiet, remote. But even here the twentieth century breaks in. On the wall of the communal laundry, where several women were washing in a tub the size of a swimming pool, filled with scummy water, a poster advertised: "Concours des Amateurs de Strip-Tease".

From Cannes we drove to Aix-en-Provence, at first through a land of red rock and rosemary and lavender bushes, with not a sign of cultivation anywhere, and then through vineyards, where the harvest was in full swing, and slow-moving carts piled high with grapes dawdled along the road. Up and up and up, and gradually the scenery changed, and great jagged white mountains, devoid of vegetation, floated in the blue sky like icebergs on the sea, contrasting with the deep red of the rocks nearer at hand. As we drove on the white mountains came nearer, and then we went for miles through weirdly fantastic rock formations—light-coloured, long, level, like a walled city, with what seemed houses and buildings—here a cathedral, there a castle; after a while one found oneself almost expecting to see people there—on and on and on it went, until we dropped downhill into Aix.

The Michelin Camping Guide lists Arc-en-Ciel camping in Aix-en-Provence in the top grade, and we found it really lived up to its rating—a picturesque place, with a little stream chattering over mossy stones under an arched stone bridge, graceful fountains, a swimming pool and all camping amenities. We had been five hours on the road when we arrived soon after midday, so we did not feel much inclination to go into the city. Instead it was pleasant to while away a peaceful afternoon exploring the grounds. A large coal-truck arrived, and as they off-loaded the coal the two dust-blackened men called a cheery greeting. John answered on an equally friendly note, but while he spoke a variety of academic French they spoke a patois, and the conversation got a little at cross-purposes, amid much laughter. Was he an American, they asked. No, said John, a New Zealander. Where was that? They had never heard of it. They should have, said John, rather wickedly, for New Zealanders were the best soldiers in the war. This they could not allow, and an amiable wrangle about the respective merits of French and New Zealand fighting men ended in laughing good-byes as they drove off. In their perky jollity they reminded me of Cockneys.

We spent two days exploring Aix, a pleasant city of cool, tree-shaded streets, tinkling fountains, and a graceful air of culture, emphasized by the surprisingly large number of bookshops. The Cathedral, very small as cathedrals go, is extraordinarily interesting, dating back to the time when Provence was Roman. The fourth century baptistry has an octagonal piscina for baptism by immersion, surrounded by pillars which were part of the original pagan temple, and there is a cloister in which no two pillars are alike—some are round, some square, some fluted or fretted, others caryatids.

We took the road again, and at Tarascon came to a camping on the banks of the Rhône, picturesquely colourful with beds of scarlet geraniums, deep blue morning glories twining around tree trunks and pergolas covered with vine leaves of an autumnal red. But, gay and pretty though it looked, it had its disadvantages. Thus late in the season most of the buildings were locked up, and the one lavatory left open was deplorable.

"Never mind," said John, determinedly cheerful. "We can't expect much at this time of the year. If we'd come earlier it would have been better."

"Yes, it would," retorted Gerard. "Then instead of one filthy lavatory we'd have had a choice of six filthy lavatories."

It was Saturday. John went off alone for a walk, and came

back with the news that there was a wonderful market—why not all come along? It *was* a wonderful market—not, I was sure, an ordinary market day, but more probably an annual fête. There was a gay, festival atmosphere in the streets and the crowds of people were obviously bent on enjoyment among the many amusements offering, and the dozens of stalls selling everything from candy floss to refrigerators. We had not intended to shop, but found ourselves so caught up by the spirit of it that we staggered back to the camping laden down with clothing, toys, food, sweets, and new cushions for the caravan. On the way we met two nuns pushing a handcart, and John stopped them and asked how to get to the church. They were both quite voluble, particularly the older one, who was ancient, short, and

when she smiled, which she did all the time, displayed a single lonely tooth. She was eager to point out everything of interest in the town, and as we parted she paid John a compliment: "For an Englishman you express yourself well. I understood everything you said." The English have such a poor reputation on the Continent as linguists that "an Englishman who speaks French" is regarded as a contradiction in terms. Not, of course, that John is an Englishman, and he insists he is no linguist.

The next day, Sunday, we went to Mass at the church of Ste Marthe. When a hymn was sung we looked at each other in astonishment, and we had to keep a firm grip on ourselves, for the tune was "Auld Lang Syne". The contrast between the devout faces of the congregation and the convivial tune seemed to us the height of the ridiculous, and it was difficult not to laugh.

176

On the banks of the Rhône, surrounded by its moat, stands the perfectly preserved castle of le Roi René, and here, since there is nothing boys enjoy more than a real castle, we went later that Sunday morning. By the time we arrived it was about half-past eleven, and we learned that the guide had set out with a party of visitors on an hour-long tour at eleven o'clock. However, we crossed the drawbridge, and in an unexpected little garden within the castle walls John and I sat down to wait, while the boys and Miriam ran about, peering through the narrow slits at the town below. At last the guide appeared, and ushered out his party, then turning to us explained that the next tour would not be for some hours and he was going home to his dinner. I suppose we looked disappointed, for much to our surprise, after giving us a brief outline of the history of the castle and telling us interesting points to look for, he showed us how to lock it after us, and went off home, leaving us in possession.

What more exciting thing could happen to any children than having a real, honest-to-goodness castle handed over to them? The boys were in a seventh heaven. They tore up and down the stairs, fought imaginary battles, became troubadours and sang in the spectacle court, withstood mighty sieges, climbed to the battlements and looked out over the wide countryside for advancing enemies.

The castle, built in the fourteenth century by King René, father of Marguerite d'Anjou, has more elegance, and seems designed for more comfort and gracious living than the rugged castles of England—which is not surprising, for it was built three hundred years later. We started at the spectacle court, where once troubadours and jongleurs performed while the ladies and nobles of the court looked down from windows above, and from there explored all the rooms and stairs, the chapel, and the great hall where British prisoners-of-war were held during the Napoleonic Wars, and where they scratched many inscriptions on the walls. I copied one:

"Here we be three Davids in one mess,
Prisoners in sore distress;
By the French we was caught,
To this prison we was brought.
Sloop Zephyr, out of Hull. 1778."

There were three signatures, all with the Christian name David.

As we walked back to our lunch I noticed faded and flapping

posters for a bull-fight, and rather wished we had come a month or two earlier before the season had ended. But perhaps we would not really have enjoyed it.

The boastful Tartarin has become a folk hero in Tarascon—in all the shops picture-postcards of his exploits are on sale, together with others of the "Tarasque", a legendary monster from the Rhône, a sort of French taniwha, which menaced the town and was overcome by Ste Marthe.

The remainder of that Sunday we spent in Avignon, which is not far from Tarascon. For seventy years in the fourteenth century Avignon was a city of some importance, when it was the seat of the Papacy. The Palace of the Popes, after their return to Rome, had a chequered history, and under Napoleon suffered greatly from vandalism, when it was used as a barracks. Now partly restored, it still stands on the banks of the Rhône, looking down on the famous broken bridge, where, according to the song, "everybody dances". On sunny Sunday afternoons the palace gardens, on high ground, with a wide view of the country-side, are crowded with citizens and tourists taking the air and children feeding the swans and peacocks. After leaving the Palace we ran into a football crowd just leaving the match. Except that the sea of bobbing heads filling the roadway wore black berets instead of cloth caps it might have been any town in England.

From Tarascon we set off in the rain through Arles—interesting both for Roman remains and for its association with Van Gogh—then for a considerable distance through rice paddies, which surprised me, for I had not known before that rice was grown in France—through Montpellier, with the great arches of a Roman viaduct towering above the road, and then the Frontignan country, past miles of vineyards, and every now and then "caves" and wineshops and "tasting stations" inviting the passer-by to come in and sample the wine. It might have been tempting had not the rain been pelting down, making the warm dry interior of the car very desirable! Then uphill into desolate mountainous country with nothing much growing save patches of scrub, and down again to the Mediterranean coast.

At Vias, right on the beach, we found a camping that was still open, but "open" meant merely that the gate was not shut; all the buildings were locked up. Nothing is more drearily depressing than a seaside place out of season. The rain poured steadily down: the sea was leaden and choppy, and the long curve of white sand wind-swept and utterly deserted. We were short of food, the two little stores were locked and shuttered for the winter, and to cap it all, the mosquitoes were ferocious. Feeling there was no point in adding hunger to our misery, John and I left the children in the caravan and set off in the car to find a village where we could shop. At the first little town we came to we found the only shops open were hardware and stationery, but grocer, baker, butcher—in fact, all food shops— were shut. We assumed this was the long Continental lunch hour, and there was nothing to do but wait—and still it rained, the cobbled streets awash to a depth of a couple of inches. We huddled dankly in an arched doorway with water dripping down our necks and wished we were anywhere else in the world. At last, since John was wearing summer clothes and I at least had a light raincoat, I made a dash for it through the rain to a stationer's shop, where I bought a newspaper and asked when the shops would open. To my dismay I was told they did not open at all on Monday. So it was back to the car and off in the opposite direction in search of another village, hoping that there the closing day was not Monday. This time we were successful, and returned in triumph with provisions, to have our lunch at well after five-thirty!

The next morning the rain had stopped, but it was still heavily overcast and bleak. When we had planned to come to this place we had hoped for a few days' swimming, but in the circumstances there was no temptation to linger. We packed up ready to depart.

"This is ridiculous," I remarked. "We're leaving the Mediterranean now and we haven't even had a swim in it. At least I'm going to paddle", and I pulled off my shoes and ran down the beach. Miriam, Godfrey and Nicky followed me. It looked desolate: grey sky, grey sea, in the chill wind the long stretch of sand empty save for a discarded sandshoe and a broken beach ball. We ran into the waves expecting a cold shock, and to our surprise the water was caressingly warm—we regretted that we had not been swimming after all! But it was too late—already John and Gerard had hitched the caravan and were standing by the car waiting for us. So it was off on the road once more.

Gradually the sky cleared, the sun came out, and our spirits rose. The road lay first through miles and miles of vineyards, then through hilly arid-looking country which reminded us of pictures of Spain—not surprisingly, for we were very near the Spanish border.

179

At Carcassonne we went to the municipal camping ground, which was a triangle, half grass, half asphalt, behind the grandstand of the sports stadium. One side was bounded by a railway line, and another by the stone wall of a building with barred windows, from behind which we were suddenly startled and horrified to hear eldritch shrieks and screams. We all stopped what we were doing and stared at each other.

"What on earth is it?" gasped Miriam, white-faced.

"Some kind of machinery?" suggested Gerard.

"I've never heard a machine make a noise like that," said John. "It sounds animal or human, not mechanical."

"Perhaps it's a bull-fight arena," said Godfrey, hopefully. "It might be the bulls."

"The building isn't big enough," I said.

The banshee screams continued at intervals, chilling the blood and striking terror into the heart, but at last they stopped, leaving us feeling a little shaken. We were just recovering from that when we became aware of another noise—the sound of many footsteps and the chattering of voices—and we were surrounded by about a hundred schoolgirls and a couple of teachers, all in track suits or shorts, who had come to the stadium for their physical education class. They ran about, hopping, skipping, jumping. Gerard at the time was putting up the tent, and all the girls formed a circle and danced round and round him, much to his embarrassment, which seemed to amuse them; then, when a train passed, they abandoned the game, and ran to stand in a row waving, while the soldiers who filled the carriages waved back. It all seemed much more informal to me than a British school "Phys. Ed." lesson.

The shrieks from behind the barred windows continued at intervals, and at last John and I could contain our curiosity no longer, and walked around to the front of the building to see if we could find out what it was. Big double gates opened on to a courtyard, and there were two small notices, one saying "No Admittance to the Public" and the other, as far as my French could make out, "Owners of animals must call at the office and introduce them to the concierge." I had a fleeting mental image of a farmer leading up a beribboned piglet and making a formal introduction to the concierge, who bowed graciously in acknowledgment! On the way back we asked the custodian of the stadium, who told us it was an abattoir.

The next morning we were still at breakfast when the school-

180

girls arrived again—not, I think, the same ones. Two of the girls left their group and came over to the caravan. When I spoke to them they made it clear it was not me they wanted to see, but Miriam, who was about their own age. The three of them stood there, Miriam frowning in the effort of carrying on a French conversation, the other two giggling, then she dived into the caravan, to emerge with a safety-pin. One of the girls had broken the elastic in her gym shorts, and was asking for help.

Carcassonne is a city within a city. The central hill is crowned by the ancient and historic walled town, carefully preserved and where necessary restored to its medieval condition, while around it, like the white round the yolk of a poached egg, sprawls the modern city. In old Carcassonne the only visible anachronism is

the traffic-lights on the drawbridge. It is a romantic city indeed, with its many candlesnuffer towers, its battlements and antique buildings, its ancient Cathedral with the now-empty tomb of Simon de Montfort—*"our* Simon de Montfort", as John remarked. (Odd to reflect that the Father of the British parliament was French!) Carcassonne has had a violently stormy history. From Roman times on it was the scene of battles and sieges; in the thirteenth century it was a centre of religious wars when it became the stronghold of the Albigensians, and was repeatedly attacked by Crusaders, so that the besieged inhabitants were reduced to starvation.

"It's a photographer's paradise!" exclaimed John, plying his camera furiously, as we walked about its cobbled streets, and made the circuit of the walls, looking out over the countryside

181

and into the huddled city. We visited the Cathedral, the Inquisition chamber, and the outdoor arena where plays are sometimes performed against a background of real towers and walls; and we were delighted to learn that people still lived in the houses and the little shops were open. Much more fun to do my daily marketing here than in the modern city below! When I went to the bakery for bread I was asked did I also want "la spécialité de la cité". Who could resist? Of course I wanted it. It proved to be a flat round pastry filled with raisins and peel. In the wine-shop John was so engrossed in the delightful task of making his choice among so many wines he did not hear the man ask me where we were from, nor my reply. Handing him his change, the shop-keeper said, "So you're from New Zealand?"

John stared at him in astonishment.

"So you're a magician!" he said.

Chapter XVII

VINEYARDS, vineyards, miles and miles of vineyards; and hundreds of pickers at work filling with grapes the baskets on their backs, which were later emptied into carts. We had followed the harvest for months—through Germany and Austria it had been wheat, rye and barley, in Italy and France, grapes.

We had passed through Toulouse, and were bowling merrily along when we were stopped by a road block. Great, wicked-looking spikes had been laid across the road, points upward, and police armed with sub machine guns stopped and searched each car. It was the kind of adventure we could well have forgone, and as a matter of fact we must have looked harmless, for when we moved up to the barrier they simply waved us on.

At Montauban we stopped at a camping with the absurd name of Petite Versailles, probably so called because of the microscopic belvedere on a mound in the centre. Even if it did not quite measure up to so grandiloquent a name, it was a pleasant enough place, shaded by great oaks which, with every breeze, sent a fusillade of acorns rattling down on the caravan roof. On the same property was a youth hostel, and as evening approached a number of hitch-hikers, many of them sporting the flags of their native countries, arrived to stay overnight.

"Look," I said, indicating one young man. "The English cartoonist's idea of a Frenchman!"

"He can't be real!" exclaimed John.

The young man in question wore a beret, a little pointed beard, and a sharply pointed moustache; and though the effect was weakened somewhat by the khaki shirt and shorts and heavy tramping boots, down to his shoulders he might indeed have been a caricature of a Frenchman: so our surprise was all the greater when he turned around revealing the flag on his haversack—Japan!

In the evening we went into Montauban to a cinema, and afterwards drove back to the camping cheerfully discussing the film; but all the chatter died away when, right at the entrance to Petite Versailles, we ran into another road block. This time, in the dark, and without the caravan, we were subjected to a more thorough check. One gendarme stopped us, and rather alarmingly stuck his gun in the window while he questioned us; another barred the gate to the camping and let us through only when his colleague signalled him to do so. We went to bed that night full of speculations as to what it had been about. A few days later we read in the newspapers of the arrest quite near there of some O.A.S. terrorists.

From Montauban we drove along a road the guide-books list as "picturesque", but all we could see was fog and the lights of oncoming cars. All day we went on; once or twice the fog lifted briefly and we were in sunshine, but it soon closed in again. During a bright spell we passed a tobacco plantation, and long sheds where the leaf hung to dry. Then we ran into a road block of a much pleasanter kind than the earlier ones.

Turning a corner sharply into a village, we were halted by a group of youths waving a huge tricolour flag. They all carried brooms, and wore bows or sashes of red white and blue, and funny hats. As we pulled up they all crowded chattering around the car displaying badges with "1964" on them. John said, "You are too early", and they chorused, "We are going to do our service."

"Quel service?"

"Militaire."

"Ah," said John. "A bas la militaire."

Everybody laughed, and they stood aside to let us drive on. It had been a jolly little episode, rather like a students' Capping Week prank, and they seemed very likeable boys.

At Bordeaux we were at first the only campers, save for a party of dark-skinned people who spoke a language we did not know. They had a chubby, bright-eyed little boy of about three, who wore a dummy on a cord about his neck and alternately sucked the dummy and smoked cigarettes which his mother lit for him. He attached himself to John, and the two of them sat solemnly carrying on the oddest conversations, neither understanding a word the other was saying. The little boy had apparently never seen anyone smoke a pipe before, and he found it highly amusing. Every time John lit up he chuckled infectiously and rolled on the ground with mirth; then he found a curved stick he called his "pipa", and, carefully imitating John's attitude, pretended to puff it.

184

Our first night in Bordeaux was bitterly cold, and we realized, with winter coming on, sleeping-bags and summer clothing were no longer adequate. All our warmer clothes had been left in storage in London. So the first thing in the morning we went into the city and spent some hours shopping for blankets and thick sweaters.

The impression I carried away of Bordeaux was of a city of flowers. There was a huge flower-market, all masses of carnations, gladioli, violets and Michaelmas daisies; there seemed to be an unusually large number of florists' and seedsmen's shops, and many people in the streets were carrying flowers. In the Cathedral the French Gothic seemed very austere after the exuberance of baroque and rococo in Italy and Austria; but there was a very beautiful marble Madonna, smiling proudly at the Child in her arms, and a picture of Christ before his accusers which I was sure was by De La Tour. On a day of brilliant sunshine we drove through the Médoc to the coast, for John was anxious to see this region of vineyards and pines, and long beaches where the Bay of Biscay waves roll in to white sand-dunes, setting of the novels of François Mauriac.

Between Bordeaux and Poitiers the pines and vineyards gradually gave way to fields and forest in all the brilliant colour of autumn—red and orange and tawny brown, pale gold of poplars, scarlet of hips and hawthorn berries, and here and there, in striking contrast, bright green clumps of mistletoe among the branches.

We spent one night at Poitiers, on the top of a cliff, whence we could see at sunset, to our right, the city, and far below the river, dotted with clumps of water-lilies. Each golden poplar along the banks was perfectly mirrored below, and on the quiet water a man sat in a boat, fishing. A peaceful scene.

The next morning, in a grey drizzle, we went on, through a gently rolling country of vineyards, ploughed fields, crops and cows. Even on such a lowering day the golden autumn foliage gave an illusion of sunshine. Once we passed a United States Army camp, and, shortly after, a grim reminder of war. What must once have been a small town was now only a field of rough grass and dandelions, with rows of forlorn little flights of stone steps leading nowhere. Each flight once led to the door of a house now vanished, and people came and went about their homes. Now all is gone, and among the dandelions only the steps remain to trace the course of what were streets.

185

About midday we arrived at Saumur, and camped on an island in the Loire. Saumur, site of the French Cavalry College, during World War II was the scene of an epic battle. When the Germans were advancing, officers and cadets, with little equipment and that obsolete, determined that for the honour of the college the enemy should not be allowed to cross the Loire, and at terrible cost held them along a twelve-mile front for three days, a feat which was almost miraculous.

The grey castle of Saumur, standing crowned with its conical towers high above the river, loomed mysteriously through the misty rain. We joined a party of visitors to see the museums it houses, and it was a joy to find our guide was a real enthusiast. Too often guides in historic places content themselves with perfunctory, learned-by-rote descriptions, but this man dwelt lovingly on each exhibit and was eager to share his excitement with others, so that he made the tour through room after room of china, porcelain, antique furniture and tapestries a thrilling experience. He spoke only French, but, except for ourselves and two Englishwomen, the party consisted entirely of French people, and John translated as we went along. At last we came to the part of the castle that houses the Horse Museum. None of us is particularly interested in horses, and left to ourselves we might have passed it by; but it was obvious that here above all was where the guide's heart lay, and his bubbling enthusiasm was so persuasive that we found ourselves completely absorbed in his descriptions of saddles, equestrian armour and horsemen's equipment through the ages. Finally, we were taken into a large hall near the top of the castle surrounded by the skeletons of famous horses, going back for centuries—some horses that had belonged to important soldiers, others racehorses (including the well-known Flying Fox). At this point, the two Englishwomen, who had been getting a little agitated as time went on, said they had to leave; they had a train to catch, and had not expected the tour of the castle would take so long. John duly translated this to the guide, who said he could not possibly leave them to find their own way out, for they would be sure to get lost. If the rest of the party would kindly excuse him, and wait here while he escorted the ladies back to the entrance?

The small windows admitted very little light, for the day was darkly lowering, and the hall was dim and shadowy as we stood among the ghostly horses and armour, waiting. Suddenly the eerie quiet was broken by a loud neigh from one of the skeletons.

186

Everybody jumped as if shot, and some screamed—and then all laughed with relief as Nicky emerged from behind the skeleton horse, looking rather scared at the effect of what he had done. He had only been pretending to be a horse—how could he know people would be frightened?

John and I had grown rather tired of meals cooked in the caravan, so that night we decided to go out to a restaurant. From the Guide Michelin we chose the Gambetta, which was not particularly easy to find, being in a rather dark back street, but we were well pleased with our choice, for the food was superb. We had

      Champignons Escoffier
      Sole Meunière
      Tournedos Gambetta, haricots verts, pommes frites
      Fromages
      Pêche melba
      Saumur vins, blanc et rouge

The cheeses in particular were splendid. Michelin gives this restaurant two forks and no stars, so we concluded that if that was French cooking on a modest level, the three star variety must be ambrosial.

No doubt the Loire is beautiful in spring, but I shall always be glad I saw it in autumn. After leaving Saumur we spent several days travelling along the river, through magical scenery —châteaux and brilliantly coloured foliage all the way. We stayed at the camping at Tours, going off each day in the car, and without the caravan driving and parking became much easier. Inevitably, I thought again of the Rhine, another river with many castles and beautiful scenery, but how different—the Rhine all rugged, romantic grandeur; the Loire, graceful, fairy-tale elegance and autumnal colour the more brilliant for the heavy grey sky above. The châteaux were unforgettable—Ussé, believed to be the castle which inspired Perrault's fable, The Sleeping Beauty; Langeais, small and perfect, with its little draw-bridge; historic Blois and Amboise, and, perhaps the most exquisite of all, Chenonceaux, spanning the stream Cher, with its reminders of Mary Queen of Scots, who lived here as the wife of the Dauphin François, of Diane de Poitiers, Catherine de Medici, and other ladies of past times. Unexpectedly, while we were at Chenonceaux, the sun came out, and the long Renaissance gallery of Catherine de Medici was filled with dancing reflections from the water flowing beneath.

187

Along the banks of the Loire live troglodytes: cave-dwellers, but how different from the poverty-stricken people in the caves near Rome! It is thought that originally the Loire caves were used as wine cellars, and the owners lived in them to protect their precious goods from thieves. Now these underground homes are all part of the fairy-tale atmosphere. One feels they might be inhabited by Hobbits, by Rat or Mole, or some other of Kenneth Grahame's charming creatures. Chimneys and TV aerials appear to sprout from the fields like mushrooms, and in the face of the cliff along the river are doors and windows, sometimes opening on to porches or terraces with garden furniture and great pottery urns filled with flowers; there are neat curtains at the windows, and glimpses of comfortably furnished rooms within.

But again, lest we be too carried away by all this fantasy, we ran into a road block; again the dangerous spikes across the road, and military police with steel helmets and guns to remind us that we were not in a story-book, but in France in 1962.

We were dining by candlelight. It was cosily dim in the caravan, with the red curtains drawn and the candles, stuck in Chianti bottles, on the table.

"It gives it quite a romantic atmosphere, doesn't it?" said Gerard, appreciatively.

But it was not with any idea of creating an atmosphere that we had decided to use candles, it was simply to save our last unbroken gas mantle. We had still not found a solution to the problem of the mantles breaking on the road, and, since we meant to stay only one night at Olivet, near Orléans, our next stop being Paris, where we would be for a fortnight, we preferred one evening's dim light to opening the last carton, and perhaps being without light. It was then the Little Man struck again.

"Where's the salt?" asked John, and Godfrey said quickly, "Don't you get up, Mummy, I'll get it." He bumbled around in the dim light for a few minutes, poking through cupboards and rattling pots and pans.

"Where is it?"

"It's there," I said, "in the cupboard."

More fumbling in the semi-darkness. "I can't find it."

I jumped up to help him, and—disaster—my foot caught the leg of the table, which treacherously folded. The candles went out, food and dishes crashed to the floor, everybody leaped up with startled exclamations and tried to grasp at things before they fell. For a few moments there was chaos in the pitch darkness, till John struck a match, retrieved and lit the candles, and the boys managed to set up the table again. Then we surveyed the damage. Surprisingly, it was much less than we had expected —wine had poured over Miriam's bunk, and some food had spilt, but nothing was broken, and there was enough left intact for a meal. Perhaps it was relief at finding we did not after all lose our dinner which made this a particularly happy evening, which I remember with pleasure. We all sat quite late, talking about everything under the sun from archaeology to the New Zealand way of life as compared with the European, and ended by taking turns reading poetry aloud.

We left early next morning, arriving in time for High Mass in the Cathedral at Chartres, and after the ceremony lingered for some time in the Cathedral. It is wonderfully impressive; prayer and meditation come naturally among the representations of the whole body of Christian belief, expressed in stone and stained glass. The grandeur of the stone carvings, the wealth of saints and prophets and Old Testament scenes, is equalled only by the jewelled richness of the windows, exquisite to see from the outside as well as from within. Quite as marvellous as the stained glass itself is the fact that it has survived through wars and revolution for seven hundred years. No modern work can equal it.

The town of Chartres is an attractive place, with a striking and unusual monument to the Resistance—a huge white stone hand rises from the ground clasping a broken sword of granite.

On to Paris, through the bronze and gold autumn woods, and long before we expected it, we had our first glimpse of the Eiffel Tower.

The camping in the Bois de Boulogne is reputed to be the best in France. It is the only one which the Michelin Camping Guide gives five tents, that is, everything possible: and it really does deserve the description; but, coming to it in late autumn, we found the shops and café had closed for the winter. However, this in a way turned out to be an advantage, for had they been open we would have shopped and eaten on the camping ground, and might never have discovered Suresnes. This was once a small country town, but now is an outer suburb of Paris, still, however, retaining a great deal of the atmosphere of a village. We became very fond of it in the fortnight we were there. Every morning before breakfast Miriam walked through the Bois de Boulogne, over the bridge to Suresnes, and returned with *Figaro*, milk, and long crusty French loaves for breakfast; then later I and any other members of the family who felt like it made the same trip to do the rest of the marketing; to buy fruit and vegetables, delicious and tempting-looking cakes and pastries, and meat from the butcher's shop where hares and whole deer were hanging. Twice a week the cobbled town square, normally a carpark, suddenly blossomed with booths and trestles under long awnings, and became the market. On these days the whole family came with me, buying, or just looking at the wares on display— toys and toilet goods, underwear and socks, heaped vegetables, mushrooms and fruit, women's hats; piles and piles of rabbits, skinned except for the heads and feet; dishes of jellied tripe; fish and flowers and shoes; cakes, biscuits and sweets; cheeses of every description, ice-cream and Coca-cola—and everywhere, the loud voices of the market people crying their wares, music from a band of blind musicians, the chatter of the customers haggling over prices, or just talking together, for the market is the place to meet neighbours and friends.

On Sundays we went to Mass in Suresnes, and once we went to a church bazaar. We were enchanted to find that a French church bazaar is just like a British one—there were the familiar needlework, produce and white elephant stalls, bran tubs, and a bride doll to be raffled. The only difference, apart from the language spoken, was that whereas for British people "refreshments" would mean tea and cakes, in France it meant wine and potato crisps.

When we went into Paris we found it easier to drive to the nearest station, park the car and go in by Métro than to drive right into the city and run the gauntlet of the traffic. The first time we did this, when we emerged from the underground into La Place de la Concorde, and saw the horde of vehicles bearing down on us like a herd of charging elephants, I realized how wise a decision this had been. The terrors of Parisian traffic are exceeded only by those of Rome. While we were in Paris, as part of a Safe Driving campaign, dozens of wrecked vehicles had been parked in La Place de l'Opera to be a horrible example. Some were so crushed and mangled they looked as if they had been put through a press, and some had blood-stained upholstery. They attracted a number of curious sight-seers, but whether they had any effect on driving standards I would not care to say. In the Bois de Boulogne one evening we saw an odd incident, when two cars collided head on. No one was hurt, but both cars were extensively damaged. Both drivers leaped out, and accused each other loudly and vehemently, with menacing gestures. Their passengers joined in, and it looked as if a real battle would ensue. The crash of the impact could have been heard for some distance,

but a gendarme, only a hundred yards or so away, did not even glance up, but continued berating a small boy for riding a bicycle on the footpath.

Paris is said to be beautiful in the spring; it is beautiful in the autumn too, when the leaves which thickly carpet the ground are stirred by every little breeze into whirling, dancing eddies, and, falling on the translucent roofs of bus shelters, make ceilings of autumn-toned chintz. But it was bitterly cold. I earned derisive jeers one night when I got into my sleeping-bag wearing thick woollen socks, slacks, and a cardigan over my pyjamas, but there was a good deal of fumbling around in the dark during the night as one by one the others got up and put on more clothes. The two young boys had given up sleeping in their tent, and took blankets and sleeping-bags into the car for greater warmth.

191

Now that winter was approaching we noticed there were fewer tourists and holiday-makers camping. Apart from the ubiquitous Antipodeans like ourselves—there were still a number of other New Zealanders and Australians—the people in the camping seemed to be, for one reason or another, permanent nomads. There was a couple with a baby, travelling the world in a caravan, making short travel films for television: a Spanish family in a van which was also a mobile bookshop; a troupe of English acrobats who gave us a free show each morning as they practised tumbling and riding trick cycles; and a couple of middle-aged artists who lived in a pup-tent, painting each morning, and each afternoon gathering up some canvases and taking them away, presumably to sell.

The only really fine day we had in Paris must, I think, have been an answer to the prayers of a great many Parisians, for it was a public holiday—Toussaints, All Saints' Day, November the first. It was still very cold, but it was good to see the sun, and the children and I—John had an appointment in Paris—spent the day exploring the Bois de Boulogne. By now the trees were almost bare, and the ground thickly carpeted with leaves. Everywhere Parisians were out enjoying the holiday in the open air—families with children queueing for admission to the zoo, young couples canoeing on the lakes, fathers teaching little boys to row, men playing bowls, children flying kites. But the next day saw lowering skies again, and a fine drizzly rain. Now it was All Souls' Day, and many families were on their way to cemeteries, carrying chrysanthemums to the graves of relatives, and everywhere, on walls, on railings, on the sides of buildings, were hung wreaths of lilies and chrysanthemums, with inscriptions, such as "On this spot . . . . aged . . . ., a gallant fighter for freedom, was assassinated by the Nazis", or perhaps "fell fighting for the Liberation of Paris". They are not forgotten: twenty years after, on All Souls' Day Paris remembers.

The weather did not prevent us from seeing a great deal of Paris. We spent a wonderful day at the Louvre, where, rather to my surprise, I found the Venus de Milo much more beautiful than I had expected: we wandered along the South Bank looking at the bookstalls, and crossed a bridge to l'Ile to visit Notre Dame: we climbed the hill of Montmartre, where, from the steps of Sacré Coeur we looked out over the silver-grey city below, and where, in narrow streets made familiar by many paintings, artists stood at easels, trying to recreate an atmosphere now

192

gone. We visited des Invalides and saw Napoleon's Tomb, where I was shocked at what seemed to me a pagan deification of a mere man. John disagreed, and said it was an expression of patriotism, a glorification of France, not the man. I was not convinced; but I enjoyed the cosy domesticity of the little Marie Louise et Roi de Rome Museum.

There was one moment of sheer enchantment, which remains vividly in my memory. We had been at the Chaillot Palace, where Godfrey—always madly enthusiastic about ships and the sea—had insisted on seeing the Maritime Museum, and we left it at dusk on a drizzling evening. As we came out John said, "Come around the corner—there's something I want to show you." Rather mystified, I followed him, and found myself on a wide expanse of wet flagstones. There before us, beyond a vast pool with fountains, rising airy and graceful in the misty violet evening, was the Eiffel Tower; all the surrounding space dim save for the occasional soft orange lights just beginning to appear. The scene was unreal, insubstantial as a dream, and hauntingly beautiful, the more so for its unexpectedness.

On another occasion we went up the Eiffel Tower, and had the greatest difficulty in getting the children down again, for on the first stage a film company was setting up cameras and lights and placing stand-ins. Every time we tried to drag them away, one or other of them would say, "Please, let's stay a little longer. Cary Grant and Audrey Hepburn will be here any minute." But eventually we managed to persuade them that it might be many hours before filming actually began—even assuming the stars *were* Audrey Hepburn and Cary Grant, which we didn't know for certain. Riding home in the Métro, Nicky said, "Look, the Pussy Brigade has gone underground", and he pointed to a door marked "Poussez."

One very cold wet day, it seemed too dismal to go out. Instead, we stayed in the caravan and the children did their lessons. In an effort to keep warm I was wearing all the sweaters and cardigans I had and grubby, unpressed slacks tucked into thick woollen socks. Suddenly, John said, "I have to go out and cash travellers' cheques. What about coming with me?"

"Just wait a minute while I change," I said.

"No, don't bother. I'm only going to the Rue de Madrid; you needn't even get out of the car. There's no need to dress up."

"I'll come too," said Miriam.

Arrived at the Rue de Madrid, John parked the car and said,

"I think we'll go into the city. Come on."

"But," I protested, "I'm not dressed for the city."

"Oh, come *on*. Who's going to look at you?" and I was propelled towards the Métro station, consoling myself with the thought that it was unlikely in Paris we would meet anyone we knew, and anyway there were so many eccentric costumes about the streets that one more would make no difference. We went to a bank, to Cook's to enquire for mail, to several more places, up streets and down streets, and found ourselves in Rue St Honoré, the centre of Paris fashion. By now it had stopped raining, but the day was quite dark, and the heavy sky hung so low one had the curious illusion of not being out-of-doors at all, but under a vast low ceiling. It was bitterly cold, and seeing all the smartly dressed, richly-furred women, I wryly reflected that, however odd my appearance, at least my clothes were reasonably warm. John, however, was not so philosophical. I caught him eyeing me several times, and at last he burst out:

"Did you have to come out dressed like that? Couldn't you have worn something better?"

"But," I protested, "you told me not to change because you were not going far and I needn't get out of the car."

"Well, I had to say that," he said, "or I'd have had to wait while you changed."

Masculine logic!

That was the nearest I ever came to the Parisian world of haute couture; but I did buy a new coat in Paris, and I had my hair waved. That night John and I were going out to dinner and a theatre. When I was ready, Miriam paid me a compliment.

"Mummy," she said, "you look just like a lady."

When everybody laughed, she added, "I mean, not a camper."

John and I greatly enjoyed evenings in Paris, when we went to theatres or night-clubs, after dining at restaurants we chose from Guide Michelin. Once it was Armistice Day, and in the interval the cast of the play—still in costume—moved through the audience taking up a collection for actors disabled in two wars.

One night at a restaurant famous for its Provençal sea-food, a bewildered-looking American couple nearby called across loudly to us, "Do you speak English?" When they found we did, they asked us to join them. They had arrived by air that morning on their first visit to Europe; they knew no French, had no idea what to see or do in Paris, and were confused about French money—it was just at the time of the change-over from old to new francs, a complication which took a little grasping at first. They were, in fact, complete innocents abroad, and some even well-educated Americans can be incredibly naïve. We were able to give them some advice, for which they were touchingly grateful. They were eating salad, which was the only item on the menu they had been able to identify, and when our bouillabaisse arrived they looked very disappointed, and the husband said, "Why didn't *we* know enough to order something interesting like that! You know," he went on, "we were lucky to meet you— sophisticated people who know their way about."

It was hardly the way we would have described ourselves but it was very flattering!

Each day we had promised ourselves we would go to Versailles, and each day it rained, so rather than spoil it by seeing it in poor conditions, we put off the trip. But at last we came to our very last day in Paris—a Sunday—and still it was raining, so we decided to go anyway. We spent the whole day in the opulent grounds, tramping muddily and squishily through the rain to the Grand and Petit Trianons, to Marie-Antoinette's little stage-set village, where she and her ladies played milkmaids, and to various other parts of the palaces and gardens. We came back cold and drenched to the skin, but mercifully no one suffered any ill effects.

The next day was bright and sunny, and we could not help feeling a little put out that, after weeks of rain, Paris suddenly decided to be fine just as we were leaving.

Chapter XVIII

AUTUMN was giving way to winter. The poplars lining the roads we travelled, only a few weeks before a vibrant gold, were now bare. We were now in the cider country. On each side of the road were apple orchards, some with small, bright red apples still on the branches, others bare, and the fruit piled in crimson heaps on the ground, ready for gathering. (When we tried French cider we considered it vastly inferior to English.)

To travel along the Somme is to be constantly reminded of World War I. Every place-name recalls battles long ago, and it is a solemn thought that this countryside, now so prosperous and peaceful, once knew so much death and destruction.

It was still very cold, and, not long after leaving Paris, we ran into stormy weather again. The day became so dark that we had to switch on the lights, but in the car, the windows closed, and rugs wrapped about us, we were warmer than we had been for weeks. Cosily wrapped in our little cocoon of comfort, towing the caravan behind us, we sped through the murk to Amiens, and arrived in the city just as the rush-hour traffic was beginning to build up. Right in the middle of the city, with masses of cars, trucks and home-going buses about us, was just about the most awkward place we could have found to get a flat tyre. We all piled out, and John and Gerard effected what must have been the quickest wheel change on record, with all the honking traffic wheeling about us. The camping, we found, was a picturesque spot, facing across a lake to the Cathedral. It was clear the holiday season was over—except for us, all were permanent caravan dwellers, with TV aerials on their vans and statuettes on the window-sills, and in the morning all the husbands kissed their wives good-bye and went off to work.

Amiens is a modern, prosperous, go-ahead-looking town, dominated by one great skyscraper, which soars somewhat incongruously above the roofs of the rest of the buildings, and is a landmark for miles around. By this time—mid-November—most of the shop-windows were dressed for Christmas, and a few

197

had displays of "Catherinette" greeting cards and motifs, for the feast of St Catherine. This is the French spinsters' festival—when a girl reaches the age of twenty-five unmarried she qualifies as a "Catherinette", and parties and balls are held to celebrate the occasion.

In the cold weather we were finding the biggest problem of life in a caravan was condensation. Even in a warm temperate climate in winter when the house is warm drops of water will bedew the windows: in the cold winter of northern France, in the thin aluminium caravan, water poured in streams, not just down the windows, but down the walls as well. Everything was damp—mattresses, bedding, clothes. The curtains were wringing wet, and books and papers had to be packed away carefully if they were not to be spoiled. It seemed it was raining indoors as well as out, and I kept hoping the sun would come out, so that I could dry out blankets and sleeping-bags; but we were not so fortunate. Then it occurred to me that in this bitterly cold weather the showers, which had no hot water, were probably not much used—at any rate, I had never seen anyone go into them—so I gathered up all our sodden belongings and hung them there, leaving just one shower free to be used. It didn't help much, but it was the best I could do.

We stayed two days in Amiens. Our original plan had been to make this our last stopping-place in Europe, and to leave on the morning of 16th November for Boulogne, where we were to catch the car-ferry for England; but after discussing the matter we decided it might be wiser to push on, and spend the last night near Boulogne. We did not want to risk missing the boat through unforeseen delays on the road. So on 15th November we set out from Amiens for the coast.

Under a grey-blue sky the sea was grey-green and choppy. Among the white sand-dunes and pines were many reminders of war—remains of pill-boxes and fortifications, tangles of rusty wire, the bombed-out remains of a large factory, or perhaps power station. We spent the night at Equehen Plage, a fishing village of tiny grey stone cottages huddled together on the top of a wind-swept cliff, with far below a wide beach of white sand stretching away in both directions, and the heaving grey waters of the English Channel. The wind was blowing hard off the sea as we bumped into the camping ground, an empty expanse of grass on the edge of the cliffs. We were the only campers, the buildings were locked up, and the water turned off, so we had to fetch it from the village pump, which was presumably the only source of water for the village, for there was always a queue there waiting to fill their jugs. It was bitterly cold and the wind was biting, but there was a wonderful pink and gold sunset across the sea.

And so—our last night on the Continent of Europe. I cooked a rather special dinner, and made it a party, and afterwards we all sat up quite late talking and reminiscing about all we had seen and done in the last few months, a conversation punctuated with "Do you remember . . ." and bursts of laughter.

"Do you remember the glass-blower in Venice, and how annoyed that English woman was?"

"Do you remember that village in Austria—where was it?— where the bank-teller had never heard of travellers' cheques?"

"Do you remember those beatniks in Rome?"

"Do you remember when the Little Man moved away the bridge over the Rhine?"

It was a night of clear, cold moonlight, and the wind rocked the caravan. All night we were disturbed by a loud, irregular thumping, which sounded like distant gun-fire. The next morning we traced the noise to the working of a nearby pumping station and I wondered if a similar experience might have been the basis of the story, much publicized a few years ago, of a woman who claimed, long after the war, to have heard ghostly sounds of battle at Dunkirk.

In the early morning the sky and sea were opalescent pink and blue, and, as far as the eye could see, the fishing fleet dotted

the water—so many little ships it was impossible to count them all. Far down below on the beach women were bent double, gathering shell-fish. It must have been a painful task, groping about in the water with freezing fingers. For a while I stood on the edge of the cliff surveying the scene—the broken pill-box near at hand, the broad expanse of beach, the pearly sea beyond —and thought of all those who had lost their lives on this coast, at Dieppe in one direction and Dunkirk in the other, and I offered up a fervent prayer for peace; then turned back to the caravan to prepare for the short run to Boulogne.

Envoi

THE crossing was uneventful. When we arrived at Dover it was only about half-past three in the afternoon, but, being England in winter, already it was getting dark. And now the question arose: "Where do we stay tonight?"

"Dover, I suppose," said John.

"It's a very nice camping in Dover," I said, remembering the night we had spent there in July.

We were heading towards Folkestone.

"It's not me," said John ungrammatically. "It's the car. It has just decided to go to London."

This pleased us all, for London exerts a pull unequalled by any other city: now we were on English soil we were impatient to be there.

"Funny driving on the left again," remarked John.

"The oncoming headlights are terribly dazzling," I said.

"Yes. Why on earth don't the English use anti-dazzle ones the way they do on the Continent?"

Through Folkestone, and on through the dark, the lights gleaming on the wet roadway. It was long since lunch, and we were all very hungry, so we stopped and bought fish and chips, then pulled into a lay-by to eat them straight from the paper.

"Back in England—fish and chips," remarked Gerard, and we all laughed. This was a family joke. A year before, on the ship from New Zealand, we had teased the younger children by telling them that in England there would be nothing to eat but fish and chips. As it turned out, that was what their first meal in England had been, and they had begun to fear it was true. Now, on our second arrival in England, again the first meal was fish and chips.

In London, we went once more to the Crystal Palace Caravan Harbour, and said we wished to book for a month, but were dismayed to be told that the maximum permitted stay was a fortnight.

"You see," explained the custodian, "this park is for genuine tourists."

201

"And what tourists," I demanded, "are more genuine than us?"

However, that was the rule, and there was nothing we could do. We booked for a fortnight.

"It's a nuisance," said John. "I had hoped to stay in London. But I suppose we could stay here for a fortnight, go somewhere else for a few days, and then come back."

"We'll think of something," I said. "Anyway, here we are for the next two weeks."

But as it turned out, we were not.

The camping ground was not the gay and crowded place it had been in July. Most of it had been fenced off, and only a small area was in use. Even on that there were few people— besides ourselves, a couple of Australians and a Portuguese circus troupe, resting between engagements. (Were they, I wondered, genuine tourists?) But the shop was still open, and— bliss—the showers were really hot. Condensation in the caravan was more trying than ever. Everything was drenched.

"Look at my beautiful dry pyjamas," said Gerard, wringing them so that drops of water pattered on the floor.

It was exciting to be in London again; to see all the landmarks we greeted as old friends—Big Ben, the Tower, St Paul's; to take our washing to a laundrette; to hear English voices. Even the cindery, smoky smell of London was exciting. But water left in a bucket overnight froze solid: all the ground around the caravan was icy and slippery, and the cold and damp seemed to get into our very bones. And then one evening it began to snow. We did not know it then, but it was the beginning of one of the worst winters on record. The camping park looked very beautiful with the flakes drifting silently down, and the red lights from the nearby television mast reflected on the snow, but we were beginning to doubt the wisdom of continuing to camp.

"We could buy a kerosene-heater," John suggested, but he sounded half-hearted. When we woke next morning we found condensation was no longer a problem—instead, icicles hung from the ceiling and festooned the walls. John and I looked at each other, and burst out simultaneously, "Let's go to an hotel!"

Straight after breakfast we set out to look for accommodation, and found a comfortable guesthouse in Bayswater where children were welcome. We returned to the caravan feeling much more cheerful with the prospect of warmth and a roof over our heads.

So our fortnight at Crystal Palace was to be less than a week. Now there were two feverishly busy days. Packing for six people was a colossal task. We had to get the rest of our luggage out of storage, unpack it all, and then rearrange everything in three categories:

1. Not needed in England or on the voyage—household goods, souvenirs, camping equipment.
2. Wanted on the voyage, but not in England—summer clothing.
3. Needed at once.

It meant a great deal of travelling back and forth between Crystal Palace and the storage firm's repository, and of course mistakes were made and some things found their way into the wrong places; but somehow the job was done, and we made a couple of trips across London to our new address with our luggage.

Then came the disposal of the caravan. Now that we were about to lose the Blue Kiwi we discovered we felt a great affection for it. For six months it had been home: it had enabled us to travel much further than we could otherwise have done: in it we had experienced a great deal of happiness. We walked around it and surveyed it. Considering all it had been through it still looked well. True, the red curtains were faded, and the pattern had worn off the linoleum where it was most trodden. A deep scratch along one side was a reminder of a certain gate-post in Somerset, and dents bore witness to the force of the Ruhr Valley wind: but these were minor details. In essentials it was as good as ever. If we thought fleetingly of keeping it and taking it home with us, we knew it was not really a practical idea—back in New Zealand it was not probable that we would take caravan holidays. So the boys carefully removed from the windows the fifty or so city crest stickers they had collected, and John hitched it to the car for the last time, took it to a dealer and sold it.

So there we were, beneath a roof again. Six weeks stretched before us until we were to sail for home. Now that the fundamental problems of warmth and shelter were solved, we resolved to enjoy ourselves, and make the most of this last, glorious spell in London.

We were very sad to say good-bye to the Kiwi, but that night we had soft warm beds and gas-fires in our rooms—and never were these simple comforts more appreciated.

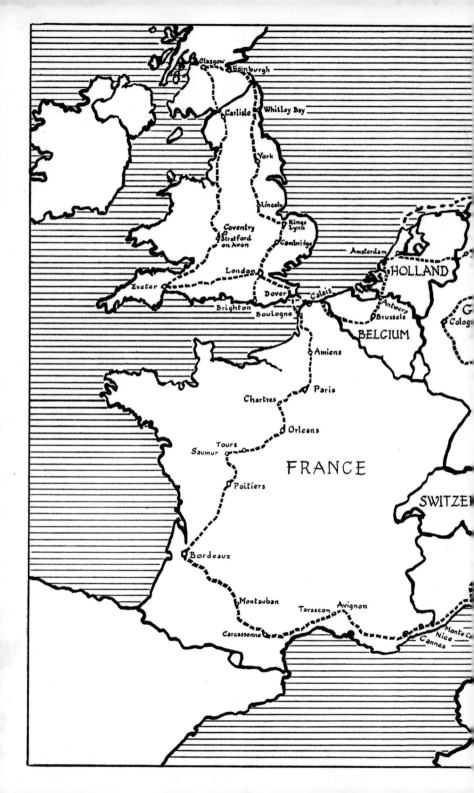